A FEATHERED FAMILY

OTHER BOOKS BY LINDA JOHNS

Touching Water, Touching Light
Spiritus
Sharing a Robin's Life
The Eyes of the Elders
In the Company of Birds

A FEATHERED FAMILY

Nature Notes from a Woodland Studio

Linda Johns

Sierra Club Books
San Francisco

The Sierra Club, founded in 1892 by John Muir, has devoted itself to the study and protection of the earth's scenic and ecological resources — mountains, wetlands, woodlands, wild shores and rivers, deserts and plains. The publishing program of the Sierra Club offers books to the public as a nonprofit educational service in the hope that they may enlarge the public's understanding of the Club's basic concerns. The point of view expressed in each book, however, does not necessarily represent that of the Club. The Sierra Club has some sixty chapters coast to coast, in Canada, Hawaii, and Alaska. For information about how you may participate in its programs to preserve wilderness and the quality of life, please address inquiries to Sierra Club, 85 Second Street, San Francisco, CA 94105.

www.sierraclub.org/books

Published by Sierra Club Books, in conjunction with Crown Publishers, New York, New York. Member of the Crown Publishing Group. Random House, Inc. New York, Toronto, London, Sydney, Auckland
www.randomhouse.com

SIERRA CLUB, SIERRA CLUB BOOKS, and the Sierra Club design logos are registered trademarks of the Sierra Club.

Printed on recycled paper.

Originally published in Canada by McClelland & Stewart Inc.

Library of Congress Cataloging-in-Publication Data
Johns, Linda.
A feathered family : nature notes from a woodland studio / Linda Johns.
    p.   cm.
Originally published: For the birds. Toronto, Ontario :
McClelland & Stewart, [19 — ?].
    1. Wild birds as pets. 2. Johns, Linda, 1945 — Homes and haunts —
Nova Scotia. I. Johns, Linda, 1945 — For the birds. II. Title.
SF462.5.J638 2000
639.9'78 — dc21   00-041965

Brush drawings by Linda Johns
Printed in the United States of America

ISBN 1-57805-056-1

10 9 8 7 6 5 4 3 2 1

For the birds, literally,
and for Mack,
a kind and generous "rooster" . . .

CONTENTS

Birds are amazing. They really are.

Since I made my home their woodland world twenty-five years ago, my life, and therefore my work, has been gradually transformed by interactions with them ranging from dignified tolerance on their part to endearing companionship between us. Though so many have come and gone, still each arrival is as intriguing and mysterious as ever. My partner, Mack, and I are not scientifically trained. We consult others when such expertise is needed. With no other haven available, concerned people bring us hungry nestlings, birds rescued from highways, cats, or window collisions, and we do our best to restore them to health and independence in their natural habitat.

It is exhilarating to open one's hands and watch a wild bird fly up easily onto a branch.

One's own spirit rises on parallel wings.

Our Nova Scotia home is enclosed by sixty acres of spruce, fir, pine, and hemlock trees mingling with hardwoods like birch, maple, ash, and beech. Poplars, chokecherry, serviceberry, and apple trees also contribute to the mix, as well as hawthorn bushes, a favourite nesting site.

Within the forest, tiny trees rise out of deep, damp moss, climbing ladders of light that lead up through the dense growth. Larger trees shelter birds, porcupines, squirrels, and raccoons. Deer nibble lichens encrusting their trunks. Enormous dying trees, some of them hollow, are hammered by hungry woodpeckers before finally falling. Recumbent, they crumble into the soil from which they arose, enriching it now for others.

An endless cycle of fascination.

Part of the forest borders on a small, round, very deep lake, lying close to a longer, much larger lake. A lake surrounded by trees, not cottages. Not yet.

A few wild meadows and cultivated fields, once woodlands themselves, join our forest to wooded hills that encircle us nearby. Hills that lure us out of the house, in every season and in all weathers, to add our footprints to the crisscrossing tracks of other creatures. To inhale the unsurpassable fragrance of damp fir boughs. To wander beside brooks that bound musically over rocks and exposed roots before dissolving suddenly in the wide placidity of the lakes.

In an area so rich with bird life, interactions are inevitable and enriching.

Especially for an artist.

Birds swoop through my paintings as well as our home. Their soaring forms emerge out of my carvings in whalebone or wood – or even in stone, where the often feathery grain enhances them.

Traditionally symbolic of the spirit, birds rendered expressively in art transcend category to elevate our thinking. Nestlings signify new thresholds of growth in our lives; they gape hungrily, suggesting our own need for nourishment on all levels.

The birds we care for teach us what they need. And when they finally leave, we discover just how much more *they* have given *us*.

But the work of caring for each individual bird and supplying them with their natural diet is intensive. Hours of dogged bug-collecting is the key, and one not to be rated lightly. Canned food is *not* properly nutritious, nor does it teach a youngster to recognize and catch natural food. And to release a babe without that knowledge is lethal.

Mealworm cultures have become essential to our lifestyle, in which insect-eaters usually prevail. In an upstairs closet, where the temperature is warm and constant, we have three large aquariums. Each contains several inches of wheat bran, and mealworms in all stages – from microscopic eggs, to worms, to pupae, to black beetles (who lay the eggs). The largest worms are gathered daily for the birds, though if there's a sudden overrun of beetles, these are added to their fare.

Fresh bran and sections of apple are fed to the mealies as needed, and because mealworm droppings build up in the bottom of the tanks, I sift each culture annually. Then I add new bran to the clean aquariums and return the mealies.

The supply of mealworms of course is governed by the demand, and this creates population fluctuations – sometimes inconveniently. How often have clusters of nestlings arrived during low tide in the mealworm culture!

A screened porch on the south side of the house is always available to the birds during warm weather. As well, I leave the light inside it on all night, with both screen doors open, and the house door closed. Moths throng into the porch all night and, in the morning, I close the screen doors, open the house door, and let the birds feed on moths – a welcome addition to the menu. Certain moths are not edible, and this the birds know instinctively.

As everyone knows, what goes in must come out – and I am often asked about droppings. I often wonder if new mothers are questioned just as jocularly – and persistently – about what they do with used diapers. I have even begun, rather whimsically, to classify people in one of two categories: those who see birds and those who see droppings.

Birds usually have routine resting places, which can have newspaper below, and in any case are easily dealt with. Their wanderings throughout the house leave inevitable spots here and there, which are also easily dealt with. We do not collar each dropping when it lands – or we wouldn't have a life. We do, however, have brief cleanups on a regular basis. And we live in a clean home.

Besides – the birds and I have always agreed that they would produce the droppings, and that I should clean them up. And though I've been lax at times, I can honestly state that they have generously upheld their side of the bargain.

Luckily, I am blessed with the sturdy support of Mack, an energetic, enthusiastic man whose delight in every arrival never stops short of helping to supply its needs. Unenviable tasks like collecting fresh roadkills for a starving raven, or cutting up beef heart and liver for a hungry owl, generally fall on Mack's more capable shoulders, to my immense relief. Buoyant and boisterous, he welcomes all challenges with unabated freshness, lightening difficulties and sheltering us all under his kindness.

It would take more than a few droppings to slow Mack down!

I am also blessed with good friends who possess wormier gardens than ours. Even after years of seeing me drive up with gaping nestlings, empty buckets, and a hopeful look on my face, they still welcome me instead of running inside and locking the door.

What's more, they help me dig.

The Animal Care Technician at the nearby university has been a staunch supplier of mealworms, as well as small frozen mammals for the saw-whet owl and, more recently, frozen trout for a raven. She is also one of our sources of scientific information.

Our home is a roomy, open design of interconnecting flyways

that at times seem to dominate the furniture and the other odd-ments of human occupation. The living room, under its pine cathedral ceiling, is graced with grey handhewn beams and a tall stained-glass window. We have more perches than chairs.

Under a south-facing window lies the indoor garden. Edged with boards and lined with waterproof sheeting, it's filled with rich woodland soil and arching plants. A large twist of driftwood provides perches, as do two tall, dead trees, chosen for their markedly horizontal branches and lugged home from the woods.

The indoor garden is the focus of the house for all the birds, even wildlings sharing it temporarily. The birds are free to roam anywhere, but the garden, with its soft soil, waterdish, seed dishes, and sheltering plants, holds the most attraction. It is an almost natural habitat, which we maintain with regular rakings and additions of woodland soil.

The "hospice" room, used for isolating birds on occasion, and for storing winter squash and sculptures regularly, opens off the west wall of the living room near the indoor garden. The summer shed for the roosters, with its large wire run, opens off the hospice.

The studio was built onto the east wall of the house, and has large north-facing windows that yield light that is consistent. Into the south wall of the studio I built a small greenhouse window with perches as well as plants. Here, many birds have enjoyed sunning themselves and watching the outdoor activities.

I isolated my studio from the rest of the house in a futile effort to establish the solitude necessary for creative work. However, with roosters and pigeons sharing it, not to mention a determined grackle, creativity had to fight tooth and nail for fulfilment.

Wonderful how creatures can impede as well as inspire. Truly, creation begins in chaos.

These, then, are *verbal* sketches from a woodland studio.

Written – for the birds.

CHAPTER 1

A FEATHERED FAMILY

April had come and Chip was ecstatic. Not that winter had been hard on her. Far from it. A free-flying indoor grackle has a full life. Each diabolic moment leads inescapably to the next, and woe betide anyone who lags behind. Only those trying fruitlessly to keep pace with her ingenuity tended to look a trifle grim in the brilliant spring sunshine.

With outpourings of ear-splitting crescendos, she pranced coyly along the windowsills, arching her black wings and tail. Shamelessly, she ogled the flocks of huge, iridescent male grackles arriving daily from the south.

Even her eyes were singing.

Utterly unresponsive to her overtures, they concentrated instead on hungrily devouring the scattered seed under the trees outside. Occasionally, two would bristle at one another warningly. They'd point their beaks skyward in silent confrontation, golden eyes unwinking. Gleaming black chests would swell enormously before collapsing suddenly with a defiant screech. Then both birds would resume feeding.

After flying hundreds of miles, food was a priority.

Between communal feedings, "musical trees" surrounding the house reverberated in squeaking, squealing cacophonies. Each branch was dotted with dozens of resting and restless grackles, preening and calling out the triumphs of another spring migration.

Chip absorbed it all, zipping from window to window, calling and posturing in alluring ways fully approved by generations of grackles. Her behaviour clarified one important issue for me: I had to stop calling her a "he," as I had all winter – and as I'd described her as a juvenile in my second book *In the Company of Birds*.

Her beautiful teal headfeathers, so striking during the snowy months, were definitely subdued compared to these wild, outdoor males. And she was noticeably smaller. Chip, the endearing rascal of many a winter shenanigan, was suddenly transformed into a young, ardent female, eager for spring courtship.

But would Chip's health ever allow her to live a normal outdoor life?

Her immediate indoor family was comprised of birds who, like Chip herself, were unable to live outdoors. Uncaged, they interacted freely each day throughout the house, a seemingly harmless regime guaranteed to entertain.

And exasperate.

The senior residents were Desmond and Molly, two fancy pigeons with snow-white fronts, chestnut backs and wings, and dark eyes. They pattered everywhere on beautiful feathered feet, in which they took obvious pride. Both birds had arrived at ten days of age in terrible health, but by the time they were well enough to be returned to their owner, they had taken up firm residence in my heart.

Day after day, they'd follow patiently behind, wherever household chores led me. In the studio, they'd snuggle down side by side in a warm sunpatch on the floor while I painted.

I encouraged their first flights by walking slowly away from Desmond while carrying Molly, so that he'd finally take wing and land on my shoulder. Then I'd put Molly down and stroll away, still carrying Desmond. Soon she'd summon enough courage to fly over and join us. Their owner had been amused at my reluctance to give them up.

"But you already have a flock of thirty," I murmured.

"I never expected to get them back from you anyway," he chuckled.

Many years later they were still with me, Desmond ever laying his heart at Molly's feet, and Molly, with increasing asperity, rigidly spurning his advances. Perhaps repeatedly seeing her own image surfacing in my artwork has convinced Molly that she's a career pigeon with no time for the usual domestic responsibilities.

Certainly her increasing crankiness towards everyone has entangled me in woolly speculations on the possibility that Molly personifies the stereotypical menopausal shrew.

One memorable morning saw Molly scoot out from under my bed, where she'd been enjoying the seclusion so dear to her unsociable heart. I was dressing, and had just pulled my sweater over my head and wiggled my arms into the sleeves, with Chip unbelievably on my shoulder through the whole process, when Molly seized my pantleg. She jerked it to and fro, cooing irritably and whacking me with her wing for emphasis. I glared down groggily at her and shook my leg, piqued at this sudden provocation.

With a curt squawk, Chip swooped down from my shoulder to my defence. Darting up from the rear, she jerked Molly's tail and danced saucily away as Molly swung around in annoyance. Released suddenly, I left them squabbling and fled downstairs muttering.

It was going to be one of those days with Molly.

A decline in Desmond's disposition would have been understandable – after all, he'd been ardently carrying the torch for Molly for the past ten years. Not even a kind look from her had fanned his unrequited fire.

On the other hand, I owed Molly a debt of gratitude. Without her rigid adherence to maidenhood, where would I have put all their babies?

Next in seniority were Bubble and Squeak, two affectionate roosters, well-spurred and resplendent in long red wattles, enormous combs, and stunning plumage. Their brooding mother had been taken by a predator when her clutch of eggs was beginning to hatch. As a result Bubble, one hour old, had come home nestled into my collar, while the eggs, wrapped in sweaters, had ridden beside us in the van. Squeak, calling from inside his shell and receiving encouraging peeps from Bubble and me, hatched later that evening in the dining room.

His was the only other egg in the clutch to hatch.

As the babes grew, it became clear that Squeak was a chicken with "special needs." His tightly curled toes required temporary shoes contrived of carpet underlay to straighten them. His ears needed periodic cleaning to unclog them, an unpleasant process to which he submitted with touching patience. Lastly, his thinner plumage decreed that he would never survive the rigours of outdoor Canadian winters. Since the two roosters were insepar-able, they both had to live indoors.

Only to select friends did I admit that we were all inseparable.

Bubble's and Squeak's personalities unfolded with their matur-ing plumage, revealing Bubble as placid and very dignified, but so enamoured of being cuddled in my lap that on occasion his bliss would overflow in drool. He was a stable, centred soul, with calm eyes, gorgeous reddish-gold feathering, and a splendid tail of iridescent dark green.

Squeak, so diametrically opposed to Bubble, was extremely sensitive and high-strung, easily excited or alarmed, and bore soft, creamy-white tweedy plumage with scant, rather stringy, barred tailfeathers. His bright eyes, keenly alert, could also suddenly soften and "smile" with great charm.

When he was cozied down in my lap, with my face on one side and Bubble nestled protectively on the other, Squeak's eyes would shut tight in unutterable bliss and deep, gentle snores would rise from his drooping head.

The morning Squeak spotted a large barred owl on a branch outside the studio window, he exploded into paroxysms of shrill clucking, violent trembling, and what could only be described as hysterical hiccups. For Bubble, a staccato of piercing squawks was sufficient, and the owl, perhaps desiring a more restful location after a night's hunting, soon swept silently away.

Chip herself was third in order of arrival – fifth in individual numbers. She had made her appearance nearly a year earlier as an unhappy, caged grackle fledgling, two weeks of age, with smelly feathers splayed by the cage bars. Her eyes were wide with acute anxiety because of haphazard and unsuitable feedings, primarily of slugs and dog food instead of worms and mixed bugs. And her coordination was underdeveloped due to her confinement.

She was a victim of the good intentions of well-meaning, unknowledgable rescuers.

I fed her worms and a variety of insects, rigidly timing her feedings to twenty-minute intervals which would approximate natural feedings by her parents, and offering only amounts that could be carried in a parent bird's beak. This technique avoided overfeeding, which can be lethal. She was given the freedom of a quiet house with freely flying birds and the delight of exploring our indoor garden designed expressly for birds. Bathing her soiled plumage in the waterdish under the arching plants soon restored her beauty and naturally clean scent, and Chip settled down to enjoy her new life.

The roosters were very gentle with her, recognizing her youthful innocence and allowing her to clamber over their backs as freely as they'd no doubt allow little chicks to do. Characteristically, mild Desmond took the addition of another housebird calmly in his stride. But pigeons certainly vary.

Molly, also characteristically, registered her blatant disapproval at every opportunity with belligerent coos of frigid hostility.

The stress of Chip's caged life, unfortunately, had taken its toll. Her damaged immune system had given rise to a chronic problem in her pulmonary system, which was most easily likened to emphysema in humans. Each time I tried to release her, she suffered an immediate breakdown in her health. I'd bring her back indoors, treat her with one small drop, three times a day, of Panmycin containing tetracycline, an antibiotic I've found to be successful with birds. When she was stabilized, I'd release her once again. However, she showed no inclination to join the migratory flocks of grackles arriving, feeding, and departing. Outdoors, amongst the ever-bustling birds, Chip lived a solitary life.

During her last release, after leaving her out for three weeks, I became aware of her laboured breathing. As she perched on my shoulder in the early morning stillness, I heard the ominous crackling in her lungs that I had learned to dread. I brought her inside immediately and dosed her with tetracycline. Later that evening, I noted anxiously that she slept with her head back and beak open to keep her breathing passages clear. Chip would never manage the fluctuating weather and stressful exertions of an outdoor grackle's normal life.

Fortunately Chip more than thrived indoors, where her breathing remained fairly normal. She had an ingenious knack of extracting tremendous enjoyment from the mundane. Chasing running water as it filled the washing machine or a sink full of dirty dishes banished tedium for both of us.

And sometimes banished peace of mind as well.

Each day became highly charged by her cheery songs and devilish pranks. In teasing one to distraction, Chip reigned unchallenged. She made friendly overtures to all visitors, from squirming babies to elders, playing with rings, earrings, and watches, accepting tidbits off tongues, exploring teeth, sampling everyone's food and drink, and riding on a variety of heads and shoulders.

However, there was an exception to her friendliness: a neighbour stopped in briefly one morning and Chip immediately fled, emerging only when he'd gone. The man was the only person of my acquaintance who was an avid hunter and trapper.

Toys became a passion for a bird of Chip's curiosity and playfulness. Soon a bizarre collection of household odds and ends found its way into her toy basket up above the coat rack. From that vantage point, she had the sheer delight of bombarding us all with paper clips, earplugs, bottle caps, corks, even hoarded pieces of pungent orange peel, long since shrivelled.

With a fresh cup of tea as a target, her accuracy was uncanny.

Chip also explored the amphibious possibilities of pens, pencils, bookmarks, crackers, popcorn, seed packages, and, alas, film cartridges, dropping them into her bath and pushing them about like little boats. Then she'd hook them out with her beak and hold them carefully under her claw.

Peering closely at her prize, she'd snap at any sparkling drops that fell, before shredding the sodden remains with manic delight. Her obsession for shredding everything from pickled beans to drying underwear drove me to desperate lengths to find more suitable sources of amusement for her.

Many a time have I slipped furtively into toy stores, emerging rather guiltily half an hour later with various inexplicable atrocities with which I'd rather not be seen. Treasures such as sinewy plastic bats and five-inch-long undulating centipedes, rubber-quilled hedgehogs that squeak when suddenly pinched (and who wouldn't?), or gigantic leering ants with waving forelegs. And a diversity of mysterious wind-up gizmos that Chip happily submerged, still whirling and spluttering, into her waterdish.

One day, I thrust my foot down into my winter boot onto something squashy that squealed. I squealed even louder and shook off the boot. Out fell a lurid green rubber tarantula belonging to Chip.

There are moments when I picture those factories in foreign lands in which people from a totally different culture work. Year after year, they produce these hideous plastic novelties in garish colours. They ship them to us in a constant stream to keep up with our demand.

How they must wonder. . . .

One memorable day, seeing my evident perplexity at the overwhelming profusion of toys, a motherly saleswoman materialized at my side, purring helpfully.

"And how old is the little dear?"

To which I replied absently, "About six months . . . here, I think I'll take a selection of these rubber houseflies."

Eyeing me askance, she took the proffered flies back to the cash register. Wrapping them in a distracted manner, she made one last effort to get a grip on the situation.

"You realize you must be very careful that he doesn't put them in his mouth and choke."

"Don't worry," I assured her. "She only swallows live ones. These are just for play."

I left her clutching the counter for support.

The ultimate toy for Chip, however, was unquestionably a tiny Japanese quail who arrived from a lab where he was considered extraneous and expendable by everyone except the Animal Care Technician. He was only three weeks old, yet fully matured. His siblings remained behind in cages, paired to produce fertile eggs for experiment. Since Japanese quail are not indigenous, Bashō, named after a favourite haiku poet, could not be released. Instead, he became our sixth resident.

As though he had indeed arrived for Chip's express amusement, she heartlessly tweaked his diminutive tail, stalked him with mock menace through the indoor garden and galvanized him with sudden aerial swoops. Bashō's sudden three-note calls, some undoubtedly in protest, I laughingly refer to as spontaneous poetic inspirations, rendered in three-lined haiku format.

His plumage is a stunning interweaving of gold and dark browns with darting accents of creamy white – a beauty reminiscent of old marbled papers.

It was pure delight to watch the two of them slipping through the garden and around the arching plants, or sharing a drink at the waterdish. Chip, always keen to try anything new, sampled Bashō's "turkey starter," a commercially produced delicacy that had accompanied him from the lab. Bashō, in turn, nibbled at white millet, niger, and other flavours in Chip's dish of mixed seeds.

But when it came to the coveted mealworms, Chip drew the line at sharing. No matter how many she'd eaten herself, I had to stand guard while Bashō ate his. It wasn't so much the urge to eat more that drove her to one ploy after another. It was the irresistible urge to steal.

Nothing gave her such unholy joy as getting away with something.

When Bashō craved mealworms, he'd patter out to the studio where I was working. There, he'd tug persistently at my pantleg until, in resignation, I would cover up my paints and bring him half a dozen mealies. After chittering excitedly and gulping them down, he'd swell out smugly and preen. His small size was seldom an impediment to getting his own way.

The roosters soon caught on to Bashō's ploy and would gather around as soon as they noticed him tugging my pantleg. I could almost hear Bubble's aside to Squeak, "Stick to the quail. He's good for extra mealies."

And of course, I always returned with extra mealies.

To watch Bashō with the roosters was delightful. Especially when he'd peck innocently and curiously at their enormous spurs. He was as safe as a chick near them. But when Squeak suddenly crowed in Bashō's face one morning, Bashō literally staggered from the impact. I could almost see his tiny ears ringing.

My own ears ached in sympathy.

When Bashō was very young he had a curious tendency to trot backwards for about half a yard before stopping. When he tried to move again, he might go backwards for several more paces before finally trotting forwards. I used to wonder if he'd lost his "operator's manual." He reminded me of Billy's car.

When I was a child, Billy and his toy car were the envy of the neighbourhood. I remember the exquisite delight of squeezing down into the seat for my turn. Grasping the steering wheel and pedalling gloriously down the sidewalk, one felt grown up at last. On one's own.

But the pedals were tricky. If you pushed down too eagerly, you were just as liable to go suddenly backwards. They had to be exactly right in order to go forwards. Sometimes they'd lock.

Watching Bashō, I sometimes wondered if his legs were hinged like the pedals in Billy's wonderful car.

Bashō's beauty and his tiny size gave everyone who saw him a craving to cuddle him, an indignity to which he would briefly submit before escaping and shaking out his plumage with evident disgust. Smitten by that same desire, I'd hold my hands out to him in greeting, coaxing him closer with false hopes of mealworms. His disappointment at being lured over only for a drivel of sweet talk was unmistakably expressed in every upright feather on his back as he stalked off.

"BUGS, not HUGS!" was his final word. Only gradually did his love of being cuddled develop, to my lasting delight.

Bashō enjoyed new experiences, and the unexpected apparition of a visiting human baby sitting on the floor beside the indoor garden one day was a sight to explore from every angle. Even the waving arms and kicking legs caused him no anxiety whatsoever. The baby, too, was entranced, his darting eyes following Bashō's scooting form.

As his father had the temerity to note, his son was having "a quail of a time"!

Chip's curiosity about the baby led her to walk brazenly up his front, pry open his mouth, and peer inside in the hopes of finding a tasty tidbit.

The climax came when the child, tiring of sifting through the garden earth, began reaching for one of the food dishes instead. His mother scrambled forward in concern. She had no intention of jeopardizing her son's future.

The dish contained "turkey starter."

CHAPTER 2

INVISIBLE PATHS

While Chip spent her April days absorbed in the comings and goings of migrating grackles, I began to enjoy woodland walks unencumbered by heavy clothing and snowshoes. Instead, I carried a light pack containing drawing materials. Early spring, with the last snows wilting in the hollows, and before the tangled summer growth baffles the curious eye of the artist, is the best time to study tree forms.

Especially roots.

For me, they have always had immediate appeal as strong gnarled toes grasping for footholds in an ever-shifting world – a reminder of our deep origins.

The beginning of our growth.

Some days, I headed for remote beaches along the eastern shore. There, torn headlands jut abruptly into the ocean. A primal world, where salty winds seldom cease and hurling waves claw boulders out of the scarred cliffs.

Cresting the bluffs, roots of stunted, silvery spruce twist and turn. They burrow stubbornly into the soil, resisting the erosion of the cliff face as it yields inch by inch to every storm. Where large sections of earth have slid down, the exposed, contorted roots are revealed as visible paths of invisible forces, paths which persisted despite the obstacles of hidden rocks within the earth. Indeed, the resisting rocks seem to have stimulated the seeking roots. To have shared in the creation of such triumphant forms.

In my paintings, using elusive colouring to harmonize with those invisible energies that create hidden paths, I weave arboreal forms around orbs of power, as life revolves around not only the visible sun but also around our inner sun. Our consciousness.

As our inner tides as well as those of the ocean respond to the moon.

As the invisible paths within our bodies revolve around our hearts.

In a more humorous vein, I've experienced other revelations of the invisible. One morning, just outside the kitchen window, I spotted a tiny saw-whet owl sleeping on a branch only a few feet above ground level. He dozed the daylight hours away, occasionally preening or peering about himself with his beautiful golden eyes. At dusk, he melted away into the darkening woods.

The following day, a little red squirrel came scampering along the ground and shot up the trunk of the same tree, only to skid suddenly to a halt just beyond the owl's branch. Slowly the squirrel retraced his way down to the branch, sniffing furiously all the while. Then he crept along to the owl's actual roosting spot and systematically examined it before finally moving on.

I was amazed that the scent of an owl could still be present fifteen hours after he'd flown away. I've held a saw-whet owl in my hands many times, pressing my face against the tawny softness, and always the plumage smelled only of freshness and feathers. Perhaps the scent of captured prey lingered on his talons. Consideration, too, must be given to a squirrel's sense of smell, which is far more highly developed than a human's.

In any case, though the visible owl had long since vanished, an invisible owl was still present.

Late one winter, a flying squirrel was live-trapped inside an attic and taken to the Animal Care Technician at the local university to be cared for until spring. I was the lucky person chosen to release the squirrel, and one beautiful afternoon I brought the cage home and set it up on the back deck. There I draped it loosely with a towel to restrict the light, since flying squirrels are nocturnal, and waited to see if the little creature would emerge from his hidey-hole box inside the cage.

Through the weeks of his confinement, he had rarely come forth, even for feedings, because of his strange, bright surroundings. Instead, when food had been placed in his cage, the box had mysteriously shuffled forward and cleverly covered the food, so he could eat with complete privacy in the dark.

Soon, where the towel parted, a furry grey face with enormous dark eyes appeared, small nose twitching at the familiar woodland scents. As dusk deepened, he stood up eagerly, pressing against the cage with evident longing. When enough light still remained for me to watch, I opened the cage door quietly and sat down a short distance away.

Gradually the squirrel eased himself out, carefully sniffing the area. I expected at this point to see him suddenly dash up a tree.

Not so.

Instead, he moved slowly towards the nearest trunk and began to climb, his nose working constantly.

Inch by inch he flowed up onto the branches, exploring the local roadways, changing from one branch to another at the same invisible intersections as the daytime squirrels, noting familiar "detours" and "overpasses" with intense care. Eventually, his greyness disappeared into the deepening twilight.

I was fascinated.

For me, the branches were merely branches. To those using them, they presented an intricate network of crisscrossing, well-worn pathways, obvious to newcomers with "eyes in their noses." Painted with a contrasting colour, they would present a defined pattern amidst the chaos of the branches.

Or would only a human perceive branches as chaotic?

Invisible paths through the visible world are to me a revelation. A reminder of the limitations of our knowledge.

I remember once stepping outside into a wintry silence of falling snow. Fields everywhere were still subtly woven with the soft greens, greys, and browns of mixed dried grasses. Where the endless passing of little wild creatures had trodden the growth, snow had accumulated, creating a crisscrossing of startlingly white pathways – more hidden paths becoming visible. Acres of vague grasses were changing into the entwining routes of a road map. Also, to my surprise, I saw large snowflakes perfectly motionless in the air wherever I looked.

How could this be?

Closer examination revealed that they were caught on barely discernable spider threads. Millions of snowy threads draped the trees, hung to the ground, joined each tree to the next, looped together stalks of dried weeds, cross-hatched the steeper slopes of my dark gambrel roof, yet free from snowy buildup. I had been living within an intricate network of invisible paths which only became visible to me during stillness and falling snow.

Perhaps, for all we know, the migratory paths through the skies are visible to birds in ways beyond our imagining.

Beyond obvious landforms and star sightings.

Beyond wind currents and the roar of coastal surf.

Certainly we've been unable to understand fully the mysterious skill behind these arduous flights, though speculation abounds.

Air travel is new to us, just as we are, relatively speaking, new to the earth. Birds have been developing their flight skills for 150 million years. The warm "robin wind" out of the south each spring, bearing waves of migrants on its strong currents, was blowing when archaeopteryx, the "fossil bird," glided through the clean Jurassic air.

How humbling to ponder this as I look out the kitchen window, insulated by glass from the soft touch of that ancient, invisible wind. I stand surrounded by a mechanized world of gleaming technological devices that isolate me from nature. From my primal beginnings.

How marvellous to reforge that link to what has never ceased to be.

Only at special moments, if one is receptive, can one be in all of time. Then it is no longer time. No longer temporal.

Then it is eternity.

The sudden rushing roar of grackles lifting into the air, the hissing flight of flocks passing overhead, sounded the same to us centuries ago. Their squeaky calls still sound meaningless to our uncomprehending ears, so little have we listened.

In many ways, so little have we learned.

But Chip, bright-eyed on the windowsill, was listening. And I, with eons of human indifference clogging my ears, was endeavouring to listen too.

Did she hear only the "visible" calls of each bird at that moment? The obvious, audible calls?

Or rather, within those calls, did she not feel a deeper thrill resonating from *centuries* of calls, a summons that does not just resound in one's ears, but reverberates in one's blood. A deep, surging, exciting call that urges each grackle to leave the egg, to leave the nest, to leave for the south, to leave for the north – the compelling call that can't be heard but that fills all one's being till nothing else can be heard.

The "invisible" call.

A call similar to that heard by the artist.

CHAPTER 3

BIRDWATCHING

"Chip! Don't you dare!" I snatched back the lid of the ink. Then I firmly recapped the bottle while she watched me with gleaming eyes.

A deadline was upon me and I was sitting at the dining-room table adding a few frantic touches to a drawing that I planned to deliver in a couple of hours. This was the last day of April, and Chip, exuberant with spring energies, was still flying from window to window, busily monitoring the returning grackles. Her wild singing resonated shrilly throughout the house while I laboured on.

How was she able simultaneously to pervade every room, yet still impede my every move?

So far she'd twitched the drawing suddenly as I worked, narrowly missed destroying it with a particularly wet dropping, snapped at the moving brush, sent the ink bottle skidding, and stuck her long beak into my ear as I hung over the work, barely breathing from concentration.

She was ubiquitous. And impossible.

Suddenly in need of a finer brush for a difficult touchup, I got up and chased Chip out of the room with whirling arms and dire "threats" – one of our favourite games. Then I dashed off and back with the needed brush. In thoughtless haste I stepped over the chair to reseat myself, my foot descending out of my range of vision. From below, Chip shrieked.

I instantly shot up with an answering cry, knocking over the chair as she zoomed out of the room in a blur. The roosters, hearing sudden distress and bedlam erupt, broke into wild, alarmed clucking at a deafening pitch, and came thundering out of the studio.

Long black tailfeathers lay scattered over the floor.

I hunted and called frantically for Chip but couldn't find her anywhere. At last, unwilling to violate her obvious need for privacy, I calmed the roosters, wiped my tears, and gathered up the feathers.

Twelve of them pointed at me like accusing fingers.

Then I sat down and stared bleakly at the drawing, marvelling that something which had been so intensely engrossing could, in a twinkling, become utterly insignificant.

Ten minutes later, Chip, looking drastically stunted without her long tail, walked into the room and paused. Then she moved over to the exact spot where the accident had occurred. She stood there silently for a moment before hopping on top of my erring foot, where she remained, quietly preening, for about forty minutes.

We were still friends.

As the last days of April dissolved into May, the ripening sunlight lingered longer each day, warming the awakening land. Vanquishing hidden pockets of snow. Now red-winged blackbirds, cowbirds, and starlings mingled with the grackles, eagerly devouring seed with appetites sharpened by the rigours of migration.

Tail-less but triumphant, Chip hailed them all as they arrived.

As well as the seed scattered daily under the trees, there was several months' accumulation of whole oats emerging from the dissolving snow. These are the least-favoured seeds of my winter regulars, the blue jays. Oats, however, are a special delight for returning grackles, and I marvelled at the speed and nonchalance with which each grackle spun the oat in his bill, shearing off the hull before swallowing the kernel.

I recalled the long minutes I had spent trying clumsily with resisting fingers to hull a single oat in order to teach Chip when she was a youngster. I laboured so long with each seed that I could never hold her attention through the process. Her reluctant acceptance of the riddled remains lacked the enthusiasm of one who had accomplished the feat herself. Chip finally learned to hull oats by watching grackles up close on one of the window feeders.

Attached to the southeast dining-room window is a shallow wooden box, my most popular feeder. Near it is a huge, maternal spruce. Bursting with seedlings and broad in the hips, it surges with vitality up beyond the roof. Year after year, this tree shelters multitudes of creatures.

I call her the "Great Mother."

From the safety of the spruce, blue jays reconnoitre the skies for sharp-shinned hawks before venturing onto the window feeder. In hot weather, they sprawl luxuriously on top of the seeds, basking in the delicious heat of the sun. Sometimes there are five jays at once, if the territorial restrictions of the breeding season are past.

During the winter months, there's a particular branch favoured by mourning doves, where they rest between feedings. Falling

snow gently mounts up on their backs and heads, showing beautifully the protective insulation of their opalescent grey plumage.
Under their snowy coverlets, they doze.

Peeking out of the upper reaches of the spruce, rosebreasted
and evening grosbeaks can be seen, as well as the more sober-
coloured grey-and-white juncos, and a fascinating variety of sparrows and warblers. Flitting from tip to tip through the branches
are tiny chickadees.

And even tinier kinglets. Sheltering one briefly in the cup of
my hands one day left me in awe. I could barely sense his touch. It
was like holding a puff of warm breath on a frosty morning.

Brown creepers spiral diligently up the trunk of the Great
Mother. Ever-charming nuthatches, both white- and red-breasted,
inch their way downwards.

One day I watched a minute ruby-throated hummingbird sun-
bathing, wings and tail outspread against the dark-green needles.
His scintillating plumage, like wind rippling over grass, created an
unbelievable shimmer of iridescent beauty.

The lower branches of the huge spruce reach down and outward like a huge skirt. Safe within this enclosure, shy ruffed
grouse feed on the seed that is scattered there. Occasionally a wary
deer will peer out.

The rarest bird I've seen nurtured by the Great Mother was a varied thrush, usually a resident of the Pacific coast. He arrived one stormy Easter and eagerly devoured the blueberries that I scattered for him beneath the snow-laden branches. After the skies cleared, the blue shadows of new snowdrifts heightened the orange touches in his glowing plumage.

Robins and grackles often fill the Great Mother with hidden music. Short-eared owls have startled me out of sleep, screeching from a branch near my bedroom window. Squirrels leap from the roof to the tree, from the tree to the feeder, with enviable ease. Below, foraging raccoons lumber cautiously up the far side of the trunk. They peer around it curiously when I step outside for a look at the stars.

Drifting off to sleep in the winter nights, I can hear the thump of flying squirrels dropping out of the Great Mother onto the feeder. If I watch them in the lamplight, I see them eating cautiously, their large, luminous eyes ever vigilant. At a sudden alarm, they instantly disappear. Unexpectedly they reappear.

They blink on and off like furry fireflies.

Unfortunately, my daily passings through the small dining room invariably scattered the birds from the window feeder. I resorted to crawling through, well out of their sight, which was not easy when carrying a mug of hot tea. Especially if the telephone suddenly rang.

With triumph, one day, I mounted one-way glass on the window frame. Now in great delight I can photograph mourning doves with their sky-blue eyelids; a parent junco hulling seeds and thrusting the kernels into a fledgling's mouth; the rosy interior of a blue jay's throat as he lies outstretched in the sunshine.

I can see the eyelashes and feathered eyelids of a dozing bird, the minute tongue cleverly manipulating a seed, the subtle ripples in the sheen of sun-touched plumage.

Warm "bird breaths" on a cold day.

I can also closely examine an ailing or injured bird and determine the possibility of rendering assistance. Or monitor a newly released one.

Sometimes, as I watch creatures who can't see me, I compare one-way glass with the transformation we call death. Separation is illusion, an ancient spiritual tenet supported, to the relief of empiricists, by research in particle physics. Existence is change, and perhaps those who have experienced that next great change now participate as though on the other side of one-way glass.

In the same way that the feeding birds cannot see me, the one-way glass of our limited view prevents us from sensing their presence, whereas much has been made clear to them and now they can see both sides.

CHAPTER 4

EYES

The greatest delight of one-way glass for me is in seeing the softness in birds' eyes, that warm gentleness, that rarest of expressions which a human, suddenly spotted by a wild bird, never sees.

An expression without fear.

Once, at day's end, I was sitting on the house roof, a favourite roost, savouring a glorious sunset over the western hills. Below, Bubble and Squeak were waiting patiently under the porch light beside the back door. At last, as the fire in the clouds faded into glowing embers, I turned away reluctantly and began to descend.

Not just bodily, but refolding my inner wings as well.

Dusk was gathering under the trees and I was unwilling to jeopardize the roosters. Soon, raccoons would be on the prowl.

Just as I touched ground, I realized that there was a magnificent ruffed grouse, that favourite target for "sportsmen," fifteen feet

away, feeding on the scattered birdseed. Seeing me, he began to melt away into the darkening woods.

But hesitated.

He watched the roosters approach me in welcome. Slowly, I picked up Squeak and sat down, cuddling him in my lap and hugging Bubble under one arm. I refrained from looking directly at our wild visitor, but watched covertly as he stood eyeing us for several moments before resuming feeding.

Gradually, he crept closer. Then closer, nibbling steadily. Soon he was only a few feet away, where the seed was most plentiful.

Though the grouse undoubtedly noted my least movement, nevertheless his unceasing watchfulness seemed to be projected in every direction but mine. I thrilled at the calmness in his eyes. It was an expression I was privileged to see only because of the assurance given him, however unintentionally, by Bubble and Squeak.

I remember glancing out of the window one day in early spring. Resting on the ground directly below were three migrant robins. They spotted me and would have flown, but at that same instant County, the special robin about whom I wrote in my first book, *Sharing a Robin's Life*, landed on my shoulder. The eyes of the wildlings immediately softened.

During those moments, we were all robins.

The eyes of birds became doorways for me that enriched my thinking. County's, in particular, continually fascinated me. Their depth, which I could never hope to fathom fully. The fringe of minute eyelashes. The tiny encircling feathers raying out into larger ones, then into larger again. Ripples in a still pond.

The ever-changing shape of her eyes radiated happiness, sauciness, curiosity, annoyance, alarm, affection. And moods beyond my capacity to interpret.

The expression was indescribable when she snuggled down in her nest over her babies.

One day, I strolled outside to the outhouse, pondering how, in artwork, I might elevate that beautiful eye, so dear to me in the particular, onto a plane of universal significance. As I sat on the "throne," still holding County's image in my mind, I saw a spider. In one reality, it was on the floor at my feet, but it appeared simultaneously in another reality.

As the "secret spinner" in County's galactic eye.

Within her eye, in a womb-shaped darkness, I rendered the sparkling highlight as the eight-rayed cosmic spider spinning out the spiralling energies of creation – yet another linoprint inspired by County.

Only the cobwebby outhouse was omitted.

Nearby, a little lake lies in stillness. Dark, pointed spruce and undulating maples and birches encircle its calm beauty. Like eyes, stars stare down impassively from the heavens and glimmer in the dark water. A sudden breeze, scattering the "lake eyes," blows like the disturbing breath of that universal dragon, our human limitations. It ripples our placidity at every turn, yet by ceaseless resistance, develops our vitality. When I float out upon the water, with stars above and stars below, I experience tangibly that great unity behind apparent diversity.

I'd be moved by that same sensation when I'd gaze very closely into the limitless depths of County's eye. Dark as water under the midnight sky, yet I'd see starry thresholds within, as though her eye were a portal.

CHAPTER 5

SPRING URGES

By mid-May, Chip's new tailfeathers were becoming visible below her coverts. With increasing interest, she'd reach around to them, first from one side and then from the other, carefully preening the tips as they emerged and lengthened. Though she'd still swoop through the house quite quickly, she'd lost the twisting dexterity needed for headlong speed. The continual need to compensate for diminished steering and braking abilities had affected her velocity, but not, thankfully, the sweetness of her disposition.

Meanwhile, a celestial phenomenon was about to add its mysterious magic to the unfolding ritual of spring. One beautiful day, the sun seemed to pause in its brilliant journey overhead through the sea of infinite blue. The vibrant sunlight began to sicken.

As a strange midday dusk deepened, the eeriness increased. Migrants feeding busily beneath the trees became uneasy. Sudden calls and short flights of alarm broke out.

The total eclipse reached its dark climax with the union of the sun and moon, the circular conjunction of the alchemical dragon's head grasping its tail in its mouth. A self-devouring peak.

Time paused.

Through protective glass, I watched with utter fascination the strange ring of fire flickering overhead in the non-daylight that yet was a spring afternoon – truly, a paradoxical union of opposites. Perhaps, in the distant future, each day in our world will seem like an eclipse when the sun's fire, self-devouring like the ecliptic dragon, has burned down to cosmic embers.

Then, as I watched, the self-fertilization of the dragon's union released the sunseed. Light began to grow in the celestial womb. Slowly the world brightened again.

As though in harmony with the universal renewal, Bubble and Squeak, like true solar birds, crowed.

Everywhere, the fecundity of spring reinforced the symbolism so dramatically portrayed in the heavens. Beside a river swollen with the rushing waters of dozens of tributary brooks, I gathered edible fiddlehead ferns, tightly curled like unwakened embryos. Their expanding spirals echoed the growing warmth of the sun. The creative resurgence of life after winter's long suppression. The unwinding scroll of the seasons.

Even the whirling orbit of living, glowing Earth through dark, death-like space.

In the river shallows, a wading grackle hooked out minnows with a natural dexterity that would make fishermen envious, swallowing each fish headfirst in one effective gulp. Above the water, tiny myrtle warblers turned and swooped through the twinkling spring sunlight, flashing their yellow rumps as they dashed erratically after flying insects.

One morning, bobolinks, back from their prodigious migration to and from southern South America, surrounded me with song as I passed through the greening meadows on my way to the woods. I was plotting a painting in which clouds of eggs were an integral part, and planned to sketch salamander eggs. An old rutted road through the trees held long, irregular furrows of water. In them, salamanders annually laid eggs, suspending them in pulpy clouds of jelly.

To my distress, however, I found several clumps of eggs scattered on the ground. The deep bite of all-terrain vehicles had gashed the puddles, hurtling out eggs to dehydrate. Perhaps to die.

I instantly became a midwife.

Collecting hundreds of eggs, I immersed them gently in off-track woodland pools, being careful not to overpopulate any particular one. By adding eggs to pools in which no more than one mass floated already, I was using locations chosen not by me, but by salamanders. Only they could sense the suitability of an aqueous world in which to launch their young. Not just the obvious factor of depth would guide their choices, but perhaps also acidity, richness of nutrients, camouflage, or other considerations beyond the perceptions of a well-intentioned helper from another species.

Gently I set the last of the embryos afloat in their new watery womb, at a safe distance from thoughtless bikers. Then I sat back on the bank among unfurling leaves and pondered the symbolic significance before me.

In the traditional imagery of alchemy, salamanders, creatures of water, are depicted within flames.

Water in fire. Opposites in union. The ultimate achievement.

Salamanders living in flames were fire spirits.

I reflected that here, in the stillness of a woodland pool, I was seeing a reversal of alchemical illustrations: within the watery element was the fire. The life spirit of each salamander being, flickering within its floating egg.

Fire in water. Opposites in union.

Meanwhile, on the home front, spring energies were rampant. Outdoors, feeding among the garrulous crowds of migrant birds that were arriving and departing daily, were three charming "ladies-in-waiting," pregnant red squirrels whose bellies had grown in unison with the buds on the trees. Although they were usually content to dine companionably together, now tempers flared frequently. They'd glower at each other, spluttering with indignation. Then they'd chase one another so furiously that they'd dash blindly right between my legs. Or gallop over my feet, tripping me up.

It astounded me that any creatures so bulging with babies could bolt up tree trunks and hurtle across branches with such reckless audacity.

One morning, when all three were eating at agreed distances, glaring at one another in a markedly unmaternal manner, I noticed that one had finally been relieved of her familial burden. Before long, all three squirrels had regained their girlish girths and were obviously nursing their young.

Two nurseries had been established in separate outbuildings, where I was challenged the moment I entered by an abusive outburst of chatter. I noticed the third nest in a nearby tree cavity, a location that I easily avoided.

Like new leaves on the trees, baby squirrels were evolving with that universal beauty of young life everywhere.

Indoors, energies were also rising and finding release in more unexpected ways. Bashō the Japanese quail, in his search for amorous relief, had taken to leaping ardently and enthusiastically onto my outstretched hand. Then he'd grip my skin in his beak while drumming his feet, the proffered mealworms temporarily forgotten.

Lust was all.

With that casual indifference so characteristic of courted females in the avian world, I would take the opportunity instead to stroke his outspread plumage and delight in the gorgeous interwoven patterns.

Occasionally, he would vent his feelings on my foot. Or, to my intense embarrassment, on someone else's foot. If visitors were present, delicate explanations became necessary.

Especially to puzzled children.

Since he was so tiny and walked more than he flew, shoes were a source of identification for Bashō, much as faces are for humans. He was so familiar with my particular shoes that the sudden apparition of a strange pair was always exciting.

The arrival one afternoon of a tall male visitor with shoes the size of fishing dories brought out questioning squeaks of near alarm. Bashō cautiously circled him on tiptoe, neck outstretched warily and eyes round with disbelief.

Fortunately, the visitor's ignorance of quail body language spared him the rosy flush that suffused my own face at that moment.

Several people at once, each with a different type of shoe, would rouse such intense interest that Bashō would be overcome with exhaustion after they'd left. Eyes closed and legs thrust limply out to one side, he'd lie, dozing in seclusion until he felt restored.

As one who, beset by earthly frustrations, seeks austere self-discipline, Bashō began to spend several periods each day running. Choosing two particular terminals, and varying them occasionally, he'd complete lap after lap between those points by the half hour, trotting steadily with the dogged concentration of a marathon athlete in training. If anyone stepped in his path, he'd chitter with evident annoyance and make a detour.

"Tourists!" he seemed to mutter as he pattered by, lacking only a sweaty undershirt with a number on it.

His energies became so charged that he'd leap up a foot into the air with uncontrollable eagerness when I descended the stairs holding mealworms. During nights, he began sudden bizarre flights in utter darkness, rebounding off walls and ceilings while I groped frantically for a light switch. For his own safety, to say nothing of my peace of mind, I was compelled to set a padded cage-like cover over him as he slept. Even then, I would hear him periodically bashing himself against it when I awoke in the night.

Truly, Bashō's name had become a double entendre.

Once, Bashō's romantic aspirations were nearly consummated. Chip's own spring fervour had driven her to gathering "nesting" material from all over the house. She'd swoop from window to window, calling to the male grackles, an untidy wad of string, shredded paper, and plant fibres held alluringly in her beak. At times, she'd carry such billowings of shredded paper towels that she'd be fluttering erratically through the air, wholly unable to see before her, and groping for the perches as she hovered above them.

One day she discovered, hanging beside the kitchen counter, a crocheted bag which contained a ball of string. Since a bit of string emerged from the top of the bag she was able to pull out lengths quite readily. She pulled out more and more, and I entered the room just as she'd discovered that her feet were entangled in it.

I was horrified.

I rushed towards her but she instantly took wing, only to fall to the floor as the unwinding string snagged in the bag. I tried to grab her but she thrashed frantically. I jerked out extra string to ease her and reached for her again. This time she shot up, flapping desperately, only to be felled in front of the woodstove. There she lay, her feet tied together, her wings and tail still outstretched.

At that same moment, Bashō emerged from under the wood-stove where he'd been napping, only to find a female bird sprawled enticingly before him.

With a squeal of enthusiasm, he hurled himself on top.

Chip squawked and struggled, but Bashō ardently gripped her neck feathers, spread his tiny wings for balance, and struggled to keep his footing.

Choking with laughter, I finally held Chip and pried Bashō off. He was actually trembling with excitement. A tuft of grackle feathers was still clutched in his passionate beak, and he growled with annoyance at the disruption. Chip fled as soon as I untangled her feet, but Bashō strutted about everywhere, peering for her hopefully.

It was difficult to decide which of the two had greater need of sympathy.

Fortunately, Chip's friendship with Bashō remained intact after this assault, but her nesting longings were growing as quickly as the young leaves that trembled in the soft spring breezes. Out in the screened porch, she absorbed courtship rituals and myriad sounds of new life flourishing everywhere. As I sat there with her, I could hear baby starlings inside a ventilator atop a nearby barn excitedly cheering every arrival of a food-laden parent at the nest, then diminishing into drowsy *chr-r-r*s when they were left alone once more. I wondered, too, how many more nestlings she could hear than I, and how strongly she was affected.

Each day rang with trilling finches and bobolinks, while frogsong permeated the starry hours. A male ruby-throated humming-bird hovered at the feeder, driving off other males and ardently swooping before the females with highspeed aerial displays.

Chipmunks, freed from the long tyranny of darkness within their winter burrows, scampered through the sun-warmed rows of young peas that greened the garden. Outside the garden fence, and too close to the tomato plants for my peace of mind, a plump groundhog mowed steadily through leafy variegated goutweed with the singlemindedness of a child with a plate of cookies.

Banks of forget-me-nots surrounded the house with a beauty I find unique to blue flowers, and each day was exquisitely sweetened with the nostalgic fragrance of apple blossoms. Nearby, a tangle of arching roots and broad leaves held a secret from the whirling world around them – in a tiny nest underneath, four helpless, downy babies were snuggled below the warm wings of a protective mother junco.

Indoors, Chip began in earnest to build a nest.

Her manic shredding of the string mop compelled me to bring her handfuls of damp, dead grass, which she welcomed eagerly. As the work progressed, I added twigs and lichens. I also moistened the earth in the indoor garden so she could incorporate mud to hold everything together, but she showed little interest in using it.

She divided her courtship displays between the wild grackles beyond the windows, and me, arching her wings and newly grown tail amid an outpouring of seductive squeaks and warbles. When she wanted to mate, she suddenly froze in front of me, crouched with her head up, her eyes fixed and her tail raised, while I gently stroked her back. Then she vibrated her wings in a short blur as though finishing a bath.

Speaking for myself, I found her wholly irresistible.

Finally one morning, Chip's usual high spirits were subdued and she lay in her new nest, beak open and her eyes closed in an inward-looking aura of stillness. Her breathing became laboured and punctuated regularly with small grunts – but no egg arrived.

Later in the day, she resumed her gathering activities and added finishing touches to her nest. This time it featured shredded cushions and a plastic bag; a plastic drinking straw followed shortly by the paper sleeve that had enclosed it; a roll of paper labels which I was trying to use and had to retrieve twice; a plastic photo sleeve and a package of postage stamps; a cartridge of writing ink.

Her nest now resembled an eccentric yard sale.

By nightfall Chip's cycle was definitely peaking. She was so drowsy and weary that, for the first time in my memory, her impish eyes lacked their usual fanatical gleam and mirth.

At seven-thirty the following morning Chip laid her first egg, a beautiful aqua colour with the irregular dark markings so helpful for camouflage.

Immediately afterwards, she soared in long, exhilarating flights throughout the length of the house before returning to stand on the edge of the nest with dancing eyes, doting on her prize. Then she stepped in and wriggled down over her egg, suffused with the sudden dignity and maturity of a new mother. For the rest of the morning she brooded off and on, discarding her usual teasing nature as though it belonged to her juvenile phase.

But later, as if unable to constrain her charged energies to the monotony of steady brooding, she began, illogically to me, to pile on more and more "nesting material," packing it well into the existing structure with vigorous kicks. Pieces of yarn, grocery receipts, even an elaborate bookmark mysteriously vanished into the maw of the nest.

I'd be the last to suggest that I know more about building nests than a bird, but surely even the most creative ones aren't built *on top* of the eggs.

By the end of the day, a prolonged probing through her heap of collected litter failed to reveal the egg, and I assumed that it had been crushed and incorporated into the walls. I had already expressed the metaphysical unity of a brooding bird and her nest in my artwork, but this irreverent fusion of egg and nest broke all previous records.

The next morning brought a second egg, which I hastily photographed lest it go the way of the other, but Chip grew calmer and showed no inclination to continue nest-building. For the next couple of days she showed no interest in brooding, either, but roamed restlessly from window to window while I watched with deepening concern. Her attraction towards the male grackles now seemed tinged with desperation.

For weeks I had been weighing the issues involved with releasing Chip. My love for her was never a barrier to her freedom, since her happiness was paramount. I could open the door for her no matter how I felt. What had been holding me back was her latent sickness, controlled but never eradicated by tetracycline.

Not only would she be at risk, but, if she raised a family,

would the nestlings receiving food from her mouth also be at risk? I had made inquiries, but no one knew any more than I.

Another serious consideration was Chip's strong trust in humans. If she got into difficulties, she might seek help from a human. Someone who might violate her trust. Or even cage her as a curiosity.

Though I often lay awake at night pondering Chip's situation, in the end I decided reluctantly to yield to her pleading. The stress of frustration could initiate another bout of sickness anyway. Her trusting nature, too, would have to be risked.

Thus, on a beautiful June morning, I coaxed a startled Chip outside on my hand.

As the full implications of my actions suddenly dawned on her, she hopped onto my head, paused, then lifted into a tree, gazing around as though newly awakened. I glided back into the house so I wouldn't discourage wild grackles from coming closer. From the windows I watched eagerly.

As soon as a few males arrived to feed, Chip flew to them in great excitement, going from one to another, posturing and singing before them shamelessly.

Maidenly modesty would never cramp her style.

Hours later, when I strolled into the screened porch, I called Chip's name half-heartedly, not necessarily expecting her to be within range. To my astonishment, not only did she answer, she flew out of the serviceberry tree onto the feeder. Excitedly I opened the door and she hopped briskly onto my hand, then flew into the house. After bathing and eating she indulged in a little after-dinner devilishness – tossing cutlery off the counter and pruning a few cherished houseplants – before drowsily retiring for a nap.

Regarding her outside venture, she maintained a discreet silence.

I, on the other hand, was bursting with questions: Did she meet anyone "interesting"? Was she rejected? Would she want to go outside again? Would she rather stay in? I railed against our linguistic limitations.

Very early next morning, Chip sat for a long while preening on the side of my head as I lay dozing in bed. Still wondering if she would leave, perhaps forever, I savoured this special moment together. The pressure of her warm feet on my face. The gentle rustle of her feathers by my ear. The aura that enclosed us.

Would Chip stay?

CHAPTER 6

SUMMER SOLSTICE

The magic of summer solstice was upon us, the beginning of that paradoxical waning of sunlight just as spring accelerates into the fullness of summer.

For me, each solstice has great significance. I welcome these pivotal times of the year with a ritual fast and vigil. Exchanging my usual comforts for solitude and introspection enriches my life.

And my work.

Therefore I fasted throughout this June day in acknowledgement of our gradual descent into darkness. All night I sat on a nearby hilltop, my thoughts as paradoxical as the turning of the year, for my mind mused instead on the rich new life around me.

High above, the dark skies were sown with scatterings of bright celestial seeds. From the marsh in the east, the continuous ringing of spring peepers mingled with the deeper, sustained trills of American toads. Barred and long-eared owls called from woods to the south and west of me. To the north lay the huddled darkness of my home among the trees, filled with, and surrounded by, sleeping birds. Under the waxing moon, the silvery meadow around me whispered with mysterious rustlings of the invisible. The pattering of unseen feet passing. The aeolian strumming of tall grasses.

I stood in the centre of myself.

The centre of my hilltop.

The centre of my world.

In my hands I held smouldering herbs. Their pungent, purifying aroma mingled with the gentle breathings that moved over the land, uniting us all. Uplifted, I honoured the great mystery of which I was a fragment.

Then, in stillness, I sat awaiting the dawn.

Closing my eyes, I breathed in the sweetness of the cool, damp air. Heard the buzzing cries of a nighthawk darting overhead. Felt the touch of moving grasses.

Opening my eyes, I marvelled at the startling brilliance of each meteorite as it flared across the heavens. At constellations rich in mythic history, still wheeling slowly to an ancient cadence around the pole star.

As I sat, I knew that the three young skunks who had been born under the shed would be on the move with their foraging mother. Each dusk I'd seen her emerge and lie down guardedly while her excited babies tumbled over her or played nearby. Then she'd collect them together and melt away into the gathering darkness. Her hearing and sense of smell maintained unceasing vigilance. But her nearsightedness allowed me one evening to move close enough downwind to photograph her charming family.

An outside houselight twinkling through the trees reminded me that moths would be flitting all night through the open door and into the brightness of the screened porch. There, in the morning, I would shut them in and open the door to the house so that Bashō and Chip could rejoice in moths for breakfast.

Competition between them was as fierce for moths as for

mealworms. Of necessity, I became the referee, since the moths lay upon the screens well out of Bashō's reach. Whenever I caught one, I'd hold it down to him. There'd be a quick gulp and a puff of moth dust. Then Bashō would be tugging impatiently at my pantleg for more. Chip's delight lay not only in catching her own moths but in snatching them out of my fingers as well, with exasperating dexterity. She was always quicker than I.

The night hours lingered on my hilltop.

Remembered images of spring twinkled in my mind's eye like the stars above me: a tiny spring peeper poised near me on a tarragon leaf as I planted lettuce seeds. The delicacy of chokecherry blossoms, their singular fragrance. The unearthly wail of loons echoing over the stillness of the misted lake. A hummingbird hawkmoth hovering energetically over the sweet rocket blooms. The rich sheen of a groundhog's fur as he basked in the sunshine.

Cursing that rich sheen after discovering severed tomato plants.

I shifted restlessly and refocussed on more pleasant memories.

The almost palpable perfume of sun-warmed lilacs. Towering stalks of creamy rhubarb flowers, surrounded by clouds of tiny dancing insects. The first swallowtail butterfly. A silken foal with mild, wondering eyes. Unfurling ferns under the studio windows. Slim beanstalks bearing new leaves.

Beanstalks bearing *no* leaves. Just slugs.

I shifted again.

The heady exhilaration of spreading pungent horse manure on garden beds. The painfully sweet carolling of robins at dusk. A rufous flash of fox slipping silently into the woods. A blizzard of windblown blossoms whitening the ground. The curious sight of an eclipsed moon with the earth's shadow taking a bite out of the bottom. The unsettling rumble of approaching thunder.

The corresponding rumble of my nervous system.

An early memory surfaced, of myself and a large dog squeezed under a tiny table during a thunderstorm, both of us howling, while our combined trembling rattled the crockery above.

I chuckled nostalgically, then glanced warily around the horizon. No large clouds were blotting out the stars, so I resumed my recollections.

And recalled the tiny dark toad who hopped casually away from my unmindful foot, which was descending onto him in the garden. The four starling fledglings from the barn ventilator nest *chr-r-r*ing softly in the trees beside the house. Morning dewdrops on spider webs, twinkling like stars caught during the night.

Throughout the darkened woods around my hilltop, nestcups of all sizes glowed with quickening life. Brooding mothers dozed lightly, vigilant ears tingling in every feather. The surging spirit of renewal pervaded even their nightly sleep with latent energies.

However, like the darkness that completes each day, like the solstice sun declining during the season of renewal, even like the rocks impeding growing roots, the universal "dragon" of arrest ever opposes the rising spirit.

As birds return by the thousands, seeking suitable habitat in which to nurture their families, the distress of rising roadkills tempers our delight in this migratory ritual. And though one acknowledges without question the right of hawks to sustain themselves, still one's unreasoning heart is moved by the sudden death of a familiar favourite that has been so magically restored after a stupendous journey of thousands of miles.

But the fiercest dragon by far is a well-fed housecat seeking, not food, but the unthinkable torture of smaller creatures for amusement – perhaps a nestling unable to elude the piercing teeth. Perhaps a nursing squirrel, rabbit, or mouse, whose babies then dwindle into starvation.

One of my lifelong campaigns is to give away small, copper "cowbells," the most effective alarm bells I've discovered, to kind-hearted cat owners willing to take responsible action to reduce such unnecessary suffering amongst wildlife.

As I sat in the cool night air, marvelling at the starry mysteries above me, I recalled that this spring a new hazard had presented itself. A new wrinkle to the eternal dragon. A fortnight earlier, a woman had coated a pole that held her hummingbird feeder with a sticky substance to deter ants. Unfortunately, a female purple finch had come into contact with the pole and her struggling wings had become stuck to her body, rendering her absolutely helpless.

Following directions from a mutual friend, the woman had cleaned the feathers with lanolin-based hand cream, followed by a water rinse. Then the bedraggled bird had been brought to me.

I had released her into my "hospice" – the room off the living room reserved for such avian emergencies. It had begun as a carving studio, and still contained my supplies, but a yearly succession of needy birds had driven me to carve outside instead. The little finch settled in well, eating a variety of seeds and managing short flights among the branches that I had installed permanently at varying levels.

The first finch song that rippled sweetly out of the hospice sent Bashō scurrying for the deepest recesses of the indoor garden. Low, buzzy growls floated out from amongst the leaves. Eventually he asserted himself and poised staunchly out in the open, crowing his defiance.

Chip, however, was curious. She perched near the hospice door, peering in with gleaming eyes. Given half an opportunity, she could create enough consternation to downgrade a "convalescent" finch to "permanently disabled."

I locked the door firmly.

Early the following morning I picked up a stunned song sparrow on the edge of a busy highway. One wing and the side of his head were both swollen but, thankfully, no bones were broken. He joined the purple finch in the hospice. There, until their release shortly before the solstice, both birds had lived in harmony, eating well and flying more strongly day by day. A selection of seeds and grit, fresh water daily for bathing and drinking, privacy from humans, and protection from predators were all they had required.

My deepest regret was the unfortunate disruption to their family lives at this crucial time of year.

During those same days I noticed a weak pine siskin near the silo feeder that held niger seeds. His eyes were groggy and his body slumped. When the other siskins and goldfinches left to roost for the night, he managed to eat a little, but tumbled off the perches several times. Exhausted finally, and persuaded no doubt by the deepening darkness, he composed himself to sleep on the lamplit vine that clustered around the window beside the feeder.

This would never do.

He needed protection from nocturnal predators, yet I didn't dare bring him indoors in case he had a contagious illness. In the end, I slipped outside, lifted him gently off the vine, and laid him, calm and unprotesting, to rest on a soft cloth inside a box, carefully closing the lid. The night was warm so I left the box inside the screened porch, keeping both doors closed, so he might cross that next threshold in peace, not torment.

In the morning, his spirit had indeed departed, and I buried the remains beneath evergreens of renewal.

As the moon drifted through the stars above my hilltop, I recalled glimpses I had caught of the dragon of arrest seeking fulfilment up in the skies.

One afternoon, in a dramatic aerial display, a sharp-shinned hawk crossed the sky, challenged both in turn and simultaneously, by swallows, grackles, and starlings as his threatening shadow clove through their nesting territories.

The hawk swooped this way and that, trying to elude his pursuers. He rolled over in flight with talons unleashed. Outraged cries filled the skies as the birds swept past overhead. Their wings hissed loudly in the watchful silence below.

Another day, I witnessed a starling, followed hotly by a demanding baby, chasing away a crow.

At times I find it difficult to reconcile myself to the dragon's bite. Late one afternoon, I had just emerged from the woods near the house when suddenly I heard piercing shrieks. Looking up, I saw a sharp-shinned hawk fly past only fifteen feet above my head, a beautiful blue jay fledgling gripped in his talons. The youngster was screaming terribly, and the parent bird was following, also screaming.

But the dragon had the last word.

For the hours of daylight that remained, the parent blue jay sat in a tree just outside the studio window, calling over and over and over again. Piteous, heartbreaking cries that drove me to play loud music I didn't want to hear, while simultaneously wearing ear protectors designed to muffle the roar of heavy machinery.

Still her cries pierced my heart.

In the night, when all was quiet, I heard them yet within me. Saw the talons puncturing the babe. Felt the pain and fear.

The ubiquitous Tree of Life is formed of creatures whose energies rise and fall like sap through the trunk. Our entwining spirits branch out continually. Like leaves we fall, enriching the roots. Like buds, we are renewed.

Those who pass through the dark silhouette of the hawk lift into flight on other journeys, transfigured.

The dragon opens doors.

And is always present. Perhaps as a sharp-shinned hawk. Perhaps in the desperate struggle that lands or loses a piece of art. Perhaps as disease.

Even perhaps as the desire to abandon my fasting vigil, which I was resisting as I sat throughout the night hungry, tired, and cold, on my hilltop.

A friend of mine once blessed me with a humorous insight into this painful reality of life devouring life. I was feeding live mealworms to Chip and Bashō in turn, a daily ritual which I am forced to tolerate out of necessity. He smiled, but with great understanding.

"Just think of them as mealworms learning to fly," he said.

It was perfect.

From the darkness of my solitary hilltop beneath the watchful, Argus-eyed heavens, I could see the eastern horizon beginning to brighten, much as my painful memory of the young blue jay brightened when I remembered the greater vision of which he forms a part. I flexed my chilled limbs and rocked on my toes, trying to generate even an illusion of warmth.

As the sunlight grew stronger, my feeling of harmony also deepened. My forty-hour fast and my nocturnal vigil had strengthened and enriched me.

The welcoming, down-to-earth clamour from the birds that broke over me as I entered the house balanced the austerity of my night, and a nourishing breakfast followed, joining both worlds into one.

Just as the solstice had joined spring to summer.

CHAPTER 7

STUDIO DISTRACTIONS

Chip's nesting drive came to a boil again, and her restlessness grew so acute that once more I opened the door for her. Again she lifted into the trees, ardently pursuing the males, though I was certain they'd long been paired with mates. She remained out through the next three nights, visiting me once or twice daily for mealworms or moths, lingering companionably on my shoulder before departing again. She refused to enter the house but would wait until I had reentered and returned with a few mealworms for her. Then she'd disappear until our next visit.

Late on the third day of her outdoor life, Chip landed on me as I left the house. I turned back to get her the usual mealworm offering but, to my surprise, she rode indoors on my shoulder. While I searched through the bran in the aquarium, Chip hopped down and quickly selected her own mealies. As I dropped several in front of Bashō, she immediately stole two in her familiar devilish way.

After a drink in the indoor garden, she followed me to my usual chair in the screened porch near the open door.

She showed no desire whatever to leave.

Instead, she preened quietly on my shoulder in her characteristic way before falling into a sound sleep. But breathing with her head tilted back. Her beak open. In the silence I heard again the ominous crackling in her lungs with every breath.

Chip was sick once again and had come home to stay.

I immediately offered her a little crumbled tofu coated with tetracycline-based medicine, which she ate without argument. By the next morning she seemed noticeably improved and refused her medicine. I feigned an indifference I certainly didn't feel and suddenly seized her, catching her totally off-guard. Then I dribbled the antibiotic down into her protesting throat.

Six hours later, when another dose was required, she in turn caught me off-guard by swallowing doctored tofu with every indication of enjoyment.

But I knew better.

The fourth session erupted into a frenzied free-for-all, until I finally threw a shirt over her in the confines of the screened porch. Once again, I forced the medicine into her mouth, a single drop without tofu.

Clearly these tactics would never do. I reflected grimly that we had sixteen drops over four days yet to anticipate. After a few days' respite, a second treatment over three days would be necessary. Even granting Chip's delight in games, and especially in outwitting me, the stress of physical capture would still offset the benefit of the medicine.

Besides, she was a poor loser.

After the last scramble, she'd left in a fury, sulking for hours and pointedly ignoring me. With her cleverness, I would need sixteen different ploys just to complete the first treatment. Each trick would work only once, and I knew my limitations.

The solution, when it finally pierced my mounting exasperation, was ridiculously simple. I coated Chip's first mealworms of the day with tetracycline and presented them on a take-them-or-leave-them basis.

She took them.

Thereafter, she was given doctored mealies at appropriate intervals, with only occasional treats of uncoated mealies in between. Soon all indications of sickness had vanished and Chip and I were buddies once more. But she chose to remain indoors.

It wasn't long, though, before I realized that one part of Chip had never returned. She still delighted in monitoring the wild grackles from the windows but not, I was relieved to see, with the acute desperation of earlier days. I sensed that she understood and accepted her physical limitations, since she reverted once more to her many indoor interests.

But often, perhaps when she was teasing Bashō in the indoor garden, or sampling supper off my tongue, or jumping down onto the clothes in the washing machine as it filled with water, or indulging in any one of a number of entertaining pursuits, Chip would hear the voice of one *particular* grackle. She'd explode instantly into shrill answering shrieks, then tear off to whatever window gave her the closest view of Prince Charming.

Chip had given her heart.

In time, even I managed to distinguish his voice from those of the other grackles, a higher, sharper sound, and we'd often watch him together, Chip positively pressed against the glass. When he began to bring his youngsters to the dining-room feeder, little did he know that Chip was ardently steaming patches on the one-way glass with her breath. None of the other grackles had ever had this effect on her.

Remembering bygone days when my own youthful eyes had been glued adoringly to the embarrassed recipient of my thumping heart, both Chip and her chosen one had my utmost sympathy.

Meanwhile, my efforts to maintain some sense of progress in my artwork were being severely challenged on all sides.

Indoors, Chip eased her pent-up energies by darting about the studio and distracting me beyond reason. Clearly understanding the invisible boundary I insisted upon around the acrylic paint, she would deliberately seize beakfuls of it whenever my vigilance momentarily waned. Finding it difficult to wave my arms like a windmill and paint at the same time, I'd finally snatch up a broom and drive her off in a hailstorm of curdling threats. Routed temporarily, Chip would whisk into the indoor garden and rinse her beak in Bashō's waterdish.

Only later would I discover with horror that his sole source of drinking water was now a strident green or repulsive purple.

At the beginning of one particular day, which is seared on my memory, Chip added her own inimitable touch to a finished canvas. She pranced cockily across the wet varnish and defecated on it while I was cleaning the brush. As I worked frantically to clean the mess before the varnish dried, I felt grateful that at least she hadn't touched the newly primed canvas as well. At that moment, she shot past my face, gripping a wad of paper towel coated with wet white primer. Unable to leave the varnish mess, I could only wail helplessly.

When I finally did thunder after her, I found that she'd shredded the soggy towel with typical grackle thoroughness all over the living-room floor and furniture, as well as over herself. White smears mocked me from every direction.

This was definitely one of those days.

I finally returned to the studio, only to find her mangling the bristles on a new brush. As I leaped forward to rescue the brush, I crushed several sticks of imported willow charcoal that she'd tossed on the floor. Cursing hysterically, I chased her out with a broom. Then settled down in rigid desperation to paint.

Wrapped finally in creative bliss, I failed to notice that Chip had returned until I was rudely awakened by her knocking a glass of juice all over my paints. Goaded beyond my limits, I hurled at her everything I could lay my hands on.

Including, in the heat of the moment, a brush I had just loaded with paint.

With fatal predictability, it passed by her harmlessly, splattered instead off the wall outside the studio door, and skidded across the carpet in a brilliant trail of thalocyanine blue.

Not satisfied yet, Chip tried another familiar ploy – remaining quietly out of sight until, in unspeakable frustration, I covered the paints and went looking for her.

Peace meant mischief.

Therefore I was only marginally surprised to find her ingeniously shredding wallpaper in the dining room. After a minor skirmish, I continued to the kitchen, where I discovered that Bashō's bag of turkey starter, which I had unthinkingly left on the counter instead of returning to the fridge, had been ripped open in several places. Pellets were scattered right through to the living room. Cooked macaroni and rice, set aside for the roosters, also lay in sticky clumps as far as the eye could see.

Had there been a fly on the wall, I'd have been deafened by his mirth.

Outdoors, distractions were just as plentiful. But not so disastrous.

Three litters of charming, adolescent squirrels, cocky and independent, now swarmed around the house, scampering under my feet, scrambling all over the feeders, and chattering incessantly. I'd squirt them with the plant mister, opened to its most aggressive setting, whenever they hung upside down along the silo feeder wolfing down expensive niger seed. Priced as it was, I preferred to reserve it for finches and siskins. The squirrels were welcome to share anything else.

One morning, when I carried seed over to the flip-top feeder with the glass sides, I found one young squirrel inside and another on top preventing him from getting out. Their antics were endlessly amusing.

Raccoons, on the other hand, failed to enchant me.

Their big woolly behinds overflowing my little wooden feeders were indeed humorous. Their deft fingers picking up handfuls of birdseed intriguing. Even their masked faces and chronic expression of guilt entertaining.

What failed to enthrall me were the scores of muddy paw prints smeared so revoltingly over the windows most of the year. Or the loathsome mounds of excrement I found in the outside waterdish every morning. Or the nightly screeching that repeatedly jolted me awake as six or eight corpulent raccoons bounded merrily all over the roof outside my bedroom window – not unlike college students on a spree.

In the wee hours, one's tolerance is at low tide.

Grimly I began setting the live-trap. Although there were days when I caught and released squirrels, cats, skunks, and even blue jays, lured equally and incomprehensibly by stale peanut butter, still I managed in time to move fourteen raccoons out of the immediate area. Peace and cleanliness prevailed once again.

Wherever I looked, nature distracted me from my artwork. Yet nourished it too.

Looking out the studio window, I watched as a chickadee clung to a crocheted plant hanger, collecting a huge beakful of fluffy yarn fibres to line a nest.

When I checked on the roosters, I saw, on the branches above them, sleek waxwings gathering serviceberries.

As I walked out to the mailbox each day, I was surrounded by daisies, bladderwort, yarrow, butter-and-eggs, sweet rocket, clover, thistle, buttercups, and so many more. All coming and going in their season. All sweetening the air with heart-piercing fragrance.

Lingering by the open window one evening, I listened to a barred owl hooting from the hills. His throaty call added a final touch to the beauty of a full moon in a clear sky, as fireflies twinkled among the trees.

One morning I looked up from a drawing to see a junco trapped under the garden netting that protected the pepper plants. As I released her, I felt my inner self, in empathy, take wing with her away from the menace of the net.

Sometimes I'd pause, paintbrush in hand, just listening. Bubble and Squeak would crow, their strident calls echoing down the valley. Then they'd pause. From the lake, I'd hear loons calling. When they paused, the roosters would crow again. The loons would respond again. I couldn't help wondering if they were communicating with one another.

Around the feeders, communications were definitely at a peak. The raucous cries of young grackles, clashing with the strange whinnies of blue jay fledglings, furnished a year's worth of vocal discordance over a few weeks.

Out the studio window I glimpsed a grackle youngster flying strongly across the sky, a watchful parent off his starboard stern. Having raised so many nestlings myself, I actually felt a vicarious parental pride in his progress.

One evening I followed a sudden desire to drive to the shore. A brilliant afterglow lit the western sky above the ocean, while glowing stars and planets heightened the deep blue-black of the eastern sky. Small, luminous ponds sprang up abruptly in the shadowy fields as I passed, revealing the indescribable beauty of water holding the light long after the land has darkened.

As our spirits still hold the light though our bodies fade into darkness.

During a routine trip to buy groceries one morning, I drove

beside a long lake covered with hundreds of white water lilies. On my other side, the power lines blossomed with rows and rows of white-fronted tree swallows, both juvenile and adult. Marvellous how one simple observation can brighten one's day.

Or one's evening.

Slipping outdoors for a brief walk after supper, I was startled when a sparrow suddenly shot out of a bush beside me. I peered down through the dense branches and, to my utter delight, spotted a tiny nest with speckled beige eggs. Then I hurried on, not wishing to alarm the sparrow by lingering. But the secret nest stayed in my memory – and reappeared in my artwork in many ways.

One day I was holding up a thick plank of birch wood and pondering a carving idea. Suddenly an adult junco and her baby landed fleetingly on the end of the swaying board while the mother hastily thrust food into the baby's throat. Then they both swooped off. A brief moment of magic.

Another time I was drawing a lakeside tree when my attention was caught by a young osprey trying to feed himself. He flopped down into the water repeatedly, trying to grab a fish with his talons. Evidently his aspirations were still ahead of his skills. With obvious difficulty, he hauled himself out for the last time, still fish-less, and sat morosely on a low branch, drying his sodden plumage.

One could only sympathize.

Everywhere, innumerable distractions lured me out of the studio, intriguing observations of the natural world that heightened with the fullness of summer. Adolescents of many species were trying to make their own way with successful or fatal results.

And sometimes a little participation from a sympathetic artist was helpful at these crucial times.

CHAPTER 8

A ROBIN YOUNGSTER

About seven o'clock one evening in early July, a two-week-old robin was brought to me in a very weakened condition.

Since at this age she would normally be out of the parental nest, being taught the principles of survival by her father while her mother built a second nest for a second family, I concluded that something drastic had happened to "Dad." Since her head was not noticeably dark, as is characteristic with young males, I realized that this youngster was a female.

She lay totally inert in my hand, eyes closed, unable to sit upright. I found no cat saliva or any indication of injury, but her crop, that food-storage chamber in the breast, felt empty and bony.

She was on the brink of starvation and dehydration.

I forcefed her raw egg yolk beaten up with avian vitamin powder and a little tetracycline, shooting it slowly into the back of her throat with a syringe, and popped in occasional mealworms with my fingers for more solid fare. Due to her age and her crucial condition, I timed her feedings at twenty- to thirty-minute intervals, to approximate natural feeding intervals, carefully restricting her to small amounts so that she wouldn't be threatened by overfeeding. As the little robin's energies began to rise, I started to include earthworms as well.

Although songbird nestlings are usually fed from sun-up to sun-down only, I fed this youngster until past eleven o'clock that same night. By then, she was sitting up quite perkily in my hands, her large eyes bright with that beauty and depth so characteristic of robins'.

Soon she was looking much more alert than I was.

Taking this as my cue, I tucked her into a warm box by a lamp, cuddling her into a nest of towels, which I hoped she'd find reassuring. Then I laid another towel gently over the top of the box, leaving a small area open for air circulation, and turned off the rest of the lights.

Finally, I crawled wearily into bed.

In only a few short hours I, like any other robin parent, would need to be ready to serve a normal, hearty breakfast of worms and mixed insects to my hungry young.

The following morning, the little robin continued to improve, gaping voluntarily for food instead of resisting all my efforts as she had the previous night. She sat up energetically in my hands and hopped slowly and curiously across the carpet when I set her down by my feet. I felt pure delight in watching her bathe happily in the waterdish and carefully tend her plumage.

When I listened closely, I could hear a slight click in her lungs with every breath, the effects of chilling and malnutrition, but I felt confident that persisting with tetracycline would vanquish any incubating illness.

Chip's initial reaction to this new arrival was undisguised jealousy and annoyance.

She snapped repeatedly at the interloper, her headfeathers bristling. The situation called for a continual outpouring of affection and reassurance from me to Chip, and soon she became, if not particularly friendly, at least tolerant towards our visitor. When I acknowledge the special deep love I have for all robins, and Chip's powers of perception and sensitivity, I don't wonder she was jealous.

Lulled by his diminutive size, I was astounded by Bashō's reaction.

When he spotted the robin hopping slowly across the floor, he hurled himself on her with a menacing growl, gripping a mouthful of plumage and shaking her, while his own back feathers stood upright aggressively. The robin shrieked and struggled.

I immediately flung myself into the fray, quickly untangling them. Then I cradled her protectively in my hands, murmuring reassurance into her soft feathers while I glared hideously at Bashō. Undaunted, he still bristled indignantly and stalked about searching for the vanished enemy.

The floor was clearly Bashō's particular territory, so the robin and I retreated to the "hospice" room and closed the adjoining door. For those times when I wasn't available as a bodyguard, she would need this haven in which she could recuperate in peace.

Fortunately, Bubble and Squeak were as tolerant of this youngster as they'd been of Chip in her juvenescence. They often slumbered in my lap while the little robin sat cozily on my finger and Chip gazed coldly from my shoulder.

However, one evening, when the robin tired of immobility, she suddenly hopped down onto Squeak's back, arousing only a sleepy glance from him as she paused there. Then she clambered awkwardly across both recumbent roosters and slid down onto "Bashō's floor."

There was an almost audible "AHA!"

A tiny, but vigilant, quail suddenly scooted out of invisibility straight onto his prey. A wild tussle erupted, the robin shrieking and flailing, Bashō hanging on grimly and growling. Bubble and

Squeak were bounced rudely off my lap, squawking their protests as I scrambled to the rescue, while Chip, ever delighted to contribute confusion to any sudden diversion, swooped round and round the antagonists, screeching shrilly.

Whatever remnants of peace still floated above the turbulence were ruthlessly shattered by my own vehement imprecations directed against anyone foolish enough to live with birds.

But outnumbering these moments were others diffusing unforgettable harmony.

When Bashō was busily hunting fallen moths out in the screened porch, I'd temporarily close the connecting door and set the robin down on the dining-room carpet. There, Chip would dance playfully around her, gently tweaking her tail and obviously encouraging her to try a game of "chase." It was warming to see the robin's own innate playfulness gradually emerge.

The two of them would be so enjoyable to watch that I'd wonder contrarily why more people didn't choose to live with birds.

The little robin progressed rapidly.

Soon she began catching her own meals in the "bug box" – a dishpan I had stocked with various worms, insects, and spiders in a few inches of damp dirt. Unfortunately, she now rejected the sluggish earthworms that she could so easily pick up.

And I could as easily supply.

Instead, she preferred the flat brown centipedes that whizzed dizzily around the perimeter of the pan – creatures moving too rapidly for her to catch as yet.

And too rapidly for me, some days.

This left her with sowbugs, caterpillars, mealworms, and other slower-moving insects. They fell within the limited range of her developing capabilities, and began to teach her proficiency in hunting.

Whenever I dabbled my finger in the waterdish, creating shimmering ripples of light, the moving water would entice her over and she'd drink eagerly with engaging adolescent awkwardness.

During the young robin's recuperation, I was obliged to deliver a load of artwork to a gallery some distance away. This also involved hours of setting up a show, then remaining awhile to speak to viewers brave enough to venture near.

Accordingly, one fine morning the van was carefully stacked to the roof with large canvases and a complicated assortment of boxes containing carvings, sculptures, and framed works. Then I added a well-stocked bug box, a bottle of water, a waterdish, and avian medicine. And last of all, a small, draped box containing a puzzled young robin.

Upon stopping in the gallery driveway, my first task was to lift her out of the box for a feeding. To my surprise, she did not emerge in her usual sunny humour.

She came out glowering.

Unfamiliar confinement, the constant roar of the engine, and hours of lurching over the winding shore road had taken their toll. She gripped my finger with tense toes and flatly refused food.

Time, however, was pressing for me, so I reluctantly forcefed her a couple of mealworms before she finally consented to eat on her own. I murmured gently to her as I slipped a drop of medicine down her throat. Finally I offered a soothing drink of cool water. Gradually, her eyes cleared, and soon her usual twinkle reappeared. She relaxed and began to preen.

But at this moment I noticed inquiring faces appearing at the gallery windows. Curious eyes searched the van.

The show must go on.

With great unwillingness, I eased the little robin back down into the detested box and covered it once again. At least an hour passed as I carefully unloaded and unpacked artwork. When the last piece was finally out, I converted the interior of the van into a temporary aviary. I set a flat dish of water out for drinking and bathing, as well as a bug box teeming with "wrigglies," and another dish that held the coveted mealworms. Trees shaded the van from the intensity of the summer heat, screened windows provided cross-ventilation, and all traffic, human or vehicular, was pleasantly distant.

As a makeshift aviary, it had much to offer.

But the little robin, freed finally, fled as far from me as possible. She utterly ignored the delectables surrounding her – and she utterly ignored me. Instead, my last peek through the van window as I headed indoors showed an otherwise beautiful youngster in an infamous temper, preening every feather with an air of icy contempt.

No need to worry about the van overheating!

I consoled myself with the reflection that this regrettable chill between us would at least further the independence necessary for her return to the wild in the near future. Indeed, after our trip to the gallery, although the sweetness of her nature quickly returned, she also began to show a distinct longing to leave the house. Her self-reliance quickened so magically that within three days I carried her outdoors and watched with mixed feelings of regret and delight as she soared up strongly into the trees.

A few days later, I sat outdoors under the big serviceberry tree in the rooster run. Squeak, unable to resist an empty lap, immediately leaped into mine and settled himself comfortably. Bubble soon joined us, and we sat companionably together in the warm, sun-dappled shadows, watching butterflies and hawkmoths busy among the flowers.

In the tree above our heads appeared an adult flicker. She moved from branch to branch, gathering serviceberries and feeding two ever-hungry babies, who followed her closely with soft squeals of enthusiasm. As the roosters and I continued to sit in stillness, gentle activities gradually unfolded all around us.

At my very feet, a little parent siskin hulled niger seeds, feeding the pulp to two minute babies, who stood before me on unbelievably tiny toes.

To my left, I watched the beauty and fluid movements of a chipmunk steadily filling his cheek pouches with grain. When he finally trotted off, his bulging cheeks wider than his body, I wondered how he'd ever squeeze through the tunnel to his lair.

Adult grackles, unwilling to feed near me, chucked warnings continually from the trees where they sat with their fledglings. One of the adults, I noted with interest, had the usual long black tail – but edged on both sides, surprisingly, with pure white tail-feathers.

Above me, two mature robins leaped and grabbed the hanging berries with their beaks, letting the impetus and weight of their follow-through snap the berries free. Then they'd pause on a branch, holding their booty and glancing about cautiously before swallowing the sweet fruit and leaping towards another.

At a short distance, a northern waterthrush slipped in and out of the shadows, pausing periodically and teetering his tail gracefully.

Then, to my great joy, I noticed a solitary robin fledgling also eating serviceberries above me, and as soon as I gained a clear view, I knew it was our little one. Her face and expression were unmistakable. Judging by the energy and success with which she was "catching" berries, she was surviving very well indeed on her own.

Only ten days earlier, she'd been on the brink of starvation.

CHAPTER 9

MIDSUMMER MEDITATIONS

The midpoint of July had passed.

Around and through me I could feel that the frenetic energies of spring had peaked and paused. Though the pivot between increasing light and increasing darkness had technically passed at the time of the solstice, shorter days and longer nights were now so noticeable as to penetrate even my duller human perceptions.

I felt a deepening stillness, that sense of nature looking inward and meditating. A sense, almost, of melancholy.

The land lay quietly breathing. Quietly resting.

Even the very trees seemed overfed and drowsy, and totally disinterested in growing more leaves. The energetic songs of nesting birds had dwindled to brief calls that only augmented the inner and outer silence. Now the monotonous piping of fledglings prevailed instead. Even the rich carolling of robins around the edge of the meadow at dusk had diminished to occasional calls.

One poignant evening, as I stood listening, they failed entirely. Instead, only a solitary song sparrow could be heard, his cheery bubbling call reduced to three bleak notes.

The tipping of the balance, the change from drive to decline, pervaded all life with equal strength and intensity. Though only the latter days of July were passing, though the heat of summer yet prevailed and would do so for several weeks, still the sobering touch of autumn could be felt at the very heart of existence.

The dog days of summer were numbered.

As if to reinforce the slowing of spring growth and running waters, a marked shortage of rain also oppressed the land. Week upon week of hot arid weather had left roadside greenery dusty and drooping. Forests, teeming with new life, were dangerously dry. Though some wild fruits, like raspberries, responded to the heat with bowed canes of large juicy berries, others, like blueberries, barely evolved.

In the vegetable garden, I noted with a sigh that the tomatoes seemed inclined to emulate the blueberries.

Outside the kitchen window, I often watched grackles standing motionless for short periods of time in the waterdish, no doubt cooling off. Only occasionally would they flurry the waters into quick, refreshing baths, although Chip, indoors, bathed thoroughly several times a day.

The well was so low that I watched her with envy.

To my astonishment, Chip not only continued to indulge in sunbaths, she would actually slip between the window glass and the drawn curtains where heat was especially concentrated. There she'd sprawl happily, every feather raised, soaking up sunshine like an English tripper on the Mediterranean.

Dense midsummer growth shaded the southern windows, absorbing the worst of the heat and tempering the hot breaths of air that glided through the screened porch. Deciduous trees always seem to cluster closely around the house in the summer, an optical trick generated by their expanding leafiness. In the winter, they step back and let the pale sunshine pour through the windows. Even the surrounding hills feel nearer the house in the summer, yet recede in the winter, leafless and aloof in their snowy undulations.

One hot, breathless morning during the drought, I walked through the woods on a familiar pilgrimage, absorbing the heady aroma of sun-warmed fir. Gone was the usual rich dampness of the early hours.

Within and without me I felt the silence. The stillness.

I arrived finally at the foot of the Tree, a gigantic white ash, hundreds of years old, that rises up unbroken through the leafy roof of the forest like a pillar of the sky. Three of us once managed to stretch our arms far enough to hold hands around the great bole.

It became the Tree of Life at the centre of a living circle. The nucleus in a single cell.

The deep folds of its enormous base are covered with dense green moss, deep and springy. On this day I noticed with delight that hundreds of beautiful, iridescent teal beetles glowed against the sun-dappled greenery like living jewels.

I sat down on the ground, wedging my back into one of the deep clefts of the bole, and sank into stillness, permeated by the ageless strength of the Tree. Absorbed into its presence. Sheltered and safe within its curve. As I sat, I sensed, not the passing of time but rather, *nunc stans*, the eternal now. Past and future seemed not to be defined by the present, but to have returned to their rightful realm of illusion.

My breathing became the breathing trees, the breathing land. Even the forest beings, the sun-bright warmth, the infinity of sky above me. The common unity of all energies diffused a healing inner glow, a vitality within apparent stillness that transfigures the inner world as the golden radiance of late afternoon sun kindles the visual world.

The following afternoon, rain began to fall gently, increasing finally to a joyous downpour that cleansed and permeated the lethargic land. Celebratory birdsong rang out from within the dripping trees, while parched air gave way to refreshing coolness.

Indoors, the drumming on the roof throbbed with the primal richness of ancestral rhythms.

Rain, the fertilizing union of sky and earth, the watery equivalent of the sun's fire, had restored the balance. As if to reinforce this unity, a magnificent rainbow emerged later in the east in response to the light from the west, linking terrestrial and celestial worlds with a translucent bridge of beauty.

In the morning, my joy became somewhat tempered by the discovery that the dwindling number of slugs in the vegetable garden had also been replenished.

CHAPTER 10

DOVE OF PEACE?

O n the same day as the rain of renewal, a mother and her young daughter arrived on the doorstep with a fledgling yellow-bellied sapsucker in need of help.

As I gently held the little creature in my hands, I was entranced by his innate beauty. Intricate patterns in black and white covered his body, except for his wine-red throat and forehead. His two most prominent tailfeathers were very firm and spiky, holding the promise of an excellent prop in his future journeys up tree trunks. The inner sides of these tailfeathers were barred in black and white, while the outer edges were solid black. His slim, needle-like bill looked very efficient for poking into even the tiniest crevice for hidden bugs, and his large dark eyes were wonderfully expressive. He was truly one of the most beautiful young birds I'd ever seen.

But his prospects didn't seem very hopeful.

He could beat his wings easily, but his legs sprawled uncontrollably, though I could feel movement in the toes. He would break out in sudden, short spells of biting, wing-beating, and desperate struggle as though in pain and/or frustration at his helplessness. He also breathed jerkily through his mouth instead of normally through his nostrils.

I forcefed him mealworms and then concocted a mixture of sesame-seed oil, peanut butter, and ground sunflower seeds, which he nibbled eagerly off a spoon. I also dissolved a little honey in water, and this he quickly learned to drink from a cup.

Truly, his spirit was willing.

The day that the young sapsucker arrived also brought a frightened wild pigeon with a drooping wing. He'd been rescued, struggling helplessly, from the side of a busy roadway by a compassionate woman who was later refused assistance by a less compassionate veterinarian.

The uniformly dark plumage of this pigeon led me to dub him, rather unimaginatively, "Smokey." His voice was as yet juvenile, a shrill piping rather than soft, throaty cooing, which told me that, although his appearance was as adult as any "downtown" pigeon, he'd been hatched just this spring.

I taped his wing to his body in as natural a position as possible, leaving the sound wing free for balance, and offered him a drink of water, which he eagerly accepted. One side of his head was swollen, and the eyelid drooped, but no other injuries were indicated. I could only hope that he'd suffered no internal complications.

However, when I offered him mixed pigeon grains, Smokey flatly refused to eat.

After several hours more, I finally injected a blend of raw egg yolk and powdered bird vitamins into his throat with a needleless syringe. Then I dusted him with rotenone powder, a natural

deterrent against parasites, and loosed him into the solitude of the hospice room.

By the following afternoon, Smokey still hadn't eaten, preferring instead to stand by the hour, partly hidden behind a wide plank of carving wood that leaned against the wall. With only his head behind the plank, Smokey remained absolutely motionless, no doubt feeling securely hidden. He reminded me of a young child, head hidden and eyes tightly covered yet with body wholly visible, playing at hide-and-seek.

However, Smokey needed nourishment in order to survive. I hoped that maybe Desmond and Molly could help.

I shifted Smokey into the studio and placed him on newspapers on top of the big drawing table, his dishes of food and water beside him. Then I set a large wire cage over him, in case territorial disputes arose. Also, I wished to isolate his waterdish from the other birds in case he was infectious. To my unbounded satisfaction, Smokey perked up almost immediately upon seeing other pigeons contentedly dozing, cooing, and eating on their own special shelves high above him. And freely flying. Neither of the two studio residents approached the new arrival, but they all eyed one another curiously.

And later, when Desmond and Molly began to eat, so did Smokey.

I've always liked common pigeons. I remember sitting on a park bench in Copenhagen with pigeons on my lap, arms, hands, and shoulders. Even on my head. Dozens more were circling, hoping for landing clearance. Even other tourists who were photographing me as a curiosity failed to spoil my enjoyment of the birds.

Once, wandering through one of Halifax's ancient graveyards, I came across a pigeon huddled in the drizzle near a blackened headstone. Within twenty minutes, the pigeon was lying in my lap at a friend's house, sipping honey water with every appearance of enjoyment. He lived with me for several weeks, gaining strength and often sitting on the arm of my chair during the evenings. When "Walter" pigeon was well and strong, I released him.

At night, in cities, I love to see huddles of sleeping pigeons on ledges high above the traffic's clamour. A gentle contrast.

Sometimes they can seem whimsical. I recall a Buddhist friend describing a temple in India. Riding round and round on large, slow fans in the ceiling were several pigeons, no doubt enjoying the cool breeze.

Because of the Buddhist regard for all sentient beings, they were welcome.

Unfortunately, the little sapsucker wasn't doing as well as Smokey.

Beginning the day after his arrival, he refused all food, and his suffering was so evident – and probably irreversible – that I respected his withdrawal and chose not to forcefeed him. The decision to let go of this life was his to make and not mine to question.

He still craved water though, which I offered frequently, and I held him quietly for long spells, sensing somehow that he absorbed

comfort from my warmth and presence. His laboured breathing and periods of struggle cut me to the heart, and I longed fervently for his release. I never doubted how marvellous and exhilarating that moment would be.

Such a brief journey. And such a difficult one.

Each time I lifted the cover on his box, I expected to find him dead. His body was obviously shutting down, and his legs were utterly useless, but his spirit shone as strongly as ever. To my despair, his eyes were still deep and bright, and he began to indicate a desire for food, although he'd swallow very little each time.

This seemed all wrong. I was caught between prolonging his suffering if I fed him and starving those bright eyes if I didn't. I felt he needed a gentle push in order to begin the Crossing and this was accomplished with carbon dioxide carefully administered by the Animal Care Technician at the university.

Without panic, without struggle, the little sapsucker finally took wing.

Smokey, on the other hand, was settling in very well to life on top of the studio table, and was eating regularly. The eventual removal of his protective cage may have given him greater mobility, but it also revealed Smokey's inordinate talent for getting into difficulties.

He began by falling onto his back in his new, larger waterdish, where he flailed helplessly, unable to right himself with only one free wing. With even greater ingenuity, he wedged one end of a set of sharp trammel points, kept for creating circular canvases, under the tape around his body. At the same time, he tangled his toes in loose threads from a fraying roll of canvas. He persistently caught his claws in his body tape and fell. Though I trimmed the flight-feathers in order to shorten his injured wing, he still caught his foot in them again and again. Eventually I encased his entire foot in a custom-made felt "boot" that could catch on nothing, and one difficulty was resolved.

Daily life riddled by such traumatic episodes naturally failed to ease Smokey's evident insecurity, and he often remained "hidden" behind the horizontal roll of canvas suspended at the back of the table, his feet clearly visible below. Only when driven by hunger would he emerge.

Desmond and Molly coolly tolerated Smokey, if utter indifference can be so described, and in time he began venturing out into studio life – pattering around the floor to pick up stray seeds, climbing up the lounge chair to peer out the windows, even "threatening" Chip whenever she ventured too close.

One morning, when I was deeply engrossed in working on a painting, I gradually became aware of a stare boring into me from behind. When I glanced over my shoulder, there was Smokey. He was standing on the extreme edge of the table nearest me, watching me paint with utter fascination.

Would that I could see such intelligent interest on the faces of most curators.

Another day found him trotting worriedly back and forth between Desmond and Molly, each of whom, with much strutting and cooing, was vehemently defending half of the studio floor space from the other. There didn't appear to be any unclaimed territory left over for young Smokey.

A crisis was reached one afternoon when I stepped into the studio only to find a struggling Smokey flat on his back. On top of him was Molly, tearing out his feathers, pecking viciously at his eyes, and blurting furious curses. I snatched her off, shook her angrily and hurled her up into the air in a new blast of inspired blasphemy.

Mine.

Flapping wildly, she shot straight into Desmond's loft and was instantly driven out by an irate Desmond. Twisting through the air, she finally skidded onto her own shelf, panting and bug-eyed.

Meanwhile, I scooped up Smokey, who was shaking and nearly hysterical with voiceless shrieks. His maturing voice had lost its high juvenile piping but had not yet developed an adult coo. All he could manage were gasping growls, which was why I hadn't heard the attack. Both eyes were blood-filled but the eyes themselves uninjured. His taped wing was raw in patches.

Quickly I squeezed antibiotic ointment into each eye and over a sterile gauze pad, which I taped against his wing. Then I held him a long while in my lap, cuddling and soothing him, trying to restore the marginal confidence he had undoubtedly lost. Finally, I set his food and water on top of the woodbox beside my chair, and he lay there quietly for the rest of the evening.

So much for the "dove of peace" notion.

Molly's behaviour forced me to build a door between the studio and the rest of the house that would restrict her and

Desmond to the studio. The door was screened to allow heat to circulate, and I built it six inches lower than the lintel to let Chip fly in and out over the top.

Smokey was reestablished at the opposite end of the house, with freedom to roam everywhere but into the studio. The quarrel between him and Molly still seethed, and they'd march back and forth on each side of the screen door, glaring at one another, Molly cooing belligerently. Within a few days, when his adult voice finally emerged, Smokey responded with equal bellicosity. Each time their mutual dislike boiled over, they'd twang the screening with their beaks for added emphasis.

The rest of us maintained a peaceful coexistence.

Unfortunately, Smokey's wing, far from healing, remained totally inert. When I removed the tape after a month, the wing dragged on the floor, tripping him repeatedly. When he fell, particularly if he fell on top of his sound wing, he had an arduous struggle to right himself once more. As I watched him flounder through each day and assisted him time after time, I finally became convinced that amputation was inevitable. I made an appointment and drove Smokey to the local veterinary clinic.

In the waiting room, he sat on my lap, preening. Then I held him quietly in my hands during the preliminary examination. Later, as the gas mask was fitted over his head, I tried to convey as much reassurance as possible and continued to hold him as he sank gently into sleep.

While the vet worked quickly and efficiently at severing the wing from the shoulder, I tried in my heart to centre Smokey in an aura of healing and protection. Tried, too, to send comfort and warmth through my hands as I held him. Until he fully emerged from the anesthetic, I countered postsurgical chills with the warmth of my body on one side of him and a woolly blanket on the other. When he was finally stable, I offered him water, which he drank eagerly, then tucked him into my shirt and drove home.

Back at the house, when I set Smokey down on his shelf beside his food and water dishes, I realized that the defeathered skin around his stitches would be sensitive to chilling – especially with the surrounding plumage still damp from disinfectant swabbings. I immediately hung a red brooder lamp, which I had used to warm Bubble and Squeak as chicks, above Smokey, and he responded to the warmth with obvious delight, lying down and preening in the rosy glow until his plumage was fully restored.

With great relief I also noted that whenever he rose to eat or drink, he walked with ease and perfect balance at last. By the following day, he was strutting around the living room with utter confidence and cockily intimidating small Bashō.

One-winged Smokey was here to stay.

CHAPTER 11

AT THE SHORE

The northern shores of Nova Scotia are intricately woven out of the warp and weft of onshore and offshore breezes, and the endless surging and ebbing of ocean tides. Wind, water, and spinning beach grasses create ever-shifting patterns on the fabric of ancient sand. Each massive rock, seemingly impervious to the silken touch of wind and wave, is refined continually by their persistence, a reality of flux masked by an illusion of solidity.

In a continuous network of invisible paths, gliding seabirds weave in and out of sunlight and shadow, linking sea, sky, and shore in primal unity.

A huge sea turtle cresting the waves, or the glistening heads of seals bobbing closer to peer curiously at me as I sit quietly on a rock, come as dynamic accents in the great rhythmic web.

The irresistible nature of these forces is reflected in the stones and bones, shells and driftwood, that I turn in my hands, fascinated.

Each, when pondered, releases an idea or a message that infuses my work. Though a particular message may arise many times, its freshness is ensured by such elemental sources and by the uniqueness of each form.

Perception, too, freshens.

One bright, summer afternoon, sunsparkles twinkled over the sea like luminous migrating spirits. Distant sands shimmered dizzily under billows of heat. As I strolled, I chanced upon a lone, evocative twist of driftwood.

Like a prehistoric beast, truncated with arrested energies, it seemed to have crawled to a halt in our indifferent modern world. I felt its vulnerability as though its last moments were at hand. Dark energies like birds of prey were swooping around it. Its sobering message was like a cool touch from the other side of brightness, reminding me of fragile forms of beauty that are dwindling rapidly in our destiny of self-destruction.

A reminder, surely, to hold our world gently in both hands.

The beauty of shells, as well as driftwood, has always attracted me. Usually the colours of those I find on the shore echo the subtle greys and blues of local sea and sky. However, caught in rocky crevices on certain beaches are thousands of northern yellow periwinkles. Ranging from bright yellow through to orange, these tiny, jewel-like spirals suggest exotic tropical climes rather than the cool reaches of northern Nova Scotia, and even Labrador, where I've also gathered them.

Holding their bright glow in my chilled hands on blustery, rainswept days, with spindrift blowing off rolling, grey waves, reveals to me the realm of simultaneous realities in which we really dwell.

Reveals bright spirals symbolic of regeneration from living waters, held in a sacred mandorla formed by my cold, cupped hands.

Reveals the power of familiar forms elevated to a plane of universal meaning.

Indeed, even the primal bleakness of the actual weather seems to represent my fallow mind before such moments of revelation.

One day I entered a friend's house and was immediately struck by the beauty of a volute shell on a table. A sudden vision of evolving life forms touched me in response to the shell's unusual markings, and I turned it round and round in my hands with great excitement. Then I borrowed it to take home.

While I was working on the painting inspired by this shell, County, the very special robin with whom I lived at the time, was having difficulty laying her first clutch of eggs. As each day brought a new egg, it would break on arrival, and County's high spirits would be submerged in disappointment.

I, too, was in difficulties with my "egg production" – the cosmic egg in my painting.

I was unable to create a shattered-eggshell effect to my satisfaction, and each failure plunged me into despair. My concentration was punctured, too, with anxiety about County's need for motherhood and how this could be achieved.

Day after day, County and I struggled with our respective eggs. Then, on the fourth day, hers arrived safe and sound. Simultaneously, I resolved the painting.

Truly, the deepest threads of our lives were entwined.

In time, I began to combine images of particularly evocative shells with those of County's babies as we strove side by side to fulfil our creative longings.

In one vertical canvas, the journey of the spirit begins with a cluster of gaping nestlings held in a shell of primal light at the very bottom.

Other nestlings, bright-eyed and calling, radiate spring melodies from their shell nests.

One spring, the Sisters of St. Martha, whose central community was in a nearby town, borrowed several paintings to display at Bethany Motherhouse during a major gathering of their order. Sisters from the United States as well as Canada came together to discuss new policies and elect new leaders. The paintings were installed in a former chapel, filled with tables and chairs, where the meetings were to be held.

Taproot, a large canvas, hung on a side wall beside a row of tall, opened windows darkened with drawn blinds. During one talk, the speaker became aware that the eyes of many of her listeners were turning repeatedly towards the first window and this canvas, which hung beside it.

Over and over, she would emphasize an important issue and look up, only to find the attention of her audience noticeably diluted. Curious about the general air of distraction, which seemed to be increasing, she glanced that way herself and was immediately struck by what she saw.

The overall tone of the painting is quite subdued except for the lower regions, in which a large, luminous shell of light hovers above colourful corals and sponges. Moved by gentle breezes from behind, the drawn blind of the open window swelled slightly, then sank back, swelled and sank, over and over. In the dimmed corner of the room, this caused the huge, glowing shell in the painting to suddenly brighten, then diminish, brighten and diminish, in a remarkable, almost eerie, pulsation of light.

The Sisters were entranced, and the speaker, with laudable sensitivity, interrupted her speech to suggest that everyone, including herself, remain silent for a few minutes, absorbing this unusual vision and pondering the Divine Mystery.

It was as though the Shell had spoken.

CHAPTER 12

ADOLESCENCE

Sunny, quiet, mesmerizing with the haunting hum of crickets, the summer season slipped slowly by.

Along the roadside, thousands of yellow butterflies gathered in clusters that rose in golden clouds as I drew near. Or twinkled over the meadows like nomadic dandelions. Each day seemed stitched to the next by glinting dragonflies, darting like bright needles through the fabric of sunlight, devouring myriad flying insects.

A golden glow transformed the land each evening, lingering last upon the hills. Then the shadow of night rose out of low-lying meadows like a tide. It slowly quenched the brightness, which vanished at last from the hilltops only to reappear triumphantly in the stars. The greater shadow of night brightened by beauty.

Shadows can be fascinating.

I remember staying at a friend's apartment in Toronto and being unable to sleep. As I shifted restlessly on the couch, trying to ignore the endless clatter of traffic, my eyes were continually drawn by an array of shadows on the wall.

Finally I sat up, groped for a pencil and paper, and drew a haunting, visionary tree, suggested by the shadows. From deep, strong roots, it rose like a prophet on a massive rock. Emanating auras of light quickened the chasing waves and darkened the cliffs looming up behind.

Bashō, the tiny Japanese quail, had diverse reactions towards shadows.

When frightened, he'd slip quickly under the arching plants in the indoor garden, blending easily into the protective dimness. During quieter times, he'd merely linger there to preen, setting aside much of his usual watchfulness and absorbing the seclusion. Shadows befriended him.

But shadows didn't always suggest security.

One day he was happily engrossed in eating a moth, picking it up and laying it down over and over, chittering delightedly. Smokey, intrigued by Bashō's excitement, stalked up silently and loomed over him, peering curiously.

Suddenly, Smokey's shadow darkened all around Bashō.

With a squeak of alarm, Bashō dropped his moth and scuttled away. But a moth was one of his favourite delicacies. Trotting back, he snatched up his treasure and fled to the garden.

There, in the dusky solitude of shadows that protect, he resumed his feast.

As summer drew on, Bashō began to hold intense fascination for Smokey.

The young pigeon, though fully grown, still needed a role model, having been separated too soon from his own kin. He remained summarily rejected by Desmond and Molly, his nearest pigeon tutors. Chip, the grackle, swooping energetically throughout the house all day, was inaccessible. Bashō, however, was friendly and available.

By default, he became a parent pigeon.

Whenever Smokey noticed Bashō enjoying a dustbath in the garden, snuggling down, scratching up the dirt, and scooping it towards himself with his beak, he'd draw nearer, intrigued. Bashō, happily unconscious of everything but the glory of dust, would suddenly feel invaded as Smokey hung over him. Disturbed, Bashō would jump up and stalk off, buzzing irritably and shaking out his feathers.

Then Smokey, having memorized the procedure, would lie down, overflowing Bashō's small dusting hollow, and hook a little dirt towards himself here and there with his bill. There he'd remain, seemingly refreshed, "bathing" motionlessly with raised feathers.

The pleased expression in his eyes was not a whit diminished by my pouring out a waterbath and pointing out rather sardon-ically that pigeons don't do dustbaths. Quails do. Pigeons have waterbaths. The bright ripples before his eyes failed to have the slightest effect on him. If Bashō wouldn't climb into water, neither would he.

Even Smokey's diet became affected.

Noticing Bashō eating mealworms, Smokey would reach over and pick one up. He'd immediately drop it again in evident distaste, but as Bashō continued to devour each mealie with unabated enthusiasm, Smokey would pick one up again, forcing it down his throat in resignation. The rest of them he'd willingly forego, one per meal being his limit.

In vain would I insist that pigeons are vegetarians. Smokey may not have shared his "parent's" fondness for peculiar food, but he didn't question it.

Fortunately, Bashō enjoyed sitting in Smokey's dish, eating pigeon grain and thereby condoning it in Smokey's eyes. However, when I transferred the dish to a specially built shelf under the coffee table, a location easier for me to tidy, the seed quantity never decreased.

Soon, I realized why.

Bashō wouldn't jump up onto the shelf. If Bashō didn't eat the seeds, neither would Smokey. I returned the dish to the indoor garden, resigning myself to scattered seeds sprouting and mouldering messily here and there.

In my less lucid moments, as I watched a pigeon trying to become a quail, I pondered the possibility of Smokey requiring, in time, the services of an eminent avian therapist.

Would I, or Bashō, be blamed for Smokey's deviance?

Eventually, adolescent rebellion, the scourge of most parents, began to assert itself, and Smokey the pigeon gradually broke with generations of quail tradition.

He began to impersonate pigeons.

As the spray from Smokey's waterbath sprinkled his plumage, Bashō would withdraw fastidiously, shaking out his feathers and muttering with annoyance. But when Smokey no longer purloined his mealworms, Bashō dined in solitary bliss.

Not for him the "empty nest" syndrome.

Despite such pseudo-parental confusion elsewhere on the home front, Chip remained buoyantly free of anxiety.

The two months indoors which had followed her attempt to live outside had been clear of health difficulties. Then I had to counter another session of illness with "doctored" mealworms. Since they were now scarce, due to the natural fluctuations of my mealworm culture, I often substituted dry soy noodles. This treatment restored her lungs once again, allowing her to resume her interrupted devilishness.

With impressive dexterity, she pulled a box of unopened votive candles off a bookcase, tore off the protective cellophane, pried out all twelve candles, and extracted every wick.

Later that same day, she stole a special blade for my lino cutter when I was intently cutting a linoprint. Hours after I'd substituted a blade that was less suitable for certain effects, I discovered the stolen cutter, long discarded in the indoor garden and already beginning to rust.

A bowl of freshly picked peas from the vegetable garden offered Chip the unholy joy of twisting every pea out of its pod; then she shredded both peas and pods all over the carpet while I painted in the studio, blissfully unaware of her nefarious exploits.

The once-beautiful variegated ivy plant hanging in the dining room I managed to save by covering it with fibreglass window-screening dusted with black pepper. Not the most attractive solution, but an effective one.

One morning, her persistence in sampling acrylic paint drove me to block out her special entrance to the studio, a ploy that merely slowed her down. It didn't stop her.

When she finally wormed her way back in, I *drove* her out by uttering unprintable threats and shaking a broom. Locked securely in the hospice room, she imperturbably shredded spruce cones all over the floor and pulverized a few ripening tomatoes. Truly, some days were exhausting.

Chip's originality also led her to initiate ongoing games between us.

Each day, for months, she'd hook the metal trap out of the sink, carry it off, and leave it on the couch, under the coffee table, behind a cushion, in the garden, or in any one of a number of other locations. Wherever I spotted it, I'd scoop it up and drop it back into the drain-hole of the sink in passing. An hour later, I'd stumble over it in the studio, or in the dining room, like a beleaguered metal pawn caught in the moves and countermoves of a perpetual game of chess.

A variation of this game involved a distressing yellow finger-puppet. It was endowed with a double Janus head that leered in one direction and laughed in another on a squat body with four waving, rubbery arms. An embarrassing addition to any household.

This loathsome creature I attached to the oddest projections I could find throughout the house, jamming it onto a pointed piece of driftwood, the antler of a deer skull, the horn of a goat skull, the top of a tapered candle, a hook for coffee mugs. For Chip, no day was complete until she'd found the little monstrosity, wrenched it loose, and tossed it to the floor.

Then it was "my move" again.

Yet a third extended game involved a more aesthetically pleasing item: an antique Chinese ginger jar. This I packed as tightly as Noah's Ark with Chip's various toys and sealed with a cork. Her retaliation was to work the cork loose, toss it aside, then tug and pry each toy out of the jar till it was empty. My final move was to pick up the scattered toys and repack the jar for her to disentangle once again.

Sometimes I flaunted an unshelled peanut before her gleaming eyes, dropped it into the empty jar, and covered it with toys as usual. When she finally worked her way down to the peanut, Chip had the added delight of picking the shell apart and eating the contents. I was left with crumbled peanut shells tossed everywhere – as well as all the scattered toys.

It almost made the revolting yellow finger-puppet look good.

Over a small area of rough bricks beside the woodstove, I had laid a little doormat. The softer material protected the birds' tender feet and was easy to clean. Chip's delight was to tug back the corner of the carpet as far as she could, jump on top, and "ride the wave" as the curved turf flapped back down to the floor. She'd do it over and over with the unflagging zeal of a Californian surfer.

One day I added another dimension to her game – a peanut hidden under the carpet. From that point on, peering under every corner of the carpet for various hidden treasures became part of her daily routine.

Of all her toys, Chip's favourite those days was a hinged wooden nut, which opened to reveal an impaled wooden bug with six quivering legs.

I'd hold the closed nut motionless in my hand, my thumb ready on top, and wait, tormenting Chip with her own unquenchable curiosity. Soon she'd edge cautiously up to the nut, prod it a few times, then push the tip of her beak carefully into the crack. As soon as she'd twisted the lid up and spotted the bug, I'd snap the lid shut by pressing down my thumb.

Chip would leap back, her saucered eyes obviously suggesting that the hidden creature had shut the nut. Over and over she'd creep close and twist up the lid, only to have it slam down again just as she spotted the wiggling bug inside.

I, meanwhile, would be shaking with suppressed mirth, hardly able to see through the tears of laughter filling my eyes.

CHAPTER 13

THE WANING OF SUMMER

A feeling of transience began to imbue the last summer days with a fusion of regret and anticipation. Haunting cricketsong tinged the changing season with vague feelings of sadness, which were augmented by the first touches of fall colour throughout the woodland leaves.

In keeping with this seasonal transition, I was pondering an idea for a painting based on transience. I had roughed it in on primed canvas with charcoal, but hesitated to begin.

Something, I felt, was missing.

While mulling it over, I endured one broiling day in town doing a flurry of accumulated errands and chores. Then I dashed home and hastily devoured a cold supper. Afterwards, I sat back exhausted in the screened porch as the evening cooled, both roosters cuddled down in my lap. Chip soon joined us and, with unusual tranquility, settled down on top of my head.

I felt buzzy after such a scrambled day. Thoughts and half-thoughts chased each other like frenetic chipmunks round and round my tangled mind. Only gradually did I become aware of Chip's soothing pressure on my head. Her perfect stillness. Suddenly, all my weariness dissolved. Strength rose within me like sap renewing a tree in springtime.

I thought, then, of the painting, and instantly imagery began to flood my brain. This part, that part, all poured in overwhelmingly. Yet still I was a solid pillar of centredness, vividly connected with Chip, who was sitting in absolute stillness on top of my head.

A marvellous communication with her.

Early next morning, fuelled by intense energy, I was hard at work in the studio, trying to bring everything into visual realization.

Beyond the studio windows, the trees were shedding their brilliance, becoming gaunt tangles of branches again after months of leafy rotundity. Gusts of colourful migrating birds like blowing leaves were sweeping southward, pursuing summer's warmth, while the chilly spirit of autumn flowed steadily in their wake. Both seasons poised briefly on the pivot of the equinox before the balance tipped in favour of shorter days and longer nights.

The dragon of darkness was hungry.

CHAPTER 14

Autumn Musings

Autumn creates meditations on moulting.

At twilight, great circles of fallen yellow apples glimmer against the dusky forest floor like small, pale galaxies afloat in the darkness of space.

Wild seeds and migrating birds alike are carried along on strong autumn winds that pull the last lingering leaves from the trees.

I worked in the garden, tugging up laden potato plants, tossing their bounty into my basket, and feeling through the loose, damp soil for any strays. A sudden honking of wild geese broke out above me.

I straightened up, eyes shaded, to watch their flight across the brilliant sky. Indescribable feelings surge through me whenever I hear that centuries-old cry of the changing seasons. My heart as well as my eyes followed the fluttering formation till it finally faded out of sight beyond the southern hills.

During times of perfect stillness, when the cool autumn air seems warmed by the memory of summer, tiny blue bugs hover among the spruce trees near the house. These insects are perennial favourites of mine, which I welcome every autumn. Their minute bodies are covered in what appears to be pale-blue feathering, while their sheer lacy wings are dark blue.

Appearing only on the gentlest of days, they drift almost imperceptibly upon the softly breathing air, pale pinpoints against the withering foliage. In their warm, feathery parkas, they float past my amused eyes as though clad for winter's worst.

Discarded feathers from wild birds mingle with fading leaves fallen from the moulting trees. I picked up a tapered flightfeather, possibly from the wing of a robin. The off-centre shaft created a feather with one narrow, stiff side and one wide, soft one.

Though the feather appeared dark and opaque, up close its sheen was transparent; when I held it over an open page of a book, I could read the printed words right through the tightly woven barbs. When I held it close before my eyes, I could see the landscape through it.

How often and effectively has its stiffer edge shorn through the bright, keen air in flight after flight.

How marvellously have the carefully oiled barbs deflected cold rains from the bird's warm body.

My finger traced the feather's subtle, aerodynamic curve. The wind made visible. I pondered the inherent beauty of all feathers, derived from the perfect coalescence of form and function, and their outward beauty, found worldwide in all colours and shapes. I considered the lightness and fragility of a single feather, in Egypt traditionally associated with truth; the strength and durability of multiple soft feathers, upon which the life of each bird depends.

Somehow, an individual feather, lying in the palm of my hand, seems representative not only of an entire bird, but also of the winged spirit that impels all life forms. The invisible flight to the transcendent realm. The Great Migration.

"Before the snow flies" is an expression that cracks like a whip behind all country dwellers anxiously eyeing long lists of autumn chores. Certainly I could hear that invisible whip snapping behind me.

One final job that still remained was to wheel several hundred pounds of wild-bird seed indoors. Soon the path from road to house would be blocked with waist-high drifts. I still blanch when I recall the winter I ran short of seed.

Due to successive heavy snowfalls, my well-cleared path had shrunk to a narrow, twisty snake-trail, as wide as the mouth of the shovel. Shoulder-high banks of snow rose on either side, frozen solid. That winter had been especially hard on birds, and I was down to my last bag of seed. Weeks of snow still lay ahead, so one day I headed off to the feed store.

I returned with seven fifty-pound bags in the van, only to discover that the mouth of my footpath had been plugged solid by a passing snowplough. Snarling imprecations, I shovelled doggedly for half an hour to clear a passage, pulling the packed snow out onto the road rather than trying to hurl it up onto the ten-foot-high banks left by the plough. During a breather, I leaned despairingly on my shovel and gazed in turn at the heavy bags of feed, then at the long narrow path.

I sighed.

Golden visions of motorized wheelbarrows equipped with studded tires danced tantalizingly before my tired eyes. One after another, I saw them roll merrily away with my burdens like mechanized Sorcerer's Apprentices.

Then I shook those dreams out of my head.

With a touch of ingenuity that could only be born of desperation, I laid the first fifty pounds of seed flat on the shovel. I lashed it securely with rope, grasped the handle, and began dragging the load up the winding trail. As I laboured, the lurching shovel ricocheted continually off the icy walls of the path and jerked back at every lump underfoot.

I arrived finally at the back door, breathless, and untied the bag from the shovel. As I scattered seed, then lugged the bag indoors, branches of birdlings watched from every tree. I paused to see them swoop down on the seed before I trudged back to the road.

One bag down. Six to go.

One after another, each fifty-pound bag was pried out of the van and coerced up to the house under protest, while the path quietly refilled. Yet *more* snow was falling.

When the job was finally finished, I stood indoors at the window, my chilled hands wrapped cozily around a steaming mug of cocoa. Birds quickly devoured the fresh seed while I marvelled that the same "bare" feet they use in the heat of summer were now standing in piercing cold fluff. My boot-protected toes had been so chilled that my stockinged feet were still rubbing each other.

"But from now on," I murmured, between sips, "I must have *all* the seed in 'before the snow flies.'"

This autumn all the birdseed was soon loaded indoors, but other chores, just as pressing, still remained: kindling for several months meant splitting old boards into narrow widths and gathering fallen branches, breaking everything into stove-size lengths and bagging it.

Summer tires had to be switched to studded winter ones, and four fifty-pound sandbags loaded into the back of the van to bear down over the wheels during slippery weather.

During a breezy afternoon of wind, waves, and wild ducks, I gathered fall eelgrass, washed up on the shore, for garden mulch the following summer.

About ten sheets of plywood, essential for building stretchers for paintings on canvas, needed to be lugged up the path before the snow fell. Otherwise I would have to lurch up and over snowbanks with every sheet, buffeted by icy blasts from the north – a winter sport that is decidedly overrated.

Six cords of split firewood had to be wheeled load by load up the path and stacked in the two woodsheds. But in this chore I was enthusiastically helped by Bubble and Squeak – the fat slugs clinging to the undersides of each piece of firewood were a gourmet's delight for them.

The final produce from the garden needed to be brought in too, before any killing frosts could destroy my summer-long effort to grow a winter's supply of food. In this task I also had help: Chip and Bashō were more than willing to relieve the vegetables of any multilegged stowaways.

With resignation, I also knew that Chip would indulge her joy in shredding veggies and scattering them throughout the house with that diabolical thoroughness so typical of grackles.

In the end, however, I always feel a full woodshed and a full freezer present a smug retort to winter's worst whims.

Provided they're both filled "before the snow flies."

CHAPTER 15

TRANSIENCE AND TRANSIENTS

The fallen leaves outdoors were echoed colourfully indoors with lovely scatterings of fallen feathers. Bashō the quail plunged into a heavy moult. As his transforming plumage became a round-the-clock obsession with him, his appetite doubled, so that his daily activities were reduced to eating, resting, eating, preening, and eating.

Whenever I returned home after a few hours' absence, or when I rose in the morning, it was never difficult to deduce where Bashō had spent his time. In his wake, he left an array of stunningly beautiful feathers patterned like exquisite handweaving – or rare, marbleized endpapers in antique books. The spiky tips of his emerging plumage gave Bashō's body a hedgehoggy feel and left his skin so tender that he curtly rejected any offers to be cuddled. I knew he'd reconsider those offers once he had fully leafed out.

Desmond and Molly were also enduring a moult, and their daily preening continued intermittently throughout each night. Every morning, flocks of discarded feathers wandered lightly over the studio floor below their roosting shelves. Or rose in short flights as I swept.

But even indoors, autumn gales were brewing.

Molly's moods, so rarely benign, now bordered on outright antagonism. She skulked for hours behind the toilet, launching herself at my ankles whenever I entered the bathroom, or hurling herself vindictively onto Smokey whenever he passed the doorway.

I had been trying to reintegrate the two birds by removing the barrier between them. However, one morning, Molly rose in such an infamous temper that I had to peel her off Smokey three times before I finally lost patience and locked her into the studio. For the rest of that day, she lay smouldering on her shelf, preening and flicking her wing contemptuously at me whenever I drew near.

Smokey, with such a role model constantly before him, and affected, no doubt, by his own moult, soon began to give as good as he got. He developed a surprising degree of skill in whacking Molly with his one wing while biting at her – yet still maintaining his balance. But if Molly threw him down on top of his wing, he was helpless before her fury.

"Whoever began that nonsense about the Dove of Peace never lived with pigeons," I muttered as I pried them apart yet again, both birds spluttering verbal abuse and both beaks bursting with one another's feathers.

Chip's joy, of course, was to circle excitedly around the panting pugilists, shrieking like a bloodthirsty ringside fan. All she lacked to complete her resemblance was an open collar and a sweat-stained fedora.

One night, Molly chose to sleep in my bedroom loft, an occasional change in her routine which, given her disposition, I always regard as a holiday for Desmond. The board-and-batten railing just above the rising warmth of the woodstove was her favourite roost. Chip's nightly roost lay almost directly below, on one of the drying pegs protruding from a handhewn beam.

That night I lay in bed, reading and luxuriating in the brief freedom from household demands that is a treasured moment in a busy life. Finally, I set aside my book, put out the light, and sank into sleep.

The soft hiss of the fire and the gentle ticking of the clock augmented the peaceful silence of another rural night. The birds, too, slept.

In the early hours of the night, Molly, perhaps in preening or in standing up for a scratch, lost her balance on the railing. Toppling forward into utter darkness, she hurtled downwards, colliding with sleeping Chip in passing. An ear-splitting crash resounded as she landed beside the woodstove, thrashing wildly among the steel pokers and shovels that lay on top of the bricks. Chip, startled out of deep sleep into instant terror by being knocked off her perch, and by sudden bedlam breaking out directly below her, shot straight up, shrieking. I awoke, bewildered, to the uproar of clanging metal.

I jerked upright, narrowly missing Chip, who blundered past me in the dark with flapping wings and piercing squawks.

Bashō, too, erupted into one of his rocketing vertical flights, rebounding off the ceiling over my head as I scrambled wildly to switch on the light.

As sudden brightness flooded the scene, Chip thumped down on my pillow, wild-eyed and panting. Bashō ricocheted off a bookcase and crash-landed in the indoor garden, where he stayed, crouched and motionless, every raised feather a question mark. Molly disentangled herself from the pokers with a final clatter and floundered away, leaving them in disarray on the bricks.

I stood still, blinking.

A bruised and tentative peace suddenly prevailed. The kind of tense silence that could explode at the snapping of a shoelace.

I was grateful that none of us was wearing shoes.

Sometimes, as I filled the outdoor feeders during these mornings and scattered extra seed under the trees, flocks of grackles would sweep past overhead, dozens of beating wings hissing in the crisp, autumn air. It was a wonderful sound. Exhilarating. Migratory. Rich with visions of the long trek to come.

They'd swerve above the big double spruce, where the Virginia creeper vine peered out from the very top, its bright-red leaves adding a jaunty contrast to the sombre, grey lichens and dark needles of its elderly host.

Countless robins, hermit thrushes, ruffed grouse, blue jays, flickers, and magnificent pileated woodpeckers with their shrill cries, arrived daily to savour the indigo sweetness of the plentiful creeper berries.

One morning, deeply preoccupied with a difficult painting, I stepped out the south door of the house to refill the silo feeder with mixed niger and canary seed. Up on nearby branches, siskins, goldfinches, chickadees, juncos, tree sparrows, and white-throated sparrows waited restlessly for my departure so they could eat.

As I was tipping the seeds into the feeder, my thoughts locked within the studio, I felt someone land on my shoulder. Not until several moments had passed did I suddenly realize that I couldn't be carrying my usual passenger, since Chip was indoors. Curiously, I glanced sideways and encountered the twinkling eyes of a tiny pine siskin, too eager for food to be cautious.

Later, I discovered a siskin with a drooping wing eating fallen seed on the ground below the silo feeder. Though unable to fly, he could certainly sprint. After a couple of awkward scrambles, I finally scooped him up and released him into the hospice room.

I set up supplies of seed, grit, and water, and the siskin immediately began to eat. With protection from predators, plenty of nourishment, and minimal stress, perhaps his wing would heal.

Certainly a gleaming-eyed Chip, impishly tweaking the siskin's tail as though he were one of her wind-up toys, was *not* helping. I ushered her firmly out of the room and closed the door between them.

After a few days, the siskin could manage short flights among the branches in the hospice, though his wing continued to droop. At times, his song would ripple out sweetly in tiny, high notes that contrasted sharply with the rapid, excited calls of the outside siskins.

Nearly a fortnight after he'd arrived, he was flying strongly the full length of the room, despite one wing remaining out of alignment. I then released him, and enjoyed frequent sightings of him at the silo feeder over the next few weeks, still flying well, and seemingly undeterred by rain or sleet.

One golden morning, during the full glory of the autumn leaves, an injured female robin was brought to me. Although the plumage on her body was mature, her subtle headfeathers lacked the striking eye-rings of an adult. I deduced that she'd been born in the summer and was now making her first transition into adult colouring. She'd been struck down on the Trans-Canada highway, leaving blood from superficial wounds on her beak, throat, and one wing. Some of her long flightfeathers and tailfeathers were broken, too.

But her head worried me the most.

One side was so swollen from the pressure within that the eyeball was pushed outward and her eyelids couldn't close. Not even the nictitating membrane, that flickering, transparent inner eyelid, could cover it. I longed to ease the swelling, but any cold compresses I could mentally contrive seemed to include a high risk of infection with such an unprotected eye.

The robin lay limply in my hands, suffering and unmoving.

I sat down, closed my eyes, and became utterly still. With quiet desperation, I began to delve deeply inside myself, seeking the only strength I could give her. My feelings centred on County, the special robin with whom I had shared such an extraordinary relationship, and I began to feel very strong, very solid, like a mountain. As this feeling intensified, I tried to send energy and reassurance through my hands to the wildling I was holding.

My awareness sharpened. I noticed that all the birds in the house, including irrepressible Chip, had become silent and utterly still.

Not a sound could be heard.

I deepened my concentration.

Suddenly, the robin began struggling quite vigorously. I opened my eyes and was astonished to discover that a quarter of an hour had elapsed, not just a few moments.

As the robin continued to squirm and kick, the rest of the birds immediately grew active once more. Molly flew past on her way to the loft. Bashō stretched up on tiptoe and crowed. Chip sang.

I rose from my chair and hastily laid a thick towel in the bottom of a large stockpot. Then I set the robin gently inside and drew another towel over the top of the pot, leaving her in seclusion and semi-darkness. Moving into high gear, I retrieved three lines of laundry drying in the hospice room, gathered all the red tomatoes from among the dozens of green ones ripening under newspapers on the hospice floor, strengthened certain perching branches, and spread more newspapers below them. Then I dashed outside, turning over rocks and logs in a bug-collecting frenzy.

Indoors once more, I set up a "loaded" bug box for her, a separate offering of mealworms, tied clusters of Virginia creeper berries to the branches in the hospice, and poured out a dish of water treated with tetracycline. All was in readiness for a recuperating robin.

But when I gently eased the pot onto its side and raised the covering partway, she stayed inside.

I left her to emerge on her own, which she did an hour later, only to hide for the rest of the day. Not until dusk did she reappear. My last peek found her crouched squarely on top of the mealworms, the fear eased somewhat from her one good eye.

Four days later, the swelling on her head had receded enough to allow the robin's lovely brown iris to peer out of her damaged eye. It looked bright, not blind. In utter delight, I actually noticed her using the sight from that eye in the familiar head-cocking motions of robins. The shape of her head was still distorted, but she remained active and ate heartily.

Fortunately, she had no difficulty in flying.

Miraculously, after another three days, her eyes matched perfectly, and I released her. As with the siskin, I caught frequent sightings of her thriving on her own. When last seen, she was in the company of other robins, all busily hunting insects under the apple trees beside the feeding station. When the call came, she'd be ready to migrate.

Months later, when deep snow held my world in close, white silence, I wondered if the battered robin I'd held in my hands was riding those warm, southern winds.

I hoped she was.

CHAPTER 16

GRASSROOTS CARPENTRY

When outside building projects have to be done, autumn is the season to do them. No matter what technical frustrations may arise, no matter whether boards split or bucksaws bind, at least when hammering, one flails away at nails, *not* at hovering clouds of blackflies and mosquitoes. With carpentry, there are enough borderline moments as it is.

Especially if one is working alone.

No words can adequately describe one's emotional state after what seems a lifetime of forcing a fractious board into place – a twisty board that, with very little refining, would make an excellent propeller – and to be holding it ready for nailing, finally, with grunts and sheer ache, only to discover that the hammer is just nicely out of reach.

Then there are the tight clusters of galvanized nails that one is forced to use after the single nails are all gone – the reluctant fingers that gingerly hold each clump as it's hammered apart, and are systematically stung with every blow.

And that familiar decision everyone makes: do I want this board to *look* level and *be* crooked? Or to *be* level and *look* crooked?

Nor can one ignore the persistent pricking of inch-long slivers that leads one to speculate moodily if the project is being built not with mere boards, but with indestructible planks of cactus.

Years of doing amateur carpentry, and of watching professional carpenters, have led me to conclude that what really sets us apart, besides their more polished results, is the enviable richness of their vocabulary under duress.

I can only marvel.

When the physical strength typical of the feminine gender is inadequate for a task, one's resourcefulness is challenged. If a framed floor has to be raised to a particular level, a vehicle jack substitutes perfectly for strong arms and shoulders. Even a minimal understanding of leverage can help one to pry off boards that feel cemented to their supports. Or raise framed walls that are too heavy to lift. Still, there are those peak moments of frenzied frustration when all fails. Then I turn to my male neighbours in case they lack enough challenges for their resourcefulness.

Sometimes, however, neighbours are out of reach.

One day, I climbed on top of the woodshed to measure for a roof structure I hoped to build. If all went according to plan, I would eventually be able to climb a fixed ladder joining the roof of the woodshed to a small platform beside the chimney in order to do my annual cleaning. This would eliminate the arduous task of balancing on top of a stepladder to lift down sections of flue, cleaning them, and then struggling up the ladder again to replace them.

They seemed to get heavier every year.

With this innovation, I would spend barely ten minutes dislodging soot while lounging nonchalantly beside the flue.

Afterwards, briefly dusting off my hands, I should be able to continue climbing up to a second platform on the peak of the house. There, the delight of a beautiful view would await me.

But before I could climb up the structure, I had to build it.

I completed my calculations, finally, and inched my way to the edge of the roof, amid an accumulation of spruce cones that rolled like ball bearings beneath my every step. Grasping an overhanging branch, I sat down and swung my legs over the edge, groping for the stepladder somewhere below.

To my horror, I knocked it over.

Bubble and Squeak, lingering below, squawked with alarm as the metal ladder crashed to the ground beside them. With hoisted feathers, they fled to the safety of the back door. There they waited nervously, watching the ladder and me by turns, eyes anxious and combs twitching.

For once, I gave them scant heed. At least they were on solid ground. Marooned on the roof, I was preoccupied with my own private hell.

Backing carefully away from the edge, I brushed aside the scattered cones and needles. Then I inched across the cleared asphalt to the edge once again, where I crouched with beating heart and sweaty palms.

I eyed the nearest tree. It was an enormous double spruce several feet away, whose lower trunk was fortunately bare of limbs. For one crucial moment, I had to convince myself that I was a flying squirrel. A flying squirrel without aerial membranes.

I sprang.

A split second later, I was embracing the spruce with ardent desperation, gasping my gratitude. Amid the welcoming clucks of Bubble and Squeak, I slid slowly to the ground in a crumbling cascade of bark and lichens, shaky but unharmed.

Another grey hair would replace a brown.

Although calculating the roof structure was tricky, the actual work took me only three days. With its completion, another element of rural enjoyment was revealed.

Sitting on the roof for the first time in the cool pre-dawn, I followed the gentle awakening of the sky as it slowly brightened in washes of light from the unseen sun. Soon, every fibre of my being was steeped in the full glory of the risen sun that lifted above the hills on wings of flame. Woodland colours around me quickened into that exquisite rosiness unique to clear mornings.

Birds gliding by on sweet ripples of song were edged with golden brilliance.

Dew-drenched spider webs dazzled.

As the fire of renewal continued to burn away the darkness, all of creation was kindled. Everywhere, flashes of light responded to the primal summons, while a glorious aurora of birdsong enriched the air.

Surrounded by golden clouds of steam rising from the sun-warmed roof, I mused on the word "dawn." It seemed too bald and motionless to encompass what I'd been experiencing. Instead, I savoured the subtle suggestion of transformation found in the archaic equivalent, "dayspring."

My rooftop eyrie quickly became a living book for me with every turning page, every ascent, a revelation.

The height of the roof brought me closer to the top of the big double spruce, its staid colouring enlivened by the cheery red leaves and blue-black berries of the entwining Virginia creeper. Sitting or reclining up there in perfect stillness, I enjoyed almost a companionship with wild hermit thrushes and robins as they busied themselves daily with the berries.

One gorgeous afternoon, a pileated woodpecker swooped into the spruce with a staccato of strident cries, and leaped from branch to branch seeking berries. From time to time he peeked curiously and cautiously around the trunk at me. Or, crouching, peered through the tangled twiggery, his big scarlet crest almost extinguishing the red leaves with its brilliance.

When all breezes slept, the tiny blue bugs would drift past me, their minute size and feathery fragility augmenting, and augmented by, the feeling of immense space surrounding them – the foreshortened ground below, the distant hills beyond.

Even familiar blue jays took on a startling freshness whenever the rich patterns of their outspread wings and tails glided below me, bright beauty heightened by dark earth. Viewed from the ground, their blueness is often rivalled by the sky, or diminished when one sees mainly their pale, grey-white breasts. Viewed from above, however, one wonders how their kind have survived with so little camouflage. Even the fledglings bear the same bright plumage as their parents.

But not all mornings rose in trumpets and glory.

Some crept slowly into being like pale shadows, softly transforming the land into a classic Chinese ink painting, with misty hollows and silhouetted hilltops. With silence and stillness.

Evening, too, could fade into night, with descending clouds dissolving the hills. Local folk, eyeing these misty undulations, would respond, as did their forebears, with the adage:

"Fog on the hill – water to the mill;

Fog in the hollow – fine day will follow."

On moonless nights, I would clothe myself warmly and leave the fireside, leave my books. Up on the roof platform, I'd lie down, floating between the dark, unseen world below me and the starry brilliance above. The chill beauty and infinite profusion of the stars would awe me into humbled stillness, their multiple radiance heightened by the utter blackness of a sky unbleached by city lights.

Moonlit nights also had unforgettable beauty. When heavy frost or a fluff of snow whitened the shingles, I would be marooned above a wonderful glitter of icy-blue sparkles.

Stars above and stars below.

Looking down, I would feel a cozy contrast in the golden warmth diffused by the light beside the door.

Some nights were so cold for moon-viewing that, when I lay flat, my chilled face felt warmed whenever woodsmoke from the nearby chimney breathed over me in soft, slow streams. Whiffs of smoky fragrance usually added another facet of enjoyment.

Unless the wind changed.

Then I might be prodded back down the ladder by acrid fingers of dense smoke.

Nothing, however, marred the thrill one night of a bright, transparent sky encircling a full moon in all its charismatic radiance. Below me, five deer grazed in the moonlit meadow beside the house. Next morning, I looked out on a world so crystallized by frost that the silvery moonlight of the previous night seemed to have stuck to everything and been left behind.

Building the roof structure was only one of my autumn projects. A new outhouse was next on my list.

The present one, worn and weathered, leaned wearily to one side, sliced by gaping fissures through which the brazen wind probed. Goosebumps rose where no one wants goosebumps. Merely sitting down on the split, warped seat boards had developed into a hazardous procedure.

Festoons of cobwebs, nearly rigid with dust, hung drearily from the rafters or clogged the recesses of the board-and-batten walls.

Bats frequently roosted in the crevices and fluttered sleepily whenever the door was opened.

Since the slowly sinking floor, now below ground level, was totally unsafe, one needed the multilegged dexterity of a spider in order to reach the seat without stepping down. Appropriately, ideal models scurried everywhere for anyone quick-witted enough to adopt their techniques.

Even raising the round cover off the seat hole was an experience. Attached firmly to the underside of the lid was a large, soft globe of developing babies guarded by a determined mother spider at least three inches in diameter – including her great, striped legs. As long as I set the lid aside carefully each time, she seemed unperturbed by my intrusions.

For my part, however, eons passed before the spider family was finally grown and scattered.

The roosters were thrilled when I began demolishing the outhouse. My careful efforts to avoid injuring insects and spiders as they were exposed were persistently nullified by Bubble and Squeak, who wolfed down the dispossessed with deep clucks of joy.

After a week's work, the new building was in place. Solid. Gleaming. And, to the satisfaction of two replete roosters, bug-free.

Set into the door was a window with an intricate Tree of Life design, which I'd cut out with the jigsaw and then glazed. For the back wall, I'd made a diamond-shaped window of deep-red glass with a rising bird form. The bench seat was covered with thick polystyrene for warm, splinter-free seating.

Now, instead of sculptured cobwebs, hatching babies, and multilegged pandemonium whenever I wrenched open a sagging door, I twitched open a balanced door. Cleanliness and peace prevailed. Wildlife posters decorated the walls.

For an outhouse, it was almost boring.

One final difficulty now needed to be resolved.

A small footpath, connecting my house to the road, undulated down in a northerly direction from the house across low, bushy ground before rising again at the roadside. With every winter storm, drifts of snow filled in the path nearly to waist level. The terrain was too rough for such contrivances as snow blowers, could I have afforded one.

The only way out was to keep shovelling.

On dewy summer mornings or rainy days, the raspberry canes, tall grasses, and wild rose bushes that bordered the path would lean across it, laden with drops. When I left the house, I'd be soaked to the waist by the time I reached the van. Visitors would arrive at the house in the same condition. Though I'd trim the edges of the path in dry weather, somehow one good rain always seemed to close it in again.

Since it was on the north side of the house and well-shaded by trees, the wet was prolonged all summer, as well as the ice in the spring. A solution had to lie somewhere.

But *where*?

Finally, after twenty years of dogged shovelling, treacherous footing, and sodden knees, my sluggish brain produced an idea. Helped by the indefatigable roosters, as well as a friend who unexpectedly offered a few hours' help – which I seized before he could change his mind – I built a sixty-foot hemlock boardwalk. It spanned the lowest land and created a walkway that was level with the road and the house area. Gone, now, was the worst of winter shovelling. Gone, too, were the icy patches underfoot in the spring and the wet legs throughout the summer.

And gone were the clutching barbs that tore passing grocery bags and released their contents to be retrieved in scratchy scrambles under the bushes.

Now I could lean down casually for a succulent raspberry or inhale the incomparable sweetness of a wild rose while remaining dry. I could lug large paintings to and fro without soaking or scratching myself or their wrappings.

In autumn, I could move load after load of firewood or birdseed in the wheelbarrow along the boardwalk with little effort, instead of struggling up the bumpy slope of the path where tree roots lay like "sleeping policemen" to slow me down.

In winter, accumulated snow could be easily thrust off the edges with a push shovel. Best of all, most snow would be blown off.

Bubble and Squeak took great delight in strutting like kings along the boardwalk or scratching for bugs in the cool, damp soil underneath it. Tirelessly they accompanied me back and forth between the roadside woodpile and the woodshed.

Now whenever one rooster stopped suddenly in front of a fully laden, moving wheelbarrow, I could skid to a stop without snarling – starting up again would be so perfectly easy.

CHAPTER 17

WINTER SOLSTICE

Early one December morning, before the light had risen, I peered out the window to see Orion, a winter constellation, striding high in the sky before the house. At his heels, like a quarry overtaken and passed, hung a crescent moon, waning as though signifying autumn's decline. Indeed, the Winter Solstice, which I would acknowledge with a day and a night of fasting, was near.

I shivered and laid a fire in the woodstove. As the flames snapped and crackled around the softwood kindling, I mixed a hot cocoa in the kitchen. Then I placed hardwood logs on the fire, closed the stove doors, and turned to the manuscript with which I began each day.

A minute insect hovered near me as I worked, flitting about on nearly transparent wings. I worked carefully around the little creature whenever it landed on the pages – and also repressed any sudden, bug-swallowing yawns! However, in a heedless moment of haste, I reached for the dictionary and blundered into my tiny companion. Appalled, I apologized repeatedly as the fluttering wings and legs tried to untangle themselves.

Then I held out my hand hopefully.

To my delight, the tiny bug immediately landed in the centre of my palm, smoothed down each wing, and to all appearances seemed fine. I found those moments a fascinating interaction between species.

When shafts of sunlight were piercing the trees, I looked out into a bleak world. We were indeed poised on the threshold of winter. The solstice would touch the next sunrise with special significance.

In the early light, I strolled back from the outhouse through a leafless, whitened world. Frozen apples still hung from branches or were wedged by squirrels into crevices in the spruce trees. Only a few weeks earlier, as the sun's warmth had dissolved a heavy frost, I'd watched hundreds of yellow birch leaves dropping steadily in the windless silence. On the blue-white ground below, a golden glow had spread. Now the inexorable snow had extinguished their brightness.

Not a bird called. Nothing moved.

I climbed up to my rooftop eyrie, moving gingerly onto the slippery, glittering boards. The distant hills no longer glowed with autumn's fire but bore cool, subdued hues of greys and mauves, blues and browns. Only the leafless hardwoods seemed to respond to the sun's awakening warmth with their familiar, rich, reddish beauty. At the very top of a nearby beech hung a spiderweb, swelling and slackening in moving currents of air that I couldn't detect. The resident spider was so minute that I pictured him being catapulted, web and all, into the next county during one of our sudden autumn gales.

A movement caught my eye and I glanced up.

A transfigured blue jay passed overhead, darkly shadowed. Along the wingtips and outspread tailfeathers blazed a brilliant edging of bright light, transforming a familiar bird into a vision.

In the upper meadow, two deer grazed, their russet coats kindled by the sun's rays. Below me, in the alder bushes, two large ruffed grouse poised effortlessly atop the thin, swaying boughs, twisting off buds and eating them. In the Great Mother spruce, red-breasted nuthatches twitched rhythmically from branch to branch, diligently combing the greenery for insects. Or hopped head foremost down her venerable trunk. Chickadees, kinglets, and tree sparrows mingled with the nuthatches in their sprightly search for food. The melancholy cooing of a pair of mourning doves permeated my whole being as I sat, lost in the ancient beauty of a new sunrise. Lost in my observations and reflections.

Above, a great eagle floated.

I climbed down from the roof with numbed fingers and toes, but paused as I was about to open the house door. Clinging all over the wall and door near the porch light were hundreds of small, drab moths with no distinctive markings on their wings. Like faded autumn leaves. Then I noticed a stalk of dead leaves rising out of the ground. Hanging within the curved stem near the top of the plant was another drab moth. Had I not just seen the others, I would have mistaken this moth for a dead leaf, so perfect was the camouflage.

Somewhat reluctantly, I gathered a handful of the moths from the wall and entered the house. Breakfast had arrived for Chip and Bashō.

Later, I swept out the studio in preparation for a day's work. Gently I began to peel the plastic sheeting off a tall, clay sculpture which was still at the wet stage.

Out of a spiral of ocean beings transforming into avian forms rose a huge spiritbird with uplifted wings, which dominated the upper reaches of the sculpture. But as I slowly unwound the plastic, I felt something shift.

Suddenly, one of the great wings fell away.

With mounting horror I lifted off the last of the covering just as the second wing collapsed.

Both were riddled with grackle-sized beak marks.

Tingling with wrath, I slowly turned the wooden base on its ball bearings. As the sculpture revolved before my shocked eyes, I discovered in the entwining clay forms the gashes of dozens of exploratory beak proddings, culminating in the mangled remains of one of the fish tails. At that moment, Chip bounced down jauntily onto my shoulder – but shot away in alarm as my first bellow shattered the quiet sanctity of the studio.

Morning had indeed broken.

Fortunately, the other housebirds tended to be involved in less detrimental activities – ones less likely to land their necks in the trembling hands of enraged artists.

One-winged Smokey spent much of his time in the studio greenhouse window, which he reached by jumping up a "ladder" of stools and boxes set at reasonable levels to one another. Though he couldn't fly, he had developed an impressive ability to jump three times his own height. A similar set-up in the dining room gained him access to another window with a different view of outside activities.

I found him there one day, close to the glass and obviously fascinated by the swirling flakes of our first snowfall. It was Smokey's first experience of snow.

He seemed very adult now, very independent. Not only did he tussle heroically with Molly, but he also routed mild Desmond on occasion. It was his attitude to Bashō, however, that particularly intrigued me.

Bashō, having weathered Smokey's parenting needs, seemed now to have become the recipient of his courtship gestures. The cooing, bowing, and circling so familiar with interacting city pigeons was now being directed at a puzzled Japanese quail. Bashō, trotting single-mindedly back and forth in his marathon runs, would be disrupted time and again by an ardent pigeon who wouldn't accept a curt refusal as the final answer. He even pursued Bashō amorously throughout the indoor garden. Helpless with laughter, I'd see question marks hovering over Bashō's head as Smokey lumbered foolishly along behind him.

Smokey was one pigeon that could be described as a "pelican in the wilderness."

Bubble and Squeak were now settled in the studio for the winter, a dustbath in a cardboard box substituting for the headier pleasure of bathing outdoors.

One morning, a mother and two little girls stopped in for a visit and I noticed that the roosters, usually so tolerant of human "chicks," were cool to these two. This was a puzzler, since both children were perfectly well behaved.

Though irrepressibly giggly.

At one point, the woman and I slipped off to the studio, leaving the girls and the roosters in the living room. When we returned a short while later, we found each child coiled up in a chair, feet tucked under them so protectively that I knew toes had been nipped. Both roosters were patrolling back and forth before their prisoners as though daring them to leave their chairs.

On the coffee table lay a plate of large chocolate-chip cookies. Each little girl had her hungry dark eyes fastened longingly on them over the roosters' heads.

But the cookies lay hopelessly out of reach.

Bubble, hearing our approach, turned away momentarily from guarding one child. She instantly shot out of her chair, collared a cookie, leaped back into her chair, and covered her toes. Bubble spun around and resumed his vigilance. But the little girl munched blissfully while her sister watched with envy.

"Truly, that one will seize her destiny," I thought with a smile as I bore two protesting roosters off to the studio.

When I returned, the cookies were disappearing rapidly and Chip was delighting the girls by landing on them and eating crumbs out of their hands. Bashō, too, had arrived for his share, and harmony now prevailed. A climb to my rooftop eyrie crowned the morning, and all the visitors left rather reluctantly for home.

In the cold predawn of the Winter Solstice, I dressed warmly before leaving the house to await the sun's first rays. Fasting had increased the significance, in my mind, of the birth of light, the beginning of longer days and shorter nights.

"May my understanding increase like the light, and my shortcomings decrease like the darkness," I thought, ruefully smiling.

For me, the New Year begins with the Solstice, the calendar date of January first having less significance. Thus, my fast parallelled the failing year, the failing light, and became a time for purification.

When the light was renewed, I would literally break fast, that is, breakfast. Nourishment on all levels would coincide with the rising energies of the New Year.

I kindled a tightly woven bundle of herbs at the hearth, the heart of my home, smoke ascending the *axis mundi*, the world's axis, to connect all levels of being as one. Then I sweetened each room with smouldering fragrance. Leaving the house for the chill darkness outside, I climbed onto the roof to await the sun.

An early raven approached me on the roof. As he passed overhead, he glided on unmoving wings, one foot casually scratching his chin, a droll trickster reminding me that humour is vital to the sacred. As though in accord, I noticed squirrels chasing each other and stopping to mate.

In one particularly humorous instance, I watched a female digging in the snow for seeds. She stood eating them with obvious enthusiasm while seemingly indifferent to the male behind her ardently mating with her, as though spring were imminent.

Moments later, a moth fluttered by, a living symbol of metamorphosis, of transformation. Which seemed suitable at such a time.

I recalled an earlier morning when I had discovered, on the pavement in front of a store, a huge *Cecropia* moth. Customers jostled in and out of the door continually. Cars drove up, drove out. Horns blared. When I peered closely at the beautifully patterned wings with their distinctive orbs, they fluttered faintly.

The creature was alive!

Unable to leave it where it could be trod on at any moment, I carried it home and laid it gently in a box of fresh leaves. I also misted the greenery lightly with a plant sprayer and placed a few drops of honey water nearby. By nightfall, she had laid many eggs. When she became increasingly restless, I released her into moonlit darkness, and watched her flit briskly away. Perhaps she seemed stronger because her cargo of eggs had been unloaded. When they hatched, I set the tiny caterpillars outside on suitable leaves to begin their own journeys.

The great moth and her living legacy lingered for years in my memory and surfaced often in artwork. I would try to combine the traditional metamorphic symbolism of moths with their natural attraction to light, and so transform them into thresholds, portals beckoning us forward out of inner darkness into the bright vitality of change. Of growth.

As though in tune with my thoughts about light, the eastern sky grew noticeably brighter.

The first bright rays touched my face, joining the end of autumn to the beginning of winter.

What would the next season bring?

CHAPTER 18

CHRISTMAS HOEDOWN

For many of us, the winter season revolves around the wood-stove. In the shivery early mornings, we huddle down before it, fumbling with matches and kindling. Once a blaze is established, it becomes an unconscious preoccupation for the rest of the day. Whether one is painting or reading, cooking or cleaning, periodically a tiny bell sounds in the back of one's mind:

"Time to put in wood."

Our woodstove is a Fisher Grandma Bear, affectionately dubbed "Grannie." Wide-hipped and efficient, she stands four-square on her brick dais, her cast-iron paws adding a touch of mirth to her austerity. A metal rack adorns her split-level top.

I toyed briefly with the idea of painting her toenails a bright whimsical pink to mellow her grim, corseted figure – but didn't dare.

For years, Grannie has been the heart of this home. She has

warmed us and cooked our food, dried out laundry and icy mitts, thawed frozen suppers and liquified solid honey, provided heatbaths – in lieu of sunbaths – for Chip and other birds, dried wet firewood, and coaxed bread dough to rise.

Coaxed bread dough to rise *again* after Chip has deflated it.

When Bubble and Squeak were adolescents, they'd sprawl luxuriously on the mat beside Grannie's warmth, their eyes closed contentedly. Only for food could they be lured away. To the roosters, heat was almost food.

During the years that County the robin lived with me, dozens of wary brown crickets lived amongst the bricks underneath Grannie. During the daytime, County would hunt them for food, but nights reverberated with the triumphant cheering of the survivors.

Bashō and Grannie together, however, had to be seen to be believed.

Bashō gloried in warmth. Especially in warm toes. He'd sleep beside the stove all night, but by morning, with the fire out, he'd be feeling chilly. Sometimes, too, I'd be away most of a day, or out for an evening, and the house would cool. Particularly the floors. When I returned, Bashō would be fluffed up and morose. I'd quickly kindle a fire and, when the blaze was in full glory, open the front doors of the stove. Then I'd crouch down, pick up Bashō, and hold him in front of the fire.

As soon as the heat seeped through his cold toes and in under his plumage, Bashō was happy. He'd cuddle down in my hands, lift his feathers, and spread his wings, absorbing the heat into every pore. Finally he'd tilt onto his side, wings still opened, and thrust both feet out towards the fire, spreading his cold toes yearningly. His eyes would close in utter bliss.

I'd remain motionless, despite my cramped limbs. Not for worlds would I have moved.

Whenever I arrived home with cold feet after skiing or walking, I'd draw my chair up to Grannie's broad lap, open the doors, and toast my own toes until they were incandescent. I rarely wore a pair of wool socks that weren't scorched brown on the bottoms. Often the roosters would clamber into my lap and, with Bashō lying on the mat beside the stove, we'd all bask in Grannie's glorious glow.

Grannie was the centre around which we all revolved. Our sustainer. Traditionally, the hearth is the spiritual focus of the home. The fire is the spirit, with our pettiness burned away. The rising smoke connects the earth to the heavens. Connects the people to the deities. Connects our earthly selves to our spiritual natures.

Like the smoke of incense lifting up prayers.

Such associations strengthen the home – and the ideal of home. I find myself disoriented in hearthless houses where mere fireplaces entertain, not sustain. Hidden furnaces provide intangible warmth. Televisions disrupt and predominate. There is no centre.

In these houses, I miss the unity of warmth and nourishment. I miss the incense of woodsmoke. I miss the prevailing peace.

I miss Grannie.

One snowy afternoon, on the brink of Christmas, I sat in front of Grannie, toasting my toes. Bashō lay nearby, eyes closed, basking in the warmth. Bubble and Squeak were crowded cozily together in my lap, and Chip preened on my shoulder.

Under the introspective spell of the hearth, I was reflecting on recent changes in my life. The little house now sheltered *two* humans, as well as the birds – a major transformation, since my closest friends were usually feathered. We were a tight fit, too, perches and roosting shelves being more plentiful than chairs or dressers. But fortunately, this newest member of the family, due back at any moment, was an adaptable soul. And a most unusual person.

One who was undaunted at the prospect of living with in-door roosters. Or with a free-flying feathered prankster that sat on his shoulder at every meal, demanding tidbits. Or with warring pigeons and a maniacally trotting quail.

Or even with that greatest of challenges, a serious artist.

Mack had become an important member of the family, disclosing untold depths of warmth and humour – crucial qualities in a household where the humans were always outnumbered.

And often outwitted.

My unconventional lifestyle left no room for frivolities, so that Mack's practical courtship offerings readily impressed me – treats for the birds, waterproof mitts, a kettle that finally worked, and a warm coat. Tickets to dances would have gotten him nowhere.

We'd been casual acquaintances for several years, but since Mack's widowhood and retirement from business, our friendship had deepened into commitment and thereby enriched our lives. Mack finally let his city house and we began our life together, surrounded not by shrieking brakes but by shrieking beaks, in our woodland world.

Mack's enjoyment of new experiences flourished with unexpected arrivals, often at ungodly hours, of injured or starving birds needing immediate intensive care. Sudden squalls of temperament breaking out in the studio failed to ruffle his equanimity. His boundless energy was up to the challenge of hours of lugging artwork to and from the van, up and down staircases, in and out of galleries. He thrived on the anxieties of driving to distant shows.

Even my domestic duties were lightened, not doubled, as Mack immediately took charge of loading the woodbox, splitting kindling, shovelling snow, washing dishes, and doing laundry – for all of which he volunteered.

The man was a godsend.

He also possessed a trickster's style of humour. Following the release of my second book, *In the Company of Birds*, I had done a taped interview for the CBC at the house. The roosters, having been featured in the book, had sat in my lap during the questions with a dignity that easily relegated me to the role of their biographer. Afterwards, to everyone's merriment, they'd condescended to "say a few words" into the proffered microphone.

Not so tiny Bashō, who'd frozen, mute, in mid-stride when the gigantic, sheathed microphone suddenly appeared before him. No such apparition had ever troubled his ancestors, and instinct drew a blank.

The interviewer, a breezy, genial woman, was entranced by "the boys." "Aren't they wonderful?" she enthused, turning to Mack.

"Oh yeah," he shrugged, deadpan, "but we *are* having them for Christmas dinner." The woman stared at him, transfixed.

Then at me.

"Absolutely," I agreed, equally offhand, setting the boys down on the floor. A stunned silence held the room as I prodded their plump forms speculatively. Then I looked up, smiling broadly. "And we'll serve them coconut, raisins, pasta – all their special favourites – at the table with the rest of us!"

In the sudden mirth that dissolved us all, she bubbled, "To think I really believed him! I didn't know how I was going to finish the interview."

I was still chuckling reminiscently as I rose from my chair and left the roosters drowsing happily before the fire. Snow was whirling past the windows as I headed into the kitchen to begin supper. Soon I was chopping and stirring, hampered by an enthusiastic Chip, who had to taste everything and steal what she could.

Mack arrived shortly, stamping the snow off his boots and sending waves of cheery energy before him. Both roosters immediately abandoned the fireside and confronted him on the threshold, daring him to enter the room. They stalked back and forth belligerently with raised hackles, vibrating their stiffened wings like rattlesnake tails. No alien rooster was going to share their territory.

Or their hen.

This had become a chronic difficulty. Whereas the other birds had accepted Mack easily, the roosters never wavered in their opinion of his debased character. If he offered them ordinary tidbits in a conciliatory spirit, they'd ignore the gesture, their cold eyes never leaving his face. Only unusual, irresistible treats would be accepted. But as soon as these had been devoured, hostilities would be resumed.

It was as if they *knew* that his family name "Kohout" meant, in Czechoslovakian, "rooster."

After dinner, we switched off the electric lamps and lit the candles on the tree. As flame after flame sprang into life, the darkness slowly flowered into soft radiance. Both roosters snuggled into my lap, keeping a wary eye on the human rooster in the other chair. After nibbling on pungent spruce tips, they smelled like Christmas trees themselves. Tempting, fresh apples hung from the branches in lieu of artificial ornaments, adding their own fragrance to the festivities. To the boys' chagrin, they hung just out of reach.

Intentionally, I might add.

Our candlelit Christmas tree is especially beautiful. And meaningful. Branches that are going to bear candles are weighted at the ends in order to level them, and I use a variety of weights. Apples are one favourite: bright red, a colour symbolic of sacrifice, yet of vitality, they interact meaningfully with the green of renewal, of resurrection, found in the spruce needles. Together they reinforce the death and rebirth of the light. Of the year.

Another favourite is onions, their many layers signifying multiplicity within unity. As multiple parts of our bodies unite in one organism. As the multiple phenomena of our planet unite in Gaia.

Oranges, too, add a festive touch, their segments merging into wholeness. And decorative gourds – full of seeds, they are associated with fertility, with renewal.

We light twelve candles, for the twelve months of the year, inspiring inner as well as outer illumination.

Feathers, expressing spiritual ascent, are suspended in attractive clusters – some barred, like the changing seasons, like our changing lives. Some chestnut coloured, reminiscent of autumn. Others winter white. Still others hang in graceful curves of iridescent dark green, recalling summer, and hence resurrection. All are contributions from Bubble and Squeak, Desmond and Molly.

Chip's dark feathers carry their own devilish implications.

A garland of rosehips, shells, and beads encircles the tree, looping the branches together and binding the assemblage into one.

Crowning this evergreen of immortality is a whitened goat skull with its suggestion of transience, of the soul's passage through the top of the skull. The sundoor of ancient times.

Obsessive artists can elevate even a Christmas tree into a creation of profound significance.

Or perhaps eccentricity.

As we luxuriated in the candlelit room, Mack opened a container of maple cream. When he plunged a knife into the fudgey sweetness, the roosters immediately became interested. Both combs twitched with curiosity. Bubble stood up in my lap.

Mack ignored them.

He closed his eyes, bit into some maple cream, and chewed rapturously, exuding little moans of ecstasy to taunt the roosters. Both of them were up now, necks outstretched, eyes hopeful. Still, Mack ignored them.

He took a second bite.

Bubble could stand the teasing no longer and clambered onto the arm of my chair, his eyes glued to the maple cream. I pulled him back and remonstrated with Mack till he finally condescended to offer a tiny piece – to Squeak instead.

Squeak eyed it closely, then shook his head, which was his habitual response to anything with a fecal look. Even with both arms wrapped around Bubbs, I could no longer restrain him. He instantly snatched up the soft brown morsel. At such times, fecal resemblance is insignificant.

Rapture indistinguishable from Mack's transformed his face as he swallowed the sticky treasure. In a sudden wingburst he shot off my lap onto Mack's. Beak to beak and eye to eye with his tormentor, Bubble's demand was crystal clear.

MORE!

An enormous bristling rooster with hackles raised and spurs nearly two inches long constitutes a powerful argument – which Mack wisely refused to challenge. Chuckling, he fed Bubbs chunk after chunk of the heavenly confection till Bubble's long hot wattles were dripping with melted maple cream and his beak encrusted. Satiation finally set in. His eyes were blissful.

At this point, Squeak realized that his judgement may have been a little hasty. Overcoming his visual repugnance to the maple cream, he tasted it, and was instantly converted. Soon his beak and wattles were also coated, and the boys cleaned one another's faces affectionately.

The hen, too, finally came in for her share.

Mack's irrepressible humour had already led him to record a message on our answering machine that left first-time listeners helpless with laughter. We discovered friends were calling us at home when they knew we were in town just to hear the tape. Many of our messages were simply bursts of giggling.

For days, Mack had stalked the birds through the house, thrusting a microphone after them while they flitted ahead in alarm. In the studio, he prodded Desmond and Molly into flying off their shelves to escape him. Then he taped their whistling wings and indignant coos as they landed once again. He persistently teased the roosters until they exploded and chased him through the house. Crouched halfway up the stairs, just out of their reach, he held out the microphone while they crowed their frustration at the bottom. At dawn, he drowsily switched on the mike, trying to catch Chip's piercing calls as she swooped over our heads greeting the day.

But taping Bashō was the easiest.

Bashō rigidly insisted on an undisturbed night's rest. If anyone switched on a light, he crowed repeatedly until the light was switched off – a three-syllable shriek that sounded to our badgered ears like "TURN IT OFF!" Since the house was open-plan, his orders, issuing from the indoor garden, lost none of their imperative quality – or volume – in our sleeping loft. Mack once found his way downstairs in the dark and flashed a light for one split second to check the time.

Bashō instantly crowed.

He was a classic example of the dictatorial nature of the "vertically challenged." But the little tyrant allowed one exception to his rule.

Occasionally, Chip, for inscrutable reasons, would refuse to roost when Mack and I were retiring. Ignoring our weary coaxing, she'd remain stubbornly on the kitchen windowsill. In resignation, we'd leave the kitchen light on and go to bed. No matter how long Chip delayed, Bashō would remain perfectly silent, but the minute she roosted, Bashō's bugle would blow, shattering our sleep. "TURN IT OFF! TURN IT OFF!"

I sometimes wondered if they were in cahoots.

However, Bashō's rigidity played easily into Mack's hands. He simply slipped downstairs in the dark to the garden, switched on a light, and held out the microphone just in time for Bashō's indignant outburst.

The trickster had triumphed.

When the tape was complete, surprised callers would hear Squeak's high-pitched crow, Bubble's baritone, Chip's passing screeches in varying volumes, followed by the whistling wings and cooings of Desmond and Molly. Then the irascible spluttering of a Japanese quail rudely awakened from his sleep. Only at the end did the humans have a word:

"Everybody's home but Linda and Mack,
Leave your number and we'll call you back."

As one caller put it, "I thought I'd got Old MacDonald's Farm!"

Telephones can add havoc to lives where eccentricity is already the norm. For reasons obscure to the rest of us, Squeak detested the ring of the telephone. Should I have the temerity to answer, he'd crow over and over, making conversation impossible.

On one memorable occasion, Mack and I were sitting in the living room reading, both roosters dozing in my lap. Mack left the room in response to a call from nature and, a few minutes later, the telephone rang.

I groaned.

Then I hastily shovelled the roosters off my lap and sprang to answer the call. Squeak, outraged, shattered the room with an ear-splitting screech that he couldn't have bettered if he were being flayed. I buried my head in the overcoats hanging beside the phone and strained to hear the caller.

At that point Mack reappeared. Bubble, irritated at being dumped out of a warm lap, and already associating every unholy grievance with Mack, lowered his head, raised his hackles, and *charged*. Pandemonium erupted, with Mack scrambling around the house knocking over mugs and books, Bubble hot on his heels, and Squeak persistently shrieking.

I finally emerged, hot and red-faced from being smothered in overcoats, to find Mack treed in the loft, shouting insults at the roosters. At the bottom of the stairs, Bubble and Squeak were thirsting for his blood, specifying in verbal blasts of unmistakable clarity exactly what they'd do to him if he ever came down again. Chip was swooping at everyone ecstatically and screeching like one possessed.

Only Bashō maintained a dignified silence.

No wonder I dread phone calls.

Christmas day dawned with the countryside deep in snow, but the temperature remained mild. As we sat on the roof at sunrise, an eagle flew low over our heads, his wings passing with a *whssh, whssh, whssh* in the silence. We filled a couple of bags with birdseed and set off for the woods to share my annual role as "Santa Paws."

Snow-laden spruces dripped gently in the warm air. Brooks bursting with meltwater scampered over tangled roots and mossy rocks, their tumblings creating enchanting music. Chickadees busied themselves in the branches over my head, seeking insects, their calls chiming harmoniously with the throbbing waters.

Low over the snow a soft mist hovered.

We wandered through the woods, stopping frequently to tip a handful of seeds down a mousehole or under a log, on top of a stump or onto the outstretched palms of spruces, under a shelter of matted roots from a fallen tree.

Tracks of woodland creatures wove stories around the trees. Hurried mouseprints disappearing under a log were crossed by the pointed precision of fox paws. The stately stepping-stone paces of ruffed grouse across our path quickened where they'd heard our approach. Broad bounds of snowshoe hares over open spaces spoke of fear of the sky. Deep thrusts of diverse deer hooves around a freshly fallen tree revealed a communal feast of lichens.

We spotted a heap of crumbled spruce cones on a stump where a squirrel had dined, and I added a handful of seeds for his next visit. Then we scattered more among the nibbled apples and criss-crossing tracks under an ancient apple tree. Ludicrously, yellow apples glowed high up in the spruce trees where the squirrels had left them.

Near the lake, we found several chewed stumps of yellow birch. There was a trail relatively free from snow, where beavers had dragged lopped trees down to the lake. But two of their felled trees had caught in other trees and hadn't hit the ground. Mack pulled one down to the water for them, but when I tried to dislodge the other, I found it beyond my strength.

I marvelled that, had the tree been free, heavy as it was for me, still they would have gotten it to the lake on their own.

When Mack returned, he untangled the branches and easily pulled the tree down to the lake beside the first tree. Then we scattered a little Christmas seed at the water's edge.

I dropped my last offering down what appeared to be an occupied tree-hole and we headed back home. We were both feeling chilled, and the prospect of enjoying hot cocoa while basking in Grannie's warmth hastened our pace. Both roosters welcomed me as I entered the house, Squeak with lifted wings and bright eyes, Bubble laying tidbits at my feet and bowing.

But Mack received only a double dose of disdain.

Later, while the boys lay in my lap before the fire, and I stroked their silky plumage, I chuckled. Friends had been planning to stop in that evening, but both their children were just recovering from a common childhood illness. Regretfully, we'd agreed on a later date.

We didn't want Bubble and Squeak to contract chicken pox!

The Christmas season lingered. Friends gathered for tree lightings, little children round-eyed with fascination as the candles slowly came to life. Bashō lay with twinkling eyes in my cupped hands, another source of wonder to children. Hot punch and shortbread heightened the festivities – and Chip made sure of her share.

Outdoors, falling snow softened the nights. Shrouded the trees. Whitened the fields, transforming them into the perfection of a primed canvas, waiting. Soon innumerable tracks, two-footed and four-footed, would trace the beauty with familiar designs. Ever new. Ever changing.

We wandered among the trees at night, and across soft, sleeping meadows, white snow our only light. When we stopped to savour, to listen, only the breath of the wind defined the silence.

Above us, stars jewelled the darkness like great candles on the invisible branches of a celestial Christmas tree.

CHAPTER 19

LOOKING FORWARD, LOOKING BACK

On New Year's Eve, we sat up on the roof platform in the cold stillness. A blurred moon loomed before us in the falling snow. Glimpses of starry skies opened and closed, as clouds drifted slowly eastward. For a few moments, Orion strode boldly into the west. Dark flakes whirled before the moon's brightness, which sharpened the snowy undulations nearest us.

The silence was profound.

At midnight we raised tiny glasses of cognac and toasted the moon, its phases signifying Time. Change continual. The circle of decline and renewal.

We sipped cognac. Nibbled shortbread.

Like two-headed Janus (January), we looked back on the old year and forward to the new. In the hearth below us, the new year lifted its wings of flame at midnight, rising like a phoenix from the ashes of the old year. Though for me New Year's Eve lacks the profound significance of the solstice – of the return of the light – still a light-hearted salute to the calendar, amid choice surroundings, is fun.

Tingling with cold, finally, we climbed down from the roof – aware of being in a different year from the one in which we had ascended. Aware of a sense of perpetual renewal.

Aware, too, of transience.

Next morning, the new year dawned on beauty. We headed into the woods on snowshoes, exulting in drifts of shouting, sun-bright snow. In dark spruces hidden and remote behind the dazzle. In soothing blue shadows softening the glare.

A snipe burst out of shallow, spring-fed water in a snow-covered swamp. A deer paused with curious ears while I stood singing to him. In a hidden pocket of hemlocks, we chanced upon seven more deer browsing. They regarded us for some time until the wind changed. Bounding this way and that like ping-pong balls, they were gone.

The crisscrossing network of deer tracks reminded us of a very young visitor, who had arrived with his parents shortly before Christmas. We had all gone for a woodland walk carrying bags of birdseed. With delightful enthusiasm, the youngster had left "presents" of seeds on various "doorsteps" for the creatures. But the real magic for him had been in seeing "reindeer" tracks in the snow. Christmas Eve was only days away and he was bursting with anticipation.

After Christmas, the family came visiting again. They arrived on a cold, windy day, so we planned our walk again in the shelter of the woods. But the little fellow was decidedly unwilling to leave the warmth and comfort of the house.

"We might see more reindeer tracks," his mother coaxed patiently.

But her four-year-old groaned at the obtuseness of adults.

"Not *now*, Mom. They've all gone back to the North Pole!"

Mack and I walked on, chuckling reminiscently and watching for more wildlife. Before us, the splayed tailfeathers of a grouse had rayed the perfect snow upon landing, releasing a beaded trail of footprints that disappeared under the low boughs of the spruces.

High up in a great white pine, fresh yellow chewings on the limbs revealed a porcupine roosting complacently. A bounding white blur bolted across our path as a snowshoe hare sought protection from hungry eyes. Overhead tinkled the sweet calls of evening grosbeaks as a flock swooped past, lifting and falling like ocean swells surging towards the shore.

In the alders hung a tiny nest capped with snow. Like a moment of silence in the surrounding jubilance, it signified summer secrecy, tiny lives being nourished, a mother's watchfulness. Its intricate weavings echoed the weavings of migratory flights returning, to begin new lives again.

A sleeping nest. Woven into a promise. Waiting for the summons of spring.

We emerged from the woods as the sinking sun gilded the long fingers of snow on the spruces. Violet trunks of hardwood trees rose out of the shadowed land, opening into a glowing mesh of incandescent branches. Before us, in the east, a softened moon hung over huge mystical mountains of pink cloud. Behind us, in the west, furry pink and gold clouds glided through the sky-fields like transfigured sheep.

A sunset in both directions. Suitable for Janus's month.

We arrived home in an apple-green afterglow. Ruffed grouse, hastily picking up the last seeds under the feeders, melted away at our approach. Or shot up into the darkened trees in sudden wing-bursts. A flying squirrel vanished, leaving the suet holder spinning quietly. Our boots squealed across the frozen boards of the deck, and we opened the door with mitts that now seemed to chill our hands rather than warm them.

Grannie's welcoming warmth would soon enfold us.

Once indoors, I added wood to the glowing coals and slipped into the bathroom. More than twenty years of gusty outhouses and smelly indoor contrivances had left their mark. Now, for me, a highlight of each day was using the indoor toilet.

When Mack and I began our shared life, his city house, though unsuitable for wildling birds or a wildling artist, nevertheless possessed one alluring feature.

An indoor toilet.

Over the years, I had never fully conquered my reluctance to trudging the dark path to the outhouse. An overgrown path of leafy charm by day, at night it enveloped me in clammy apprehension. The thin beam from the flashlight illuminated only what I knew, but wherever the light passed by, I was certain that familiarity reverted to primal mysteries that flourished only in darkness – and were better not seen.

My imagination was enough to stimulate any bladder.

When I was younger, nighttime trips were rare. But as I grew older, no matter how carefully I governed my fluid intake, I usually found myself at some ungodly hour shuddering on a cold seat.

In the dark.

Mack was impressed with my courage in living alone, and with the unusual survival skills that I had developed over the years – like encouraging nocturnal wildlife. Seeing wary creatures quietly feeding during the night close to the house always reassured me that all was well. Basking in the glow of his esteem, I hated to disillusion him. In desperation, I resorted to subconscious suggestion.

Whenever nature's call wakened me, I would hitch myself closer to Mack's slumbering form and whisper over and over in his ear, "You have to pee . . . you have to pee . . ." Soon he'd waken and groan irritably.

"Darn. I have to pee."

"Really?" I'd murmur consolingly. "So do I. I'll come too."

Together we'd stumble down the dark outhouse path freed suddenly of its usual chilling associations. Then Mack, with gentlemanly deference, would feel obliged to relieve himself in the night wind, while I sat with relative comfort in the shelter of the outhouse. I felt it was an admirable arrangement.

He never commented on our synchronized bladders. Perhaps he felt they were another indication that we were made for each other.

Until one memorable night.

I had just begun my magical incantation into his ear when he suddenly opened his eyes. He glared.

"Ah . . . HAH!"

He'd been *awake*.

Within a week, we had a septic field and an indoor toilet. They cost more than a dozen roses and could hardly be considered romantic, but they did guarantee a perfect sleep every night.

For one of us.

CHAPTER 20

MICE LEARNING TO FLY

Over the next ten days, invisible signposts began to arise, identifying our next avian guest. Signs that I understood only after he'd arrived.

After years without mice in the house, they reappeared, raiding the compost bucket under the sink and the birdseed in the indoor garden. We dusted off the live-trap, baited it with peanut butter, and began to move mouse after mouse down the road. Still they persisted – and mice became part of our daily routine.

That was the first sign.

For several evenings, we enjoyed watching a saw-whet owl hunting moths and mice outside the kitchen window. In the studio, I came across an early painting of "Whoot," a saw-whet owl I'd helped and released nearly twenty years earlier. In the living room, I hung two recent paintings – of owls.

That was the second sign.

In the new, insulated rooster shed attached to the hospice, Squeak developed chills and sickness. He had always been a frail chicken, unlike the mighty Bubbs. I moved them both back into the warmth of the studio and began antibiotic treatment – leaving the rooster shed empty. Sign number three.

Had I read the signs, I would have been waiting for the call.

It came one morning from a retired surgeon. He'd found an owl in his yard, unable to fly. He'd been caring for it for three days, feeding it compost worms. The local official wildlife representative had been unable to advise him on proper feeding, and after improperly identifying it as a short-eared owl, had suggested casually that it would be kinder to put it down.

The surgeon was scandalized.

Friends had recommended that he call me, and I immediately realized the owl was a saw-whet. Its seven-inch height was conclusive. Snow lay deep over the land, meaning that mice, the mainstay of saw-whet diets, were able to travel below the snow's crust for safety. I suspected this owl was suffering from starvation, and this proved to be true.

When the owl was delivered, I lifted him out of the box and cradled him gently, trying to transmit confidence. And caring. Though frightened, he was too weak to object. He stood quietly in my hands, held against my front, trying to get his bearings. Then he slowly tilted his head up and back, eyeing me with an unwinking golden stare.

I could feel the talons relax. And calmness pervade his body.

Mack arrived, having dashed into town to buy beef heart, liver, beef strips, and turkey necks – for our "Feathered Food Bank," as he put it. Later he cut them up, packaged and froze them, a revolting job I was glad he undertook.

We dropped liver, heart, and avian vitamins into the blender. To assist the owl in casting up pellets, we added chicken feathers discarded by Bubble and Squeak, and cuttings from our own hair. In the wild, owls cast up pellets of indigestible matter, such as bones and fur, a process that cleanses their crops. We hoped our substitute roughage would be adequate.

Then we buzzed all the ingredients into a loathsome pulp and offered small dollops on the end of a chopstick to the owl. After we coaxed down the first two mouthfuls, the owl became animated, eagerly cleaning the foodstick as soon as it was presented.

He ate a mouse-sized serving.

As he fed, his eyes softened and partially closed, revealing beautiful feathered eyelids. When he was full, both eyes remained shut, and we left him in seclusion in his covered box.

In the morning, a small, tight casting of our own hair lay at his feet.

We baited the live-trap in the hopes of catching mice to feed the owl. With my lifelong fondness for mice, I was more than grateful to Mack for taking on this part of the owl's rehabilitation. We agreed that no lactating mice would be used, but would be released to return to their babies.

Next morning, the trap still remained empty, but the owl was active and hungry. We warmed the blended substitute to mouse-body temperature and offered it again. We also included extra clippings of our hair, because we felt he should be casting a larger pellet. This time, the owl didn't hesitate but ate from the chopstick as though he'd been using one all his life.

"He's ready for Chinese takeout," Mack chuckled.

While the owl dozed again, we removed most of the shavings from the floor of the rooster shed, leaving only a thin layer. In one corner we anchored a small birch tree with sturdy horizontal branches. In the opposite corner, we set the old Christmas tree, feeling that the dense spruce branches would offer seclusion when needed. Then we moved in the owl.

We soon realized that the spruce tree was *too* dense. Only after Mack thinned it did the owl finally roost in it. Otherwise, the rooster shed, cool and private, we felt, had become an ideal owl shelter.

Opinions, however, vary.

Bubble and Squeak, roaming into the hospice, peered through the low window into their rooster shed and spotted the owl. Instantly, they burst into ear-splitting squawks of alarm. Throughout the rest of the house, birds immediately slipped into hiding and silence. Over and over Bubble and Squeak trumpeted "DANGER!" while I tried fruitlessly to reassure them. Nothing I did would quiet them down.

I was hampered, too, by my giggles. The situation seemed so ludicrous. Both roosters stood well over two feet tall, whereas the owl, on tiptoe, might have achieved seven inches in height.

They could have shredded him like a bun.

In desperation, I pinned cardboard over the window and, after a few dwindling calls, the roosters finally fell silent. My ears sighed with relief. With a triumphant wingflap, Squeak crowed "ALL CLEAR!", followed almost immediately by Bubble.

In the indoor garden, Bashō emerged warily from the shrubbery, straightened up, and crowed a Japanese ALL CLEAR. Chip reappeared, and called out a North American version. In the studio,

Desmond, then Molly, being Lahore pigeons, cooed Pakistani translations of ALL CLEAR. All birds then resumed their usual activities. Would that we humans could communicate so fluently between our own nationalities.

We dubbed the owl "Doc" after his rescuer, the retired surgeon, and over the next few weeks the bird flourished. Whenever Mack opened the live-trap in the owl's room, the freed mouse dashed ahead. Doc instantly dropped out of the tree, and in a split second the mouse was dead. Doc was a sudden, efficient killer, for which I was grateful.

Remembering my friend's comment about mealworms that I was feeding to the birds, I consoled myself with reflecting that these were mice "learning to fly."

Escapes did happen, however.

Twice, when Mack was releasing a mouse, he neglected to close the door behind him. By mischance, or perhaps premonition, each mouse upon release spun around and dashed back to freedom between Mack's feet. For the remainder of the winter, they shared the house with the rest of us, boldly eating seeds in the garden each evening and flatly refusing to enter the trap a second time.

We shrugged. There were other mice in the sea.

On another memorable occasion, a mouse sped out of the trap but swerved suddenly towards the spruce just as Doc landed. The mouse, looking out from behind the spruce trunk with alarmed eyes, spotted the owl only two feet away. There could be no sudden kill now. The mouse would be living in continual mortal terror.

Sheepishly avoiding each other's eyes, Mack opened the small, rooster-sized doorway leading to the outdoors, while I guarded the owl. Then Mack chased the terrified mouse outside.

Doc glared at us in disbelief.

"I'll warm up some substitute," I murmured, and fled to the kitchen.

Whenever possible, we fed Doc one mouse a day, keeping the substitute food in reserve. Soon mice in the house became scarce, so Mack borrowed two extra live-traps. He set one in the wood-shed and the other in the former goatshed, nearby. Now, instead of having to go out once in the night to pee, he had to go out *several* times each night to check his traplines. A captured mouse could freeze in the subzero weather.

By comparison, it gilded his gloomy remembrance of our pre-toilet nights.

As soon as Doc began eating mice regularly, he cast up much larger pellets of tightly compacted fur and bones. One per mouse. His strength gradually returned, until he was able to fly silently up onto the branches, a dead mouse hanging from his beak. Except for a small death wound on the backs of their necks, the mice looked untouched.

At this point, Doc began a curious ritual.

When he had killed his mouse, he lugged it up into the birch tree and hung it, head upwards, in a crotch of branches. There it would stay for hours before being eaten.

I theorized that allowing the blood to congeal prevented wasted nutrients due to spillage. A congealed mouse might also protect plumage and prevent loss of body warmth from wet feath-ers. Whatever the reasoning, for the rest of his stay, Doc persisted in hanging his meat before dining.

With specific exceptions.

There came a spell when we simply couldn't catch mice in any of the traps. Mice are a universal favourite with predators and, living in the woods, we were up against a lot of competitors. We fell back upon the blended substitute, and Doc correspondingly produced smaller pellets, but we felt he should have as natural a diet as possible.

We bought four white mice.

The first white mouse, which Mack released at twilight, trotted forward, then stopped to forage for leftover rooster grains in the shavings. He seemed utterly unaware of the owl in the dusky branches of the tree. The instant Doc spotted the mouse he lifted his wings preparatory to dropping down. Then he paused, teetering uncertainly. Vivid question marks hovered over his head.

Mice aren't white!

He continued to watch the unsuspecting mouse with perplexed eyes. If he'd had a *Field Guide to Eastern Mice*, he'd have been flipping anxiously through it. Finally, with an almost perceptible shrug of resignation, he sped silently down and made his usual instantaneous kill.

This mouse, however, was left for hours in a corner of the floor, rather than up in the tree. By morning, the mouse had been eaten, but for the first time there was blood in the killing spot.

This raised more questions.

We sensed Doc's reluctance to eat the white mouse. Would it taste different, perhaps inferior, to a wild mouse? Also, the outdoor temperature had risen abruptly from bitter cold to well above freezing. Would this sudden mild spell have affected Doc's appetite?

At this point, we caught a deermouse and, when we released it in Doc's room at twilight, there was no hesitation. Doc not only killed it instantly but hung it up in the tree once again. To further confuse us, the second white mouse, upon release, was killed – but eaten – immediately.

How I wished Doc could be persuaded to eat tofu instead.

Tofu learning to fly?

CHAPTER 21

AN OWL FOR POSTERITY

During Doc's recuperation, we were visited by John and Janet Foster, nationally known naturalists and filmmakers, who planned to do filming for Discovery Channel. Having enjoyed their marvellous nature films on television for many years, I was in awe when they actually walked into our home loaded with equipment.

I needn't have been anxious.

The Fosters' easy manner, their innate sensitivity, and their natural gift for merging harmoniously into their immediate environment smoothed the way. We seemed to have known each other for years.

Despite having filmed every kind of creature in every part of Canada, John and Janet had also retained their vital freshness. They seemed to take as much delight in our feathered family as in more exotic species living in inaccessible corners of the hinterland.

Both of them wanted to be behind the one camera when Desmond was lolling in his bathwater, eyes closed in rapture, while I showered him with the plant sprayer. His radiant "smile" was obvious even to strangers, rendering them almost helpless with mirth.

The Fosters were honestly amazed at the gentleness and beauty of both huge roosters. In the evenings, I lay back in my chair, my feet on a footstool, while the boys sprawled languidly in my lap – which at such moments extended to my ankles. Even the Great James River Morning Rooster Romp was successfully filmed, both boys "chasing" me gleefully through the house regardless of camera, lights, and outbursts of laughter from strangers. This aerobic workout had become our usual morning ritual whenever I let them out of the studio to begin each day.

Chip, true to her unpredictable nature, was friendly to all, but persistently eluded the camera. Only after considerable coaxing did she allow herself to be filmed. Unlike her juvenile days when she positively dominated the CBC camera, her mature years found her quite coy.

Mealworms, rather than an adoring public, finally precipitated her comeback.

Doc delighted both Fosters, and proved to be the soul of co-operation. Although they preferred to film with existing light, a free-standing lamp was needed in the owl's room, its brilliance carefully adjusted so as not to overwhelm Doc. Everyone moved and spoke very quietly in order to create the least amount of disturbance, and soon all was in readiness. Then Mack offered warm substitute food on a chopstick at midday to a drowsy owl accustomed to a mouse delivered at dusk.

We all kept our fingers crossed.

Doc swivelled his head and casually eyed the offering. Mack prodded his beak gently but encouragingly with the foodstick. John quietly filmed. Janet and I watched breathlessly from the doorway.

Moments passed. We still waited.

Then, with supreme dignity, Doc hooded his eyes and swallowed the morsel. He turned a wide golden stare onto the second offering. This he accepted also, followed more reluctantly by a third. Finally, he closed his eyes in dismissal. Jubilant but silent, we backed out of the room, carrying the equipment, and left Doc in well-earned repose.

It was small Bashō, however, who won Janet's heart. He snuggled down into her cupped hands without the slightest hesitation. With twinkling eyes, he lay there most of the evening, a captivating handful of delicate beauty. Only under pressure did Janet yield her small companion to John, who was also intrigued. Bashō, sensitive to the differing energies in everyone's hands, hesitated, but finally consented. Soon he was snuggled in John's gentle hands, enchanting him too, while Janet watched yearningly.

I warned them both that I would be checking their pockets before they left.

Many of my paintings, books, and sculptures were also filmed during those two days, with the Fosters taping my interpretive commentary. Later they added their own voice-overs, revealing an understanding of my art that I can only *dream* of finding in most curators.

The resulting film was as much a tribute to the Fosters' perception, intelligence, and sensitivity as it was to my life.

And a tribute to Mack's unsurpassable homemade bread, which fortified us all during an intense filming schedule.

As the snow deepened, so did the beauty of the woods. We snowshoed along our footpaths, widening them into ski trails. Branches were snipped, windfalls and standing dead trees cut and pulled off the track. Whenever possible, we avoided cutting live trees.

High up in dense spruce areas, we spotted squirrel nests,

efficient biodegradable housing. Deer tracks crossed and recrossed our paths, suggesting new possibilities for ski trails. Stepping with great precision in single file, the feet of wary ruffed grouse traced the snow in elegant stitchery. In the mixed tracks that emerged and disappeared around us, the bounding prints of fishers lightened the sombre, stealthy stride of stalking wildcats.

So much to read in the snow.

But best of all, we liked being in the woods when snow was falling. A windless snowfall of softness and silence. A time of flakes falling thickly and steadily, blurring the receding trees. Large flakes settling so lightly on their points that we could see between them. Settling, too, on even the tiniest projections. On the irregularities of vertical bark. On spider webs. On eyelashes. Yet mounting up so rapidly that soon bare twigs swelled to many times their usual size and wove intricate white patterns of rare beauty against the textured sky.

I have often wondered at the emphasis we put on no two snowflakes looking identical. I find it difficult to marvel solely at that when, looking around me, I see no two leaves alike either. No two clouds. Not even so-called identical twins.

What does amaze me is the unity of it all. The interconnectedness.

I arose before the sun on these chilly mornings, to meditate and pursue my writing before various daily demands intruded. Often, the setting moon, sinking slowly behind the hills, shone softly through the west windows. Sometimes a crystal-bright waning crescent, with stars here and there among hurrying clouds. Soon, deep azure would transform the eastern sky as it began to lighten.

I'd kindle a fire in Grannie's capacious belly and carry a hot cocoa up to my desk by the east window. I'd also carry up Bashō, who had strong opinions on cold toes. He'd snuggle into my housecoat while I wrote and, as the warmth pervaded him, emit tiny notes of happiness. Then he'd tuck his head behind his wing out of the glare of the lamp, and doze. I'd gently rub his neck feathers while I pondered an elusive word. Often, a deermouse, cheeks bulging with stolen seeds, peered at me from the bookcase over my head.

Inevitably, I'd have to interrupt my work to answer nature's call, and I'd set Bashō under the covers on top of Mack's warm chest. Inevitably Bashō, too, would answer nature's call. Mack, still dozing, would become unpleasantly aware of a warm wetness, followed by an eye-opening aroma. At this point, in all innocence, I'd return and retrieve Bashō.

Mack, mopping himself off yet again, refused to marvel at this daily coincidence. He declared it was all a calculated plot. He'd mound the covers over himself once again and with a determined effort finally sink into sleep just as the sun's rays rose above the trees, gilding the hilltops.

A daily event that never ceased to stimulate Chip.

Her first calls welcoming the morning would shatter the drowsy duskiness downstairs. Soon we would hear whirring wings and she'd bounce down on my shoulder with beaming eyes – and piercing screeches.

Mack would moan piteously and bury his head. Chip, intrigued, would land on his pillow and turn up the volume. Mack, snarling, would thrust out his head and bare his teeth. Chip would spring into the air and zoom around and around the room, shrieking excitedly. Then land by him again, looking for more fun.

It was just Mack's fate to be the only night owl in a house full of morning risers.

Chip's views on in-house owls became clear the day she spotted Doc flying briefly around the hospice, which opens off the living room. Mack and I soon directed him back through the doorway into his own shed, but Chip had seen enough. She shot up into our sleeping loft and refused to come down.

Even for food.

Day after day, Chip stayed in the loft. Though we coaxed and coaxed, she remained adamant. She greedily watched Bashō eating mealworms in the garden but refused to swoop down and steal them – showing self-discipline I never suspected she possessed. Instead, she ate what we brought her.

At night, she slept on the lamp beside our bed and shattered each morning with welcoming shrieks – to Mack's daily despair.

Nearly a week passed in this way before Chip began short forays to the indoor garden. But the slightest noise – a dropped spoon, a sneeze – shot her straight up to the loft again. When she ventured as far as the kitchen, I was relieved. And when she dug a deep hole in a fresh loaf of Mack's bread, cooling on the kitchen counter, I knew she was back to normal.

I ignored Mack's deplorable suggestion that we vary Doc's mouse diet with marinated grackle.

Doc was physically well enough to release after two to three weeks of solid fare, but unusually deep snow yet smothered the land. Mice still travelled below the crust, and no doubt other saw-whets were struggling for survival. To free him now would be to return him to conditions that had nearly defeated him. Indoors he was eating readily and well, and showing no signs of unhappiness due to confinement.

Our final decision was to feed him until the snow had shrunk to a manageable depth, yet release him in time for the saw-whet courting and nesting season, beginning about March.

At this time, the Animal Care Technician at the university bequeathed to us several frozen mice and gerbils. We offered Doc one a day, thawed, whenever we lacked live fare. To our relief, he ate them readily.

A gerbil, being so much larger than a mouse, actually lasted two days. While twenty-four hours from a frozen mouse gave us a welcome reprieve from the constant preoccupation of catching live food, forty-eight hours from a frozen gerbil became a holiday.

No wonder frozen goods are the ultimate convenience for busy parents.

On the twenty-ninth of February, in a "leap" of faith, we opened Doc's window near dusk. Successive thaws had reduced the depth of the snow, and the saw-whet's courting season was fast approaching. After some hesitation, Doc flitted outside and landed on a nearby branch. In the outdoor immensity, he looked tinier than ever. He peered this way and that for twenty minutes before lifting his wings and slipping silently away, leaving only his memory – and his image on film for posterity.

We watched with mixed feelings: satisfied to see him restored to his natural element in good health; regretful to have seen the last of such a fascinating bird.

And jubilant at declaring a truce with the mice.

We eyed the skies, hoping that the worst of winter was now past. Hoping Doc would be able now to provide his own mice.

Knowing we would always wonder.

In Mack's shameless words, we'd have to read *Who's Who* to find out how Doc was getting on.

With Doc gone and with him our need to collect mice, they naturally flourished once again in the indoor garden. Night after night, they disturbed the sleeping birds with their scuffling and squeaking, and dishes of birdseed melted away.

"Where were they when we needed them?" we muttered, combing the house and plugging even the smallest of holes, while we caught and released mouse after mouse.

Once I was awakened, I had difficulty falling asleep again. Often the snap of the trap or the persistent rattling from a captured mouse opened my eyes. If I trekked downstairs to release the mouse outdoors, the disruption cost me another hour or two of sleep.

Mack, on the other hand, could float downstairs half asleep, open the front door to the ankle-gripping night wind, shake out a mouse, rebait the trap, trudge back upstairs, and be asleep the moment his head hit the pillow. There's no justice.

But there are alternatives.

Remembering my previous success at coercing him to the outhouse at night, I resorted to a similar ploy. When the trap woke me, I sidled closer and murmured over and over, "You have to pee . . . you have to pee . . ."

Soon Mack would groan irritably and get up. I'd sigh as though his rising had disturbed me, mumble, "Sounds like a mouse in the trap again, dear," cozy down in the covers, and fall asleep before he returned.

Though many women feel God is a female, only men have suggested that the devil is too.

CHAPTER 22

NIGHT LIGHTS

Moonlight on fresh snow is utterly magical – and irresistible. Mack and I set off one evening on snowshoes just as a full moon was rising great and golden in the east. We trekked up and down the gentle undulations of the fields, then plunged into the shadowed mystery of the woods.

There, familiarity ceased. Above us, the moon grew smaller and more remote, yet brighter, exchanging its gold for silver. Its cold radiance glittered on the snow, deepening the shadows of the trees. Dissolving distances. Heightening the hitherto unnoticeable.

We floated through long ripples of velvety dark and sudden brightness as though underwater. As though the shadows were moving and we were still. In the eerie blue light, strange shapes flowed towards us and passed, denying our presence. We had slipped into a primordial solitude. A fluid reality utterly removed from the hearty fellowship of sunlight.

Like fish rising to the surface, we ascended an open hillside. As the trees dwindled behind us, we lifted our faces to the stars. Before us, the full moon shone calmly, familiar now. Unlike the strange moon whose uncanny touch had so altered the woods. To our right, high above a valley, strode Orion the Hunter in his glittering belt, centuries-old image of undaunted energy. To our left rose a distant hillside, dignified with spacious hardwood trees, the hue of their sturdy trunks softened to a luminous grey in the moonlight. We turned around, our eyes never leaving the skies. There, above the chastened woods, glowed the Hale-Bopp comet, its glorious tail adding the final touch of magic to the night.

We sat on a log among gentle hardwoods, sipping tea from a Thermos, our usual loquacity quieted by silence and silvery beauty everywhere. The sharp hoot of a hunting owl cut through the stillness almost visibly. Stars sparkled at our feet and peered through the entwining branches above our heads.

Later, we headed for the open fields, treading galaxies of reflected moonlight and leaving a dark trail of snowshoe prints across a glittering universe.

Back home we stretched our toes towards Grannie's warmth and raised steaming mugs. Mack browned slices of his homemade bread over the coals, filling the room with the unsurpassable fragrance of toast. Through the window we watched the union of sun and moon – death and renewal in a total lunar eclipse. The passage of time, as signified by lunar phases, faded. Our utter absorption as the moon disappeared created a corresponding sensation of limbo within us.

Time dissolved into darkness. Into oblivion.

Slowly the rind of the moon began to reemerge among the stars. And the ticking of time resumed.

Extreme crescent moons are special. Their delicate beauty appears in the mysterious interval between day and night. They are outriders of the moving mass of darkness. A waxing crescent in the sun's afterglow heralds the approaching night. A waning crescent, hovering in the chill pre-dawn, lingers behind the darkness dissolving into the west.

In the icy green twilight of one winter day, I saw the tiniest moon of the year. A waxing crescent so fragile, barely a discernable curve, that its gossamer beauty will always haunt me. Like an otherworldly aspiration of greatness and delicacy, forever unattainable.

Late one afternoon, as the sun was sinking behind the western trees, we set off for the woods on skis. Snow had fallen all day and, although skiing uphill was difficult and slippery, downhill we floated. In the deep fluff, sudden landings were fun.

A great moon climbed steadily into the sky, its luminosity darkening the tangled shadows of the trees. As always, our sensation of gliding underwater was heightened. We halted beneath the enormous special Tree, which glimmered in the moonlight. A barred owl hooted, and on a whim I answered. After a few moments, a shadowy form landed on a nearby branch. The owl cocked his head this way and that, examining us curiously. I hooted again, but my first effort was the best, and the owl floated away, unimpressed.

The way home lay downhill from the Tree, and the snow was fast. With little or no depth perception in the uncanny light, we felt almost weightless as we glided rapidly down the curving woodland trails. The final slope was steep, and we shot out of the woven shadows of the trees onto calm moonlit fields with stars above and stars below.

Overhead strode the stalwart constellation of Orion. Though traditionally seen as the hunter, to me he is also a defender. At the darkest time of the year he gleams above our home. His great bow arches upwards as though protecting our pinprick personal world.

Our shelter in the trees. Our hearth of warm embers, surrounded by sleeping birds.

Wherever long fingers of light from our porch touched the frosted bushes, thousands of stars glinted, rivalling the moon-bright snow and spangled sky. Heaven and earth were indivisible, and we floated through galactic glitter.

As I glanced up at the stars flickering among the tracery of bare branches like unattainable fruits of immortality, I noted again the similarity of both ends of a hardwood tree. I chuckled at a tale from my childhood days of trees hiding their heads in the ground during winter, leaving their roots in the sky. Not until later years did I read about ancient Hindu and Christian concepts of the Tree of Life being upside down. Its sky roots were nourished by the gods. Its branches swept the earth, offering their bounty to earth dwellers.

High in the sky swung the Big Dipper, slowly turning every twelve hours, through the centuries. In northern countries, it is always visible, unlike many other constellations, and is thus associated with immortality. It shines out of a few of my paintings in which I need to place emphasis on the imperishable, the unchanging.

Years ago, on a dark winter's evening, I slipped out of the house to view the stars. I set out for the drumlin, a small sudden hill left in the fields by receding glaciers in the Pleistocene era. As I emerged from the shelter of the trees, I suddenly perceived the northern lights dancing above. I ran eagerly up the drumlin and stood open-mouthed in wonder.

I was actually *surrounded* by northern lights.

From every point on the horizon, long tongues of rosy light punctuated by stars were shooting up to the zenith high above my head. Over and over, they flared and faded, flared and faded, in living pulsations, as though driven by the beating heart of the universe.

In the concentrated brightness over my head, one elongated area of sky remained dark, untouched by vibrations of colour. It was shaped like a hawk hovering on outstretched wings. And I felt immediately vulnerable, small – like a mouse.

No longer did the night sky seem remote. Restless molten-bright energies had transformed the usual black backdrop to the stars, swelling the sky until it pressed against the shrinking earth. Even the snowy fields around me glowed pink, as though the kindled earth were responding to a primal call. Witnessing such cosmic conflagration in the utter silence of a remote hilltop increased the eeriness. And my dilating sense of isolation.

At that moment, the uncanny stillness erupted into shrill howling and yelping, like deep shudders made audible. Invisible coyotes had contributed the only possible accompaniment to such a night.

A night I'll never forget.

Another experience of northern lights, though not so dramatic, still glows in my memory. I had been visiting friends who lived on a farm at the edge of the sea. Since their driveway in winter was an experience in itself, I had wisely left my car at the roadside. Later, as I carefully picked my way back down the long icy driveway to the road, I suddenly stopped, enraptured.

Pulsations of green light, mingled with blood red, filled the northern sky, darting beyond the zenith in bursts of glorious energy. Below, on the calm salt water of a protected bay, floated hundreds of Canada geese. A continual murmuring of their voices hovered as though on invisible wings above their shadowy forms, incomparable music that completed the vibrant splendour of the heavens.

Yet another winter's night left a singular memory, though no moon, stars, or northern lights graced the night sky. Only a faint diffusion of light from the nearby town. I was crossing a field during thick falling snow. As I walked on, surrounded by silence, only the faint swish of my boots through the fluff could be heard.

Suddenly I felt something pass above me. A soft hissing on the edge of hearing. Then silence. Or did I hear anything?

I paused, waiting. Listening. The snow fell softly around me.

Then I heard it again, but more clearly with my footsteps stilled. I looked up.

A large, dark mass swept past and was gone. I waited a few moments. It swept past again, a soft hiss in the darkness. Then again. But I had finally understood.

A huge flock of crows were circling over the field on muffled wingbeats. Occasionally a single muted croak would be heard. Around and around they flew, circling silently and steadily in the falling snow, while I remained rooted. Enchanted.

And knowing I'd always remember.

CHAPTER 23

CABIN FEVER

Snowfall succeeded snowfall as winter deepened. Drifts were shaped into fantastic sculptures, knife-edged and curved with geometric precision. Even stranger configurations evolved close to the walls of the house, fashioned and refashioned by thwarted winds and whirling eddies, their invisible energies made visible.

The surrounding peace and beauty of the muffled land lured us outside almost daily on skis and snowshoes. But when sudden thaws and rains crusted the fields with ice, we were cabin-bound.

And wholly at the mercy of the birds.

Squeak's latest illness had yielded to antibiotic treatment, restoring his vitality and enabling him to assist Bubble in monitoring the movements of that third rooster, Mack. The boys stalked him throughout the house with cold disfavour, marching with military precision in what I called the "testosterone two-step." They lunged with lethal spurs whenever his back was turned, guarded

the studio doorway while I painted, sat in my lap daring him to come near.

I found their loyalty quite touching. Mack found more caustic words for it.

Every morning I wedged a fresh apple into the base of the easel and, with delighted bites, the boys devoured the entire fruit down to the stem – sometimes, in their enthusiasm, flicking bits of apple onto the canvas. But if Mack, in an effort to ease the underlying tensions, offered to share *his* apple during the evening, while we all relaxed in the living room, both roosters remained frigidly aloof.

Chocolate, however, enraptured them. Switching shamelessly to sudden overtures of irrepressible affection, they coaxed generous portions of his chocolate bar out of him. But as soon as the delectables were finished, hostilities were resumed. Mack quickly found that bribery lasted only as long as the bribes.

On one subject, however, Mack and the boys were in continual accord. Neither of the feathered roosters had ever evinced the slightest interest in my homemade whole-wheat bread. They'd pick up a morsel, as though hoping for improved flavour, then drop it with resignation. Mack, possessing more courtesy, gave every appearance of enjoying it.

But when he offered the boys tidbits of his homemade rye, they wolfed it down with tactless enthusiasm. Miffed (not to say cunning), I suggested that the menfolk should assume all the bread-making responsibilities in our household.

Which they did.

As Mack faithfully kneaded bread in the kitchen each week, Bubble and Squeak lingered nearby, supervising – and passing judgment on little samples of uncooked dough. When the hot loaves finally emerged from the oven, permeating the house with a mouthwatering aroma, the boys were first in line for their share. Rye, whole-wheat, apple-raisin-oatmeal (with raisins soaked in whiskey), even beer bread all attained the roosters' strict standard of approval.

Outnumbered, I could only agree.

Each morning, as soon as I opened the studio door, I would turn and bolt through the kitchen to the living room, with Bubble and Squeak "chasing" me excitedly. There I'd spin around and scoop them up in exuberant hugs.

This was the Great James River Morning Rooster Romp, which John and Janet Foster had filmed.

Though only two roosters were in the race, Squeak, when ill, finished last. Now, restored to his usual vigour, he was finishing second – a difference not immediately apparent to outsiders.

Some evenings, Mack would sit back picking out familiar melodies on his guitar, hoping to lull my ever-vigilant protectors. Bubble would pointedly ignore him. No "rooster" playing ever so sweetly could impress him, and he'd hunker down in my lap with renewed determination.

Squeak, however, was intrigued.

He'd wander over to the enemy's camp and stand by the half-hour, watching Mack's fingers gliding up and down the strings. He never crowed with irritability as he did the instant he heard the television. Or the telephone. He just remained quietly watching.

I would wonder aloud whether Squeak listened because he easily distinguished good music – or because he didn't.

Louder strumming would be Mack's only reply.

One evening, as I settled into my usual chair, Bubble immediately jumped into my lap, demanding hugs. He always enjoyed them, but on certain days he seemed to really *crave* them. This was obviously one of those insatiable times.

Seeing Bubbs getting all the attention, Squeak came running over to our chair and pattered back and forth anxiously. Hoping to avoid his frustrated crows, which would be bellowed at unbearable decibels, I scooped him up beside Bubble. Squeak instantly pushed past Bubbs to stand closer to my face and be first in line for cuddles.

Looking rather put out, Bubble turned away and dropped back down to the floor. Then he spotted a small heap of crumbs set aside for Bashō on top of his "doorstep" to the garden. Bubbs immediately broke out clucking in a loud, very compelling voice, calling and calling till Squeak finally left me to check out Bubble's find. As soon as Squeak began nibbling the crumbs, Bubble sprang back into my lap, pushing up to my face for hugs and cuddles, and ultimately drooling with bliss.

It was the same trick the wily Squeak had pulled on Bubble two or three times in their younger days.

Only rarely, however, could *both* roosters be tricked.

One evening, years earlier, a friend dropped in for a visit. Immersed in the Eastern discipline of Aikido, he offered to show me special breathing techniques to assist relaxation and release additional energy.

Both roosters instantly disapproved. They stalked menacingly towards him, bristling, until I hastily intervened, shooing them over to the edge of the room to watch instead. Ear-splitting crows erupted from Squeak every time the visitor spoke, while Bubble's frigid stare seemed to suggest that any attempt to steal the spoons would be futile.

Both roosters, united, generated enough tension to challenge any relaxation technique. Even their spurs looked twice as long as usual.

Despite his reception, the visitor maintained his sense of ease. Perhaps his knowledge of self-defence manoeuvres sustained him. However, having also witnessed Bubble and Squeak in action, I wouldn't have known where to place my money.

With the roosters' eyes never leaving us, and with Squeak fracturing the silence at unexpected moments, we stood in the centre of the room. The visitor stepped a little ahead of me so I could follow his lead, then focussed his concentration in inner stillness.

Slowly, he began.

The technique evolved out of deliberate movements and pauses held together by controlled breathing. Sometimes we were gathering energies from a crouching posture. Sometimes reaching out or above and encompassing. Sometimes releasing.

Over and over we glided through the time-honoured movements. My breathing began to feel integrated with each moment of being. It became a conscious centring instead of an unnoticed mechanism, generating a wonderful sense of wholeness. Overriding tensions dissolved into their proper irrelevance, and harmony prevailed.

As we finally breathed to a stop, I became aware of the silence – not to say, peace. I glanced over at the roosters and smothered a laugh.

They were standing with drooping heads and closed eyes. Squeak's head hung down nearly to the floor. Gentle snores rose from their unconscious forms.

Both were sound asleep.

Developing even the slightest illusion of relaxation could only benefit someone like me, perpetually on the rebound between the tensions of a studio and the daily demands of unpredictable creatures. I can recall instances where even a rudimentary ability to restrain myself might have averted further disaster during an already doomed day.

One morning, before Mack and I were together, I rose very early as usual to write. As I worked, I became so engrossed in my work that I lingered over it long past sunrise. Denied breakfast at their customary hour, the creatures rose collectively in revolt.

From the studio, Bubble and Squeak called over and over, banging the door for emphasis. Occasional mysterious crashes, not unlike the breaking up of furniture, also magnified their displeasure. I turned a deaf ear and wrote on. With words flowing so unusually well that morning, I couldn't have laid down my pen unless the walls gave way.

From the indoor garden, Bashō crowed in persistent crescendos, at a volume out of all proportion to his size. Desmond and Molly arrived behind me and immediately began to fight. They struck each other angrily with their wings, their shrill insults muffled with beakfuls of one another's feathers. Their claws scrabbled for footholds on the bare floor as they wrestled back and forth.

I donned ear protectors and wrote on.

Finally Chip, favouring a more direct method of registering her complaints, began bouncing down on my head, shrieking piercingly, and springing up again – a perpetual disruption guaranteed to destroy any writer's concentration. She landed each time as though she were wearing ski boots and hammered on the ear protectors like a demented woodpecker.

I laid down my pen at last.

Unwritten words, those shadowy gropings of thoughts seeking articulation, are timid creatures and often need coaxing. These shuddered and fled.

After breakfast all round, I set a wash going in the machine and buzzed through the house, doing a hasty cleanup of droppings. Winter days are short and sometimes chores are long. I was anxious to start painting before the light declined.

Though the outside thermometer had plunged well below zero, most of my windows were clear. Glittering arabesques of frost graced the less-efficient ones, as though offering beauty in exchange for their chilly shortcomings. The frozen deck-boards squeaked shrilly under my boots as I crossed them to fill my containers with birdseed.

Turning back, I skidded suddenly on the icy edge of the deck and banged my head on the large wooden feeder that hung from a low branch. My arms and legs shot out, sending up wild spewings of birdseed in all directions. They stung my face, dropped down my neck and into my boots, and sank out of sight in the deep snow. They landed everywhere but in the feeder.

I limped back into the house, rubbing my head and muttering ominously.

By this time, the wash was done. The machine drained into the bathtub as usual, while I crammed wet clothes into the spin dryer. Then I realized that the water had *remained* in the tub. Oh no, I moaned. Surely the drainpipe isn't frozen again.

It was.

Gritting my teeth, I refilled the machine for the rinse cycle, and after it had drained again into the tub, got out a large stockpot. I began lugging load after load of dirty water to the kitchen sink, while the roosters "helped."

Unable to see my feet while carrying a brimming pot, I stepped blindly, pushing cautiously against them at times. Unwittingly, I trod on Squeak's toes. He instantly screeched and I jerked back, slopping a wave of water down my legs and into the carpet. Another squawk from Bubble directly behind me as my heel came down on his toes galvanized me again, and I slopped the second wave over Squeak as well as myself.

Both roosters looked at me reproachfully.

With the gauge on my sweating forehead rising dangerously, I choked back the delicious profanity I longed to scream at the world generally, and finished the job. Then I changed my sodden pants.

In the studio, finally, I settled down to work on a circular painting that was nearly finished. It depicted a large nest woven into a core of four branches – the centre within the four directions. Falling snowflakes of varying sizes surrounded it, while glowing visionary nestlings rose above the snow-capped nest: the promise of future generations.

A whale haunted the lower regions of the canvas. Its dark, devouring implications paralleled the silent, frozen season and long nights empty of nesting songbirds. Yet the whale's association with the ocean spoke too of creative potential, of the waters of life, as do the melting snows of spring and the welcome return of migratory birds.

The painting had laid in well, but the work had been intensive – especially delineating endless snowflakes, which later danced frenetically in my dreams at night. I was tired but anxious to finish the remaining area – the actual nest. I wanted it to be composed not of woven grasses and twigs, but of migratory flights and energies studded with stars of guidance. I had less daylight remaining than I'd hoped, but plunged in confidently.

It wasn't long before my confidence changed to horror.

Then to panic.

The nest wasn't working as I had envisioned it at all. Acrylic paint dries immediately, so wiping out errors isn't an option unless one uses retardants, which I've always viewed with suspicion. I like my paints pure.

There being no going back, I painted on, faster and faster, as though leaping from tussock to tussock in a swamp. I began to rail inwardly at my idiocy, my arrogance, my habit of carrying difficult painting ideas around in my colander head instead of working out every detail first, tangibly.

I railed even louder because I knew I always would.

Still, I painted.

Faster and faster I worked, my brush darting here, darting there, all over the nest. I was crying now, and utterly furious. My panic deepened as I realized that what was emerging bore little resemblance to my original vision, yet I didn't dare stop. I couldn't bear to lose the whole thing.

Wild exhortations and imprecations began to break out as beads of sweat rolled down my face and my clothes clung damply. No dessert ever created can compete with the sweetness of certain profanities in the heat of the moment.

That day I tasted them all.

After two hours, the light was down and, in a final burst of vexation and tears, I threw the protective dustcloth over the painting.

Was it ruined? Was it a success?

I had no idea. And I knew I'd need a week before I could look at it to find out. No wonder the word "pain" is part of the word "painting." And "painter."

Exhausted, I wandered out to the kitchen and noticed for the first time that the roosters had fled the storm in the studio and were lying on the couch. They raised their heads when they saw me, but I ignored them and peered wearily into the fridge. I felt too tired to cook anything and too irritable to care what I ate. I lifted out a plate of cold pancakes and poured what I thought was maple syrup all over them.

It was herbal cough syrup. And the last straw.

I wolfed them down anyway. The stomach ache that followed seemed a fitting end to such a day.

A week later, friends stopped in, people aesthetically sensitive, and honest. They wanted to see the painting, and I left them to it.

I still hadn't peeked under the cover and waited nervously in the kitchen for their verdict.

There was utter silence in the studio.

Then, "It's wonderful," they breathed. I galloped out to join them and stared in amazement.

Within the confines of the nest, windswept bird energies wove around glowing orbs in convoluted rhythms that, at a distance, emulated the entwining components of an actual nest. It was all I'd hoped it would be.

The Sleeping Nest now hangs on their wall, but when I relive that stormy session in the studio, I marvel at real nests under coverlets of snow sleeping through wintry blasts as fierce as my own. Recalling my dementia, I wonder whimsically that the sleeping nest wasn't jolted awake.

And I wonder, ruefully, just who painted it.

CHAPTER 24

DON'T WAKE ME IF
YOU CAN'T SEE THE TREES

After a night of falling snow, Mack and I rose early one morning and climbed onto the roof platform. The breath-catching cold that had gripped our world so long had mellowed. The slumbering land seemed faintly to breathe once again, and the thermometer rose to zero.

Rays of early red sunlight pierced the grey pall in the east and kindled hilltops in the west. For a brief moment, a weathered barn became transfigured into a visionary one. Then the sun was submerged once again, and the colours faded. The sparkle vanished from the snowflakes that were still falling.

Snow clung to every twig and branch, softening the brittle treetop twigginess that surrounded us on the roof. Tall strips of snow hugged the north sides of trees and posts along the fenceline, where the winds had had their way in the night. In the morning stillness, snow spiralled down with gentle persistence.

Against a muted backdrop of falling flakes, whitened fields, and pallid sky, a huge black raven sat motionless in an elm tree. Like a spoken word within silence. Like a Japanese poem.

Below us, at the feeders, pairs of blue jays passed each other seeds. Holding to their lifelong bond with each other. Anticipating the nesting season soon to begin.

Raccoon tracks crisscrossed the roof in all directions. Each night, half a dozen woolly rascals congregated under the feeders, where they'd loll on their haunches till the morning light, eating birdseed and kitchen scraps. The hugest one we nicknamed "Bear."

When Bear rolled back onto his behind, his thick, ringed tail would protrude before him and his hind legs would sprawl out ridiculously on either side of his belly. Hour after hour, he'd sit, his black fingers feeling moodily through the litter of hulls, selecting seeds and cramming them into his mouth. His jaws never stopped working. Behind the characteristic mask, a vacuous gaze belied his constant vigilance.

But his ponderous paunch foiled sudden escapes.

Often at our approach, Bear was the last raccoon up a tree, grunting laboriously, his heaving bulk a visible reproach to all who disturbed him.

Mack, like a true trickster, often tweaked Bear's tail, adding insult to indignity.

Bear and his cronies grew quite accustomed to my quiet entries into their nocturnal world on my way to and from the roof platform. They'd look up at the sound of my voice and occasionally shuffle to one side, but seldom felt threatened enough to climb a tree. This morning we noticed a wide scattering of beautiful feathers – a grouse dinner the raccoons had enjoyed the night before. One less grouse would join the little flock of fourteen that had graced our feeding stations each day.

One night, when I still lived alone, I was undressing in the loft at bedtime. Suddenly the protective household stillness was marred by crunching footsteps on the roof outside my bedroom window.

My heart bounded like a rubber ball.

With trembling fingers I switched off the light, crept to the side of the window, and peered out. At first I could see nothing. Then what I had believed to be shadow moved into dappled moonlight and I giggled weakly.

It was a large raccoon.

Now as Mack and I sat on the roof savouring the morning, we watched our resident porcupine lumber forth to climb one of the ancient beeches along the fenceline. Of late, he'd taken to sheltering among the stacked firewood during windy times. On the house wall inside the woodshed there is a tiny, low door that opens into a woodbox inside the house. Often I'd find myself crouched down pushing firewood through the little doorway while chatting cheerily to a sleepy, but wary, porky only a few feet away.

The sun emerged once again through the dissolving clouds, and the falling snow dwindled to hovering flakes twinkling like stars around us. Warmth and brightness grew steadily. On the chimney of a neighbouring house we saw starlings toasting their toes. Most of the snow had slid off the south slope of the barn roof, leaving it bare and steaming in the sunshine. There a huddle of pigeons preened.

Creatures survive winter in ingenious ways. When I was building a fire in the woodstove one morning, I snapped the icy bark off a log. A frozen spider fell out. I was holding its fragile form lightly in my hand, wondering how many must die by freezing, when I detected movement. As my warmth pervaded the tiny body, the spider began flexing its stiffened legs. It took steps. Soon it was walking naturally, while I watched, utterly humbled by the miracle of it all.

On another winter's day, I had retreated temporarily from the bone-chilling north windows in the studio, and was reading by the fire in delicious warmth. I raised my eyes just in time to see a beautiful yellow butterfly drift past and alight in the indoor garden. Despite the brittle cold outside, the butterfly had emerged, like a redeeming spirit of summer, from a cocoon hidden somewhere in the house. A gentle reproof to winter's blustery tantrums.

I was so moved by the winter butterfly that it took wing again later that winter in a painting.

The midwinter thaw that began that morning lingered like an illusion of spring. Rains routed the snow, leaving huddled remnants hidden in hollows. On the bare southern slope of the garden I planted garlic, a chore left over from fall. Against all reason, moths floated past me as I worked. Boisterous winds tumbled the clouds and rolled them across the skies. The peaceful colours of sunset were scrambled like a painter's palette.

I watched a pileated woodpecker with flaring feathers not so much flying as being blown across the field. Blue jays tacked like sailboats, speeding in one direction while facing and flapping in another. The smaller birds wisely stayed in the shelter of the woods.

Stepping outside during still evenings to savour the stars, I'd be shaken by sudden heart-stopping explosions of ice cracking on the lake nearby. Echoing booms that seemed to bring the lake right up to the door. Jellied from the knees down, I'd be irresistibly reminded of Mack's abrupt sneezes.

One of his recent nasal blasts, delivered like a backfiring bus, shot Chip straight off her perch one night and me out of a sound sleep. Groggy and bewildered, I heard Chip crashing about in the dark and scrambled to switch on a light before she hurt herself. Mack was helpless with laughter.

I retorted with a testy ultimatum that he at least give warning before striking, as any decent rattlesnake would. I reminded him that even the roosters, before shattering the stillness by crowing, usually flapped their wings first.

Thereafter, whenever Mack felt a sneeze coming, he too flapped his "wings" – an interesting gesture that, while restoring tranquility to my life, raised serious doubts in the minds of the uninitiated who witnessed it.

One afternoon, the temperature was so mild we took supper to the shore. We set out in perfect sunshine and blue skies – only to arrive at a fogbound beach. After eating, we wandered down the sands and climbed great ice floes piled along the water's edge.

The quiet fog muffled all sounds and created an aura of mystery around the familiar. It encircled us almost watchfully, so that we walked in a small cave of visibility that continuously opened before us and closed behind us. Occasional seabirds appeared briefly, scanned us, then glided on into obscurity. Only our footsteps and the tinkling drops from the melting ice floes touched the silence. We had walked into another reality.

Then one night the thermometer plunged again. Winter's holiday had ended. It was business as usual.

I opened the outhouse door during a power outage, only to find myself gazing into a crystal cave. Frost feathers stuccoed the walls and ceiling, intricate icy plumes two to three inches high. Though enraptured by the sudden beauty, I shuddered. Then lowered myself gingerly onto the seat.

I intended to be brief. I didn't want crystals to begin forming where no one wants crystals.

From a fallen apple branch nearby rose clustered veins of ice, arching up and over into a perfect ocean wave. Hokusai's Great Wave incarnate. Similar veins of water, lifeblood of the earth, thrust up out of the ground as the frost gripped the soil, and froze in clumps like crystalline grass.

Deeply embedded in lake ice, intricate designs like miniature trees created a magical world just out of our reach – but accessible to the imagination.

Years ago, in the woodshed, I discovered other patterns that energized my thinking, though they weren't formed of ice. On the inner side of a large crust of bark, seemingly random splotches shaped themselves insistently into a sobering visual metaphor. I carried the bark excitedly into the house and began to draw from it – fleeing burning figures, a gigantic, smouldering horse's head, and disintegrating buildings all emerged from the variegated markings.

Later, an intense painting called *Nemesis* developed, of a cosmic conflagration with fleeing figures. Of a planet vandalized by aggression.

Snow again quilted the land, protecting sleeping roots from the piercing probes of frost. Insulating chipmunk burrows. Packing icy slopes so deer could wander and graze freely.

We went up to bed one night with winds bending the trees. Clumps of ice sprang from the branches and rattled on the metal roof. Dense snow blew sideways across the fields.

Mack peered moodily out the window. We hoped to go skating at the town rink after my usual morning writing was done, but the porch light revealed wild whippings of frenzied flakes. "Don't wake me if you can't see the trees," was his final word as he turned out the light.

Two days after the storm, we hiked into the woods carrying lunch in a backpack. Red squirrels flitted secretively across shaggy branches. Chickadees chimed in the treetops.

In a quiet dell of tall hemlocks, we surprised a group of six deer. Two of them were bedded down but rose quickly on our arrival. Though we froze in motionless admiration, they watched us only briefly with lifted ears and twitching tails. Then, stamping the snow decisively, they turned as one and bounded soundlessly away, vanishing almost instantly.

In a tall spruce, we gazed up into the watchful eyes of a barred owl. Later, another owl swept silently away through the trees.

A fallen nest from summers past lay in the snow, its protective unity dissolving into chaotic twigs and grasses. Borrowed materials being returned.

In a little hollow by a spring, we broke off dead branches and kindled a fire. Soon the delicious aroma of woodsmoke rose like incense into the stillness. Warmth reached out cordially from the crackling flames. We sat back on fallen trees, sipping hot chocolate and eating apples. Over glowing coals, we toasted Mack's home-made bread and saturated it with butter. Peace prevailed.

Everywhere but at home.

Chip, in high spirits and looking for devilry, found plenty of it. She began with the sewing machine and quickly discovered the knack of pulling out thread – luckily without entangling herself. She looped it gracefully around the living-room plants, encircled a lamp, and dropped the end finally in the kitchen.

On the coffee table, she tipped the lid off a dish of candies, removed most of the contents one by one, and twisted off the wrappers, scattering candies and wrappers all over the rug.

Getting into stride, she spotted the open compost bucket, forgotten on the counter. Snatching up a cluster of eggshells, she carried them off to the living room and systematically crumbled *them* all over the rug. Then she grabbed strips of cucumber seeds coated with coffee grounds and flew to the studio. With appalling dexterity, she shredded them into an unsavoury, floating mass on top of the roosters' drinking water.

Moving on to the bathroom, she detached the shower curtain, hook by hook.

Up in the loft, she tossed clean, damp underwear off a drying rack onto a floor that always seemed to need sweeping. Some items she managed to drape alluringly over the railing. Others flew over the railing entirely and dropped heavily onto filthy crumbled bark and stacked logs below, narrowly missing the hot woodstove.

In a burst of ingenuity, she unhooked the short door leading into the studio and released Bubble and Squeak as partners in crime. They immediately joined forces with Chip and hooked recipe books off a shelf. Then they tore out pages with their beaks and scratched the fragments about with their feet as though scratching through seeds.

Back in the kitchen, Chip discovered a pot of cooked macaroni that she'd overlooked earlier, during her rummages in the compost bucket. As if knowing it was destined for the roosters, she hurled out piece after piece with gay abandon, while the boys ate their fill.

Going through recipe books had sharpened their appetites.

The uneaten macaroni hardened and stuck wherever it landed. And it landed everywhere.

As a second course, Chip dug an enormous hole in a loaf of fresh bread that was cooling on the counter. Beakfuls of bread flew in all directions, though many of the morsels that hit the floor were fielded by the roosters. Evidently, however, they'd found the macaroni rather filling, and couldn't quite manage all the bread either.

As I pointed out to Mack when we returned, and were standing in stupefied horror amidst the chaos, the birds had obviously learned traditional human roles. Being a woman, Chip had redecorated the house and served out the food. Being men, the roosters had eaten and left the clean-up for someone else.

It would have been so much tidier if we'd only been burgled.

CHAPTER 25

Spring Threshold

The thermometer veered yet again.

With the seasons between winter and spring, the fickle weather produced neither snow nor warmth but drizzled freezing rain for days.

Ice coated all the tree buds, staple food for ruffed grouse. Ice hardened almost immediately on birdseed scattered over the ground. Ice crusted the woodlands, creating treacherous walking for deer already wearied by winter's vagaries.

And ice continually re-formed on walkways or car windows, inspiring new levels of profanity in certain humans – humans, like deer, wearied by winter's vagaries.

Finally one morning, the cloudbank oozed moodily into the northeast to brighten other lives with its dreary dripping. Sunshine burst over the land, vanquishing the gloom and igniting the silvered trees in eye-dazzling glory. Tiny rainbows sprang into being out of prismatic glitter. The icy coating of branches surrendered to the warmth and broke away, falling in musical tinklings on the crust below the trees. Brooks danced.

After the long silence of winter, we could hear nature's pulse beating again.

The very earth seemed to sigh and relax.

From the roof one evening, Mack and I watched deer venturing out into the meadow. A crow passed, bearing a large twig for nest-building. Below us, five skunks emerged from under the studio, their usual winter quarters. They congregated under the feeders and began searching for food.

Of one accord, we began tossing pieces of cookie among them, giggling helplessly at their varied reactions as cookies rained down out of the sky.

I tried to toss my offerings in front of each skunk. If I succeeded, the skunk immediately cornered the morsel and began to eat. If my aim was off, I usually struck a skunk on the head. He'd jump back, blundering into one of his companions, and tails, like questions, would be raised.

Mack, with his usual trickster humour, aimed only for the skunks. Whenever a fragment bounced off a skunk's back, the victim would instantly erect an outraged tail and glare around at the others. They, oblivious of any broken taboos, would continue to chew blissfully. The smitten skunk, realizing he would miss his share, would then lower his tail – but only gradually, as though not entirely convinced that he hadn't been insulted. He, too, would be blissfully chewing when the next chunk struck him.

One of the skunks was an old favourite named Sooty. Only the top of her head and the tip of her tail were white. The long stripe joining them was missing, and her back was black. Seen from above in the deepening dusk, Sooty in motion looked like one small white creature chasing another – or two romping in tandem.

Indoors, spring's energy was affecting the roosters. Very little dirt remained in the large box that I had provided for indoor dust-baths. They were eager to luxuriate in sun-warmed earth and scratch up feasts of bugs. Unfortunately, though mild winds teased the land and southern slopes were beginning to respond, ice still prevailed, and the ground remained frozen. Bubble began to get edgy. Occasional pseudo-cockfights became tainted with serious undertones.

We came home one day to a crisis.

The boys had had a disagreement, and Squeak, the smaller of the two, was injured. Over the previous couple of years, a peculiar lump had developed on his magnificent comb. This lump had now been punctured and was bleeding profusely. Blood trickled down the side of Squeak's face, and he shook his head repeatedly, splattering gore all over the studio. His chest plumage was saturated.

The fight had probably been no worse than their usual brief encounters, because the boys were now cozied down together. If the lump hadn't been punctured, the situation wouldn't have been serious.

For two hours we laboured to stop the bleeding. We tried direct pressure, antibiotic ointment, and finally unbleached flour. The lump persistently refilled and dripped blood. Flour proved to be the most effective, but every handful also dusted the bloody plumage on his chest, forming a revolting paste.

After the bleeding had stopped for half an hour, it began again. I quickly coated an adhesive bandage with antibiotic ointment and folded it around the comb, pressing it down thoroughly. The flow finally ceased.

We washed Squeak's plumage, marvelling at his patient, trusting nature, and dried him with a blow-dryer. Then I fastened a sock over his foot to prevent him scratching his comb. With lots of reassuring hugs, we bedded him down.

Bubble we also fitted out with socks in case he caused further complications and, for the first time in their lives, separated the boys for the night. An hour's scrubbing restored the studio, and we reeled off to bed ourselves, bone-deep exhausted.

Five days later I removed Squeak's bandage, which was hanging off his comb. The cut looked sealed, but in fifteen minutes began bleeding again. Though Mack and I laboured for an hour and a half with flour and corn starch, applying direct pressure, pressure above, and adhesive bandages, we couldn't stop the bleeding. Professional help was needed. Despite Bubble's shrill cries, we bundled up Squeak, carried him out to the car, and drove rapidly to town.

He lay trustfully in my arms while I caressed his neck feathers and reassured him. But his utter passivity chilled my heart.

The vet tried repeatedly to tie off the bleeding with a stitch. Then he opened the lump further, seeking for another bleeder. He cauterized twice.

Nothing worked.

Finally he decided to put Squeak under a general anesthetic and add stitches to permanently deflate the lump. To stop what he called the aneurysm.

I still held Squeak in my arms. The mask was fitted over his face, and he sank into unconsciousness. I remained holding him, trying to convey reassurance. Trying to hold onto his life.

But in vain.

In a few minutes, Squeak stopped breathing. Never a strong chicken, he'd lost too much blood to be able to withstand the added burden of the anesthetic. Devastated, I carried him home and froze his body for burial in the spring.

Numbed with grief, I stumbled out to the studio to see Bubbs. He welcomed me in his usual way, picking up tidbits and laying them at my feet, but I couldn't respond. I remained silent, sickened, leaning against the doorway. Finally I slid down onto my knees, staring wordlessly at him.

Bubble froze. He stared intently into my eyes. For several long moments, he remained utterly motionless, not even blinking, while

I told him about Squeak. Our interlocked gaze created a bridge of communication that was almost palpable. Almost visible.

I had absolutely no doubt that Bubble understood my message. He knew now that Squeak was dead. He walked silently into my arms, and we hugged long and hard.

Outside the window, snow began to fall. Large, soft flakes like feathers. No two alike. I used to describe Squeak's tweedy white plumage as snowflake plumage. No two of his feathers were ever patterned alike.

That night, in the living room, Bubbs jumped up onto my legs and, after we hugged, lay down across my knees. He left my lap bare, as though an invisible Squeak lay in his usual spot.

Maybe he did.

Over the next few weeks, I tried to comfort Bubble, to ease his obvious despondency. I coaxed him to eat his usual favourite foods, but he grieved, and food had little interest for him. He hated to eat alone and ate very little if we chanced to be away during the day. Often I brought his dish into the living room in the evenings and watched sadly as he happily ate the same food he'd left all day. He showed an accelerated interest in sharing my food instead, and ate very tidily off my plate. New foods became his favourites – stewed rhubarb and strawberries; cooked green or yellow beans, which he swallowed whole like a human sucking back a strand of spaghetti; peanut butter and honey on bread; cooked squash and carrots; scalloped potatoes; stir-fried veggies; pita-bread veggie sandwiches.

With Squeak gone he seemed to identify wholly with us, and we often took him along in the car. He rode like a king in my lap.

I wondered if he saw Squeak everywhere, as I did. And heard him. Heard Squeak's deep clucks of joy when lettuce, raisins, or warm macaroni arrived in the morning food dish. Heard his piercing crows prodding the sun to be up and doing.

Saw him standing beside me as I painted, tugging on my pant-leg so I'd caress his neck feathers with my free hand. Saw his smug contentment as he sat in my lap before the easel. Saw him asleep in my arms, snoring trustfully.

Whenever both roosters were snuggled down in my lap, Squeak had liked to curl his toes up in the palm of my hand. As they warmed, he'd doze blissfully – a ritual that stemmed from his chick days, when his whole body could lie basking in the warmth of my hand. He was sensitive to chilling.

Squeak was still everywhere. Watching Mack play guitar or bake bread. Letting fledgling birds sit on his back. Lifting his wings to me in his own special greeting.

His patience with his own problems was enviable. He had staggered about gallantly in homemade shoes as a chick to straighten his toes. His coordination lingered long behind Bubble's, so that even his ability to jump into my lap was achieved months later than Bubbs'. One wing was permanently twisted, and often hurt him when it was touched. He had chronic ear problems, which meant I had to clean his ears every week. Even his beautiful plumage took months to first develop, rather than a few weeks.

Squeak definitely had "special needs."

I'll always be grateful to that thin plumage that decreed that Squeak would never survive outdoor winters in sheds as do other chickens. Living with both roosters indoors involved me in a rich companionship I would otherwise have missed.

It filled my days with fascinating insights. Provided me with interaction at depths never known to someone who approaches chickens only to feed or to pen them.

I have been privileged.

CHAPTER 26

SPRING

Spring, I'm beginning to suspect, is an illusion. A state of mind, rather than a defined season. An ideal left over from the golden age of antiquity.

Despite the bland assurances of the wall calendar, we seem to experience only occasional days of perfection that escape bone-chilling north winds and plummeting temperatures. We weary of delicate crocus blossoms drooping dejectedly under heavy caps of wet snow. Dwindling firewood generates anxiety. Glowing photographs on seed packages taunt us.

We're bounced from one wintry setback to another, like a kayak caught in rapids, until one day we're suddenly catapulted onto the calm surface of summer. Billowing heat and blackflies enervate us, well levels drop, and everyone agrees we need rain.

Only migratory birds seem to know when it's spring.

Paradoxically, therefore, we went cross-country skiing on the first day of spring – a warm, sunny day in the open, but cool in the woodland shadows. A day crowned by a jubilant blue sky, but cursed with snow which either bogged us down in sunshine or shot us downhill in shade on icy ball bearings.

Tracks of more sensible creatures, who were using their feet, crisscrossed in all directions. The busy tread of mink, fox, deer, and squirrel mingled with the delicate meandering trail of grouse. Large, stately steps revealed the unmistakable presence of a bear out of hibernation – and more convinced than we of spring's presence.

Above our heads, gray jays peered down curiously from spruce branches. In an elm tree, nine bald eagles perched in unassailable dignity. A single grackle, forerunner of the flocks to come, flighted by.

Trout turned in a deep pool swollen by rushing, sparkling meltwater and graced with budding alders. The distinctive call of a red-winged blackbird rose out of a marshy hollow still bound by snow, where brittle, broken reeds jutted up like angular knees.

Though winter and spring seemed locked in a struggle for supremacy, we knew who the winner would be when we saw a robin and heard its "cheerily-cheerily" call. Vibrations from its ancient spring song gently released winter's stranglehold. Melted its icy fingers. Quickened the thaw tinkling musically around us.

As we turned towards home, we almost expected to be swatting mosquitoes when we took off our skis.

We wandered outside one morning, unable to resist the intoxicating sweet-and-sour smells of spring, as a warm south wind began to strengthen. A tiny vole emerged cautiously from under the studio to gather seeds. On the silo feeder above him, siskins fed each other. As we walked away from the house, grackles dropped out of the trees to feed. Their squeaky calls and iridescent plumage were echoed indoors by a gleaming Chip, who was watching from the windowsill.

Further afield, the irresistible warmth of strengthening sunlight beguiled the shallow crisp snow into melting and releasing the lower meadow. Millions of glittering sparkles sprang out from the softening crystals. The dazzle created a slight vertigo in me, a touch of weightlessness, as though I were passing through it rather than treading on it.

High in the maple that towers over the rest of the woods, pileated woodpeckers were mating. The melodic trillings of finches opened around us like musical buds. Sleek pussywillows emerged, soft and grey as spring mist. A duck rested on the beaver dam, her bill tucked behind her wing, while bright waters sparkled around her. As bright as her watchful eyes.

On the tops of the hills, icy branches of hardwoods glittered in the sunlight. A song sparrow sang from the fenceline. Shading our eyes, we watched bald eagles spiralling high in the sky in their singular courtship rituals.

Across open patches of ground, robins ran.

Paused.

Ran again.

They often snatched up food. Curious about what they were eating, we wandered towards the flock through alternating patches of snow and stubble. The dead grass was vibrant with black spiders darting this way and that between our footsteps. Food galore.

In the distance, a fox crossed to the woods, carrying a dead muskrat in his jaws. The muffled drumming of ruffed grouse vibrated in the forest. As we drew nearer the house, we watched the black, white, and yellow of evening grosbeaks brightening the trees beside the feeders. Closer still, we could see red squirrels frenetically chasing chipmunks, as well as each other. Two squirrels rolled over and over down the slope in front of the house, grappling and chattering feverishly. Territorial restrictions were a clear indication of spring.

In the warm earth near the south wall of the house grew snowdrops, each with drooping white "ears" like Nubian goats. Spears of daffodils protruded gingerly, like tentative periscopes testing the weather. The tips of their green leaves were singed yellow by earlier frosts.

But the seeds of spring are often planted in the dark of winter.

One frosty night in January we had heard horrific screeching from the field across the road. Was one creature killing another? Was there a trap holding an animal? The screams persisted.

We snatched up flashlights and headed outdoors, me well behind Mack – in order, as I pointed out, to give him a clear view.

He glanced sideways at me but made no comment.

We plunged into the ditch, up the other side, and strode quickly across the snowy stubble. The cries rang out louder. Suddenly they stopped, and our lights revealed two large porcupines, alone in the dark field – two porcupines engaged in a delicate and very private ritual necessary to the perpetuation of their species. They blinked in the brightness that interrupted their night of bliss.

We turned off our lights and returned to the house, blushing.

Now, as spring danced on the threshold, that baby porcupine would also be nearing a threshold – of birth.

On the bird feeders at night, we watched flying squirrels. Two of these delightful nocturnal creatures would sit side by side, each holding up food to eat. When one squirrel finished chewing, he'd reach over and gently take part of the other's food. When the other finished, he'd retrieve some from the first squirrel. Eventually both would be finished, they'd each pick up new morsels, and the ritual would continue.

Their soft fur, grey on their backs, white on their bellies, was so beautifully set off by their enormous dark eyes, and such intrinsic charm was further enhanced by their gentle interplay. Chip, watching from the windowsill, seemed equally intrigued.

On another occasion, I looked out the kitchen window after dark. In the glow from the porch light, a flying squirrel searched the empty feeder. I slipped quietly out the door beside him, murmuring reassurances, scooped seed out of the metal bin, and turned around. The squirrel still sat on the feeder, watching me.

I moved slowly towards him, holding out seeds on my hand. Only when it was inches from his twitching nose did his courage waver. Or perhaps his innate caution admonished him. In any case, he sprang lightly up the tree. As soon as I returned indoors, he dropped down on the seeds and began to eat.

During the days, as we worked outside, a pair of gray jays began appearing regularly. With their soft grey and white plumage and large dark eyes, they seem to me to be the avian equivalent of flying squirrels.

The gray jays frequently landed near us, watching us expectantly, and quickly taught us to carry bread or cookies in our pockets. One landed freely on our hands to pick up treats, but the other seemed warier, taking food only when it was set on a branch or tossed on the ground. They began peering through the windows at us and, as soon as we noticed them, swooping around to the door to wait. So well were we trained that we'd appear almost immediately with food.

One afternoon, I was reading indoors. Despite being engrossed in my book, I was soon aware of a sense of being watched. I looked up into the intent gaze of a gray jay outside the window. I got up obediently, and he swept around to the door. In a few moments he was standing on my hand, selecting morsels, flying off to hide them, then returning for more. Only when he had taken all he wanted did I return to my book.

The gray jays remained with us only a few weeks before moving on. We have a lot of blue jays in our immediate area, and the gentler grays seldom remain near dense populations of blue jays.

Beneath the house floor, spring energies had begun early to burst out. During February evenings, our peaceful solitude had been frequently marred by the savage snarls and squeals of raccoons in the throes of courtship. Their uproar conveyed to us not amorous amity but the shrill protests of one raccoon being gruesomely flayed by another. Often the reek of skunk would pervade the house at ungodly hours, temporarily vanquishing the lovers and lifting us out of a sound sleep on the fumes.

One night, sudden snarls erupted so fiercely that Chip shot off her perch in the dark, convinced at last that predators had invaded her sanctum. The pandemonium jolted us awake too, and we switched on a light. Chip skidded to a stop on our pillows, her eyes like platters, and flatly refused to go back downstairs. She remained on our bedside lamp for the rest of the night, and we all drifted into an uneasy stupor, numbed by skunk fumes.

The skunk emissions seemed to occur most often under the back porch in which our outerwear hung. Whenever we donned our jackets and left the house, the pervasive odour of skunk would follow us. Heads would turn in stores as we passed guiltily down aisles. We didn't dare enter a restaurant. Even opening the car door after we'd ridden to town released malodorous musk in nauseating waves.

Washing our jackets was futile. Their welcome freshness almost seemed to trigger another blast of skunk the same evening. We took to hanging all our jackets out on nearby tree branches instead of indoors, creating a gypsy-like atmosphere for callers.

We clung to hopes of an early spring, when our downstairs tenants would finally move out.

Now, in the warmer weather that began to prevail, we heard the unmistakable churring of baby raccoons under the studio floor. During the following weeks, the mother moved her kits several times to different locations under the house. They were next heard under the woodbox, then under the indoor garden. From there, they were shifted to beneath the couch, then under the stereo, and finally back under the woodbox.

Soon we'd be seeing them tumbling at their mother's feet as they followed her in her nightly quests for food.

One afternoon, during the raccoons' nursery days, I let Bubble out into the rooster run for an enjoyable scratch in the thawed earth. He basked in the spring sunshine and devoured bugs, while I tucked into indoor chores, which had accumulated alarmingly.

After a couple of hours, I felt a sudden uneasiness about Bubbs.

The feeling not only persisted but intensified, so I brought him inside. Twenty minutes later, the mother raccoon was rummaging through the wild-bird feeder on top of a pole in the rooster run.

I broke into clammy perspiration at the narrowness of Bubble's escape, for raccoons are notorious chicken killers. I stormed outside, shouting and banging angrily, trying to drive her away. She scrambled down the pole and retreated to the far end of the run, where she paused, looking mildly at me. I snatched up a stone and hurled it, but she only ran over to it in the hopes that it was food. She sniffed it, then looked up, disappointed.

Suddenly, I realized how thin she was. How desperately hungry. How well fed her babies probably were at her expense.

I felt ashamed.

We were plentifully stocked with food. Bubble, after all, had not been harmed. And birdseed was hardly decent nourishment for a nursing mother.

When I returned with food, she was nowhere to be seen, but I dropped cheese and buns in front of her den under the studio. Soon excited squeals broke out. The feast was on. Later Mack contributed fish skin and I added some of Bubble's cooked macaroni. From that day, we offered supper scraps regularly, until the family left for good.

However, because of other wandering raccoons, Bubble's safety each day became an anxious preoccupation. Only in spring do the activities of raccoons cease to be strictly nocturnal, it seems. I'd hear Bubble's alarm call, fly to the window, and see a great raccoon climbing the fence of the rooster run, his hungry eyes fastened on Bubbs. As it was, Bubble was outside only from late morning to late afternoon. This was the safest time of day – a period buffered by hours of daylight on each end.

Still, I checked on him constantly, anxieties crawling over my skin like ants.

Raccoons were a nuisance in other ways, too. They lingered in the rooster run all night, cleaning the last seeds out of the feeder and sifting through the hulls on the ground. With such thorough competition for seeds, flying squirrels, one of our favourite creatures, ceased their visits.

If I forgot to bring in the delicate silo feeder, I would find it dismembered all over the ground in the morning. Siskins and goldfinches would have to wait for their breakfast while I repaired their feeder. To top off everything, piles of raccoon excrement would be left to defile Bubble's run and drinking water.

It was Mack who provided a solution.

Years earlier, hidden in the gardens and trees surrounding his city house, he had discovered a wild duck on her nest near his small pond. Raccoons were plentiful, and he knew she stood little chance of escaping their searching noses. He quickly set up an invisible barrier around her in the same way that he protected his vegetable garden.

He drove three stakes into the ground to form a triangle, with the duck's nest in the centre. On each stake he suspended a tin can, punctured several times just below the top, leaving the lid hinged.

Then he peed into each can.

Raccoons respect territories. Boundaries are defined by urine. When sunshine evaporated some of the urine, or rain diluted its efficacy, Mack pried up the lid, refilled it, and pushed the lid down again. Odour drifted out of the punctured holes, surprisingly unnoticed by humans but well understood by raccoon noses.

That duck hatched a full brood even though raccoons were spotted every night nearby.

Surrounded by malodorous cans, Mack's garden – even the ripened corn – also escaped raccoons.

In a similar fashion, we suspended pee cans all around the

rooster run, and the results were immediate. Even the silo feeder remained untouched.

Spring's insistent momentum continued to transform lives.

Indoors, Chip haunted the windowsills, bursting with song as she pursued the returning grackles from feeder to feeder. I wondered uneasily if she would lay eggs again.

One-winged Smokey began following Bashō the quail all over the house again, while we watched, puzzled. Trying to elude him, Bashō would duck in between low plants in the indoor garden. This manoeuvre gave him only a temporary respite, for Smokey would search the shrubbery plant by plant. Soon tiny Bashō would emerge, trotting hard, with Smokey the pigeon lumbering foolishly in his wake. On one occasion Bashō's patience blew, and he stormed around and around Smokey, nipping his toes and chittering angrily. Smokey waited meekly until Bashō had finished and trotted off, still grumbling – then ambled amiably after him.

All became clear the day I discovered Smokey's hidden nest, fashioned of shredded newspapers, rooster feathers, and even a few soy mein noodles purloined from Chip's treat dish.

Smokey wanted to lay eggs!

On a trip to the city, we noticed a wild pigeon flying overhead carrying more traditional nesting material. We also discovered a wild duck in a park, brooding her eggs in a twiggy nest lined with her own down. Her aura of inner stillness and renewal created a centre of wholeness within the whirling clamour of traffic and commerce.

Under the magic of a full moon, we sat in a nearby swamp listening to the strident cries of hundreds of spring peepers – at decibel levels that assaulted our ears. Though the music and beauty thrilled our hearts, the chill air froze our bones. Our shuddering bodies were thankful to huddle once again around Grannie's welcoming warmth.

One morning we awoke once again to billowing flakes and a thick shroud of snow covering the land. Winter's last fling. Robins joined the seed-eating migrants foraging under the feeders, and we added apples and thawed blueberries to their daily fare. The omnivorous jays showed immediate interest in the fruit, and thus taught the robins not to fly off when I appeared at the door. Soon, when I gently opened it, the robins would hop towards me expectantly, and I'd toss them raisins as well as berries.

Several days of such harsh weather nearly finished our supply of frozen blueberries, but help was on the way. The passionate trilling of spring birdsong had never ceased. Soon its fervour warmed the land and the snows fled. Over the greening meadows once more, robins ran.

Paused.

Ran again.

The persistent renewal of life is inspiring.

In the woods one spring day, when snow still lingered underfoot and in the crotches of trees, I sketched an ancient, gnarled tree. Hunched among the straighter trunks of younger growth, this elder evoked a lifetime of struggle. Blotched with lichens, it appeared dead – until I looked up.

High above, lifting sturdily out of the twisted, broken body, rose slim, young branches, like tapers. They bore sleeping buds shaped like potential candle flames waiting for the fire of spring to ignite them.

In my finished painting, I added two robins, framed by twisty, old branches. The sunny radiance from each robin is melting the snow around them and kindling the candle buds at the top of the tree.

One afternoon, as I wandered through the awakening woods, I picked up a deer antler that had been shed a few months earlier – a wonderful symbol of regeneration. The carolling of robins rippled around me as I stood, musing.

Change cradles us from our beginnings. How vital for each of us to grow inner antlers for protection. How equally vital to shed them when they inhibit new growth. Fascinated by the significance of antlers, I've used them many times in my artwork.

On a grander scale, spring, with its fleeting moods and surging regeneration, seems like the response to the shedding of winter's antlers – a reflection reinforced by frequent sightings of deer playing lightfootedly in the greening meadows each spring.

A celebration of change.

CHAPTER 27

OF FLYING GARDENS

Once frost had released the earth, Mack was busy outdoors with his creation. In the fall, he'd cut down several trees to provide open ground. Then he'd used the logs to shape an unusual garden – one that had so intrigued John and Janet Foster that they'd filmed it, though it lay white with snow.

A vegetable garden shaped like a gigantic flying robin now honours County, the special robin who had once shared her life with me. The head faces east, the direction of beginnings. The outstretched wings span ninety feet between wingtips. The tail is spread in flight.

Like a true migrant, the robin garden had reappeared in the spring.

Mack laboured mightily. He chopped roots. Wrestled with stumps. Pried up rocks. Swore.

Load after triumphant load of debris was wheeled outside the log perimeters, creating a huge mound among the trees, which soon sheltered squirrels, chipmunks, and juncos. As he dug and turned the resistant earth, it began to relax and loosen.

It began to resemble garden soil.

Next we hauled feed bags of old hay from a nearby farm and scattered it evenly for humus. Then a load of topsoil was delivered to the roadside by truck – and to the robin garden by hundreds of wheelbarrow loads.

Between the topsoil pile and the garden lay a steep knoll that, with each exhausting load, became a mountain. Once the wheelbarrow was filled, we needed a running start to galvanize it and chase it successfully to the hilltop. There, suddenly getting into the spirit of things, it would shake off its lethargy and hurtle down the other side like one possessed, dragging its hapless victim in its wake. Strong arms and stubborn heels were crucial to manoeuvring a wobbling load safely down the hill and up a narrow plank into the walled garden.

Not every load made it.

We borrowed a second wheelbarrow and hired two young boys for a gruelling weekend. Fickle spring weather contributed summer heat and blackflies as the boys struggled up and down the knoll with their loads. Any alluring thoughts of quitting school to enter the work force dissolved as topsoil steadily filled out first one wing, then the other, of the huge robin basking languidly in the sunshine. After two exhausting days, even final exams looked better in comparison.

A layer of horse manure followed, which Mack and I lugged in old feed bags from a distant equestrian farm, then a second layer of old hay and a second layer of topsoil. Now horse manure was needed for the final dressing – but it still needed to be hauled.

Accordingly, one morning we piled bags and digging forks into the back of the old cargo van, which had been corroding contentedly all winter. As the engine burst into life, rattling the teeth in our heads, I opened the glove compartment for my sunglasses.

And paused, staring.

Inside lay an enormous soft mass of leafy litter. As we watched in astonishment, a tiny pink baby mouse, still blind, tumbled into view from a hidden entry. It rolled helplessly onto its back, mewing soundlessly and waving unbelievably tiny feet. The wary head of a mother deermouse reached out, gently grasped her babe, and pulled it back into the nest out of sight.

I closed the compartment gently, and Mack and I looked at each other.

Without a word, I switched off the engine. We climbed out of the van and unloaded our gear. Then we transferred everything to the car, adding plastic sheeting to protect the seats, and drove off to get a much smaller load of manure. It would be nearly three weeks before we could use the van again.

During that time, we maintained a buffet of water, mixed seeds, and whole-grain bread smeared with peanut butter in the "nursery" van to feed the mother mouse. We wanted to relieve her of the long, anxious journey from the van to the bird feeder, which undoubtedly had been sustaining her. Saw-whet owls and other natural predators frequented the area every night, as did the occasional cat. The thought of her babies waiting in vain for her return touched our hearts.

Admittedly, our actions weren't entirely altruistic: if the mother were killed, we knew *we'd* have to raise all her babies.

The very idea made us weak – and sustained us as we moved load after load of manure in the limited confines of the car.

Each day more peanut butter was licked off the bread, until the bread itself was eventually eaten. Seeds and water, too, diminished. We renewed everything regularly, until finally one morning we noticed with relief that the food had remained untouched.

The nest was empty.

We cleaned out the debris and finished hauling our manure in two enormous loads. Now the robin garden was ready for planting. Soon it, too, would be raising young.

A garden-in-progress was pure delight for Bubble. For some mysterious reason, while we were all in the garden, he never challenged Mack, and harmony prevailed. Perhaps the robin garden exuded a benign influence. If so, speaking as a harassed hen, it was welcome.

After weeks of cabin fever and grieving for Squeak, Bubbs revelled in sinking his toes down luxuriously into the soft soil. With loud clucks of joy, he wolfed down worms, much to Mack's chagrin; he wanted them for the garden, but wisely forbore to argue. Bubbs also relished the green weeds which sprang up with miraculous speed, dandelions and wild sorrel being his special favourites.

But the pinnacle of his ecstasy lay in dustbathing, and soon dusting hollows began to appear everywhere. These were small craters, which Mack whimsically called "Bubble baths" – except when they appeared in the midst of a row of new lettuce or radish shoots. Then he called them something else.

Every feather beamed with bliss as Bubble rolled in the warm, damp soil, rubbing his head well into it, shaking his wings and hurling dirt over his back in earthy cascades. For long moments he'd just lie still, his feathers choked with dirt, his eyes looking positively inebriated. After nearly an hour's indulgence, he'd stagger up onto his feet with obvious reluctance, looking like a dishevelled desperado.

Then he'd shake vigorously.

As if by magic, his tangled feathers would snap instantly into place, and out of a cloud of dust an immaculate rooster would emerge. Sunlight would rebound in bright gleams from each

feather, like wind-stirred water under a dazzling sky. To touch his plumage at this time felt like touching soft, slightly damp silk of the very highest quality. Even his eyes would glow with warmth and contentment.

How dirt, which sullied, could also *cleanse* remained ever mysterious to me.

Though his initial low opinion of Mack never varied, Bubbs still adored Mack's whole-grain bread. Commercial pita bread, a former favourite, remained his only concession to the bread industry – its only palatable product, in his estimation.

One afternoon, when Bubbs and I were headed for the garden, he spotted a chunk of white "store" bread discarded by one of the lads with the wheelbarrows. Uttering deep clucks of joy at this unexpected booty among the weeds, he quickly strode over and snatched it up.

Then, in obvious disgust, spat it out.

Strolling away, he nibbled at greens instead, while I laughed helplessly. Roosters, indeed, have their standards.

With Squeak gone, Bubble clung closer than ever to me. He often accompanied me in the van, where he rode in my lap, or, as Mack so atrociously put it, in the "cockpit."

One afternoon, I took Bubbs sketching. We drove to a special tree I'd often admired on a secondary highway. I lifted Bubbs out of my lap onto the passenger seat, got out my sketchbook, and began to draw. Bubbs waited patiently, watching the world beyond the windows.

A cold-eyed dog emerged from a nearby house, spotted the van, and circled us suspiciously. Bubbs followed the dog's movements vigilantly, clucking low, soft notes of warning.

Two guardians, guarding each other.

Finally the dog cocked a leg over one of the wheels and began to wander off, just as I finished the drawing. As soon as I started the engine, Bubble leaped back into my lap, the dog broke into shrill barking, and we drove away, the determined dog pursuing us maniacally down the road.

After we'd left him behind, we met a woman cyclist pedalling languidly towards us in the opposite lane. She glanced up with dull eyes that suddenly widened in disbelief as we whizzed by, Bubble's brilliant plumage and enormous red comb and wattles completely filling the driver's window. From the side mirror, I watched her bicycle wobble as her head spun around to watch a van seemingly driven by a chicken.

We stopped at a second tree, one with a twisted, evocative trunk, and again Bubble waited patiently on the passenger seat while I sketched. Cars passed frequently, slightly rocking the van, but he took little heed and, when I was finished, climbed back into my lap. I found a place to turn the van around, and we headed back the way we'd come.

Unbelievably, the cyclist too was returning, and again we drew towards each other. Seeing us, she skidded to a stop and stood aghast, staring openly with shaded eyes and moving lips.

I maintained a dignified hauteur as we passed, my face now as red as Bubble's from repressed giggles.

Despite the rumours we were creating behind us, we continued our drive and stopped for tea at a friend's house. In her kitchen we sat surrounded by the golden, unwavering stares of numerous cats, which roosted at various levels from the floor to the top of the fridge. Their undisguised fascination reminded me uncomfortably of the woman cyclist.

What they suggested to Bubbs remained a mystery, but he basked in my lap like a king, nibbling chocolate cookies and occasionally reaching over to prune the lush hibiscus growing beside me.

Later that evening, at home, he lay in my arms with his head on my shoulder, eyes closed and drooling happily, while I sang softly to him. Whenever I stopped, he opened his eyes and gently pecked my cheek. I'd begin singing once again, and he'd lay his head back down on my shoulder, eyes closed once more. Soon contented drool would again ooze from his beak.

One morning, with white blossoms unfurling in the great service-berry tree protecting the rooster run, and the sweet calls of bobo-links rippling over the meadows, I laid Squeak's frozen body deep into the very heart of the robin garden, facing him into the east of renewal. Forget-me-nots encircled the logs with their gentle blue.

On top, I set a large, round stone like an egg. A stone smoothed by ocean waves. White and speckled like Squeak.

Though only Bubble's call now echoed down the valley, Squeak crows ever triumphantly in my artwork, in paintings, prints, and sculpture.

In one canvas, music, portrayed as winging spiritbirds, is released in streams from his open beak. Below, a dark, slumbering land begins to brighten.

The eternal call to us all to awake.

Fugitive spring, having fully vanquished winter, now began to merge into summer, and the land blossomed.

The very bird feeders flowered with the pink, black, and white of rose-breasted grosbeaks, the yellow, black, and white of evening grosbeaks, and the ever brilliant blues of jays, as they all jostled hungrily for seeds.

Goldfinches had shed their winter disguise, which has fooled many people into believing that they migrate, and now sported their characteristic summer yellow. Purple finches, still rejecting the name imposed on them by colour-blind ornithologists, persisted in growing not purple but raspberry-tinted plumage. Fox sparrows, more accurately coined, flashed their long, rufous tails. Occasionally, a communal alarm aroused by the passing of a hawk would scatter all the birds like a shattered rainbow into the safety of the surrounding trees. Then even the sober spruces would brighten.

One day, a male evening grosbeak was brought to us with a bloody wing, perhaps the handiwork of a cat. We offered food and seclusion in the hospice, and after three days released him triumphantly into the serviceberry tree, now a bower of blossoms.

In the evenings, we watched beavers swimming underwater in the clear marshy shallows yet leaving no telltale ripples on the surface. Kingfisher voices staccatoed the still air. Fish sprang from the lake and disappeared again, activating widening circles that gently dissolved back into placidity. Common mergansers and ring-necked ducks cruised in pairs.

A sudden alarm call from Bubble one morning catapulted me out the door just in time to startle an enormous eagle off the porch roof overlooking the rooster run. No chicken dinner for him that day.

Outdoors, Mack pottered happily in the robin garden, planting seeds and setting out transplants to harden off.

Indoors, a wily Chip softened his remaining seed packets

in her waterdish before tearing them apart and scattering the contents – a nefarious act that pitched Mack into incoherent ravings about "four-and-twenty blackbirds baked in a pie!"

The robin garden began to "feather out," as cautious seedlings gained confidence in the nurturing warmth of late spring. Eelgrass, hauled from the shore the previous autumn, mulched the rows, retaining moisture and baffling weeds. Wood ashes protected sprouting beans from slugs.

Plants leafed out quickly, creating wonderful patterns of green "plumage" that were fascinating to watch. Unfortunately, the local chipmunk population was equally intrigued, and entrances to underground tunnels erupted everywhere. With accelerating zeal, chipmunks savoured the sweetness of new sunflower, squash, and cucumber plants, preferring to harvest them *before* the secondary leaves unfolded. Peas became special favourites.

Unfortunately, they were also our favourites.

Mack replanted gaps in the rows and dusted the surviving plants with hot cayenne, which was effective until rain washed it off. After a night of rain, he had to rise before the chipmunks in order to renew the cayenne. Sometimes he got to the garden first.

Oftener, the chipmunks did.

As soon as baby chipmunks were seen on their own, Mack began to live-trap any and all chipmunks and move them out of the area, regardless of their innate charm. Having devoted weeks of intense effort to creating the robin garden, he was determined that it should fly. In two days, eight otherwise delightful chipmunks were inexorably dispersed to new territories.

One afternoon, we set off for town to take care of neglected errands. I drove while Mack sat beside me, another caged chipmunk at his feet ready to be released en route. Suddenly, a squirrel dashed in front of the car, and I hit the brakes. The trap tipped over and Mack howled. He bounced about the car, clutching himself and shouting unmentionables, while I watched, bewildered.

The chipmunk had run up his leg under his pants.

Despite our differences with the chipmunks, they were still endearing neighbours. I looked out the window one morning and spotted one in trouble. His hindquarters were snagged in nylon netting, which had been left carelessly balled up and forgotten beside the garden. We tore outside to help.

The chipmunk, though wild, remained calm while I reassured him softly. Watched by those unblinking dark eyes, I worked quickly to cut the netting that had tightened around his body. He made no struggle, no attempt to bite, while I handled him.

When the last strand freed him, he instantly shot down a new burrow among the struggling snow peas. And Mack immediately set the live-trap.

Sympathy had evaporated. Hostilities were resumed.

With the sudden decline in chipmunk harvesters, the robin garden finally fledged. Neat green rows grew at all angles, in bright patterns intensified by the sober mulch. Pots of red flowers set out for hummingbirds added a cheery accent. In the deep, rich soil, all the plants thickened quickly to create almost solid plumage.

Early one morning, I sat up on the roof savouring the sweet, chill air. The sky was clear, with stars growing pale as the east slowly brightened.

Below me, the robin garden began to hover.

Though the earth surrounding it remained dark and wet, the vegetable plants, heavily beaded with dew, were reflecting the growing light above. This gave the whole robin a pale sheen and an illusion of floating.

My imagination responded with delight and quickly took wing. I saw the robin garden, heavily laden with veggies, migrate one magical night to southern lands, perhaps to alight near a remote village with struggling gardens. A village whose need was great.

Children would discover it the next morning and run to tell the news. No one would believe them until they returned with a strange, delicious food – a handful of edible pod peas.

The whole village would accompany the children to the garden and gaze with astonishment at the gift. They would bow in gratitude.

Those experienced at growing food would skilfully tend the vegetables and distribute them fairly. When the earth under the seaweed mulch needed moisture, water would be hauled cheerfully from a mountain stream. Everyone would enjoy varied bounty, as each vegetable matured in its season. When the garden was finally bare, the village would still be nurtured by root crops carefully stored while the robin rested.

Months later, at the moon of planting, the gardeners would plant indigenous seeds in the robin garden as an offering. In their own gardens, they would sow unusual seeds carefully saved from the robin, as well as their local ones.

All the seedlings, as though blessed by the traditional robin spirit of renewal, would grow quickly into strong, bushy plants. Even the unfamiliar "fledglings" born from the robin garden. Then one morning, the villagers would arise to find the robin gone.

It had migrated again.

To alight one magical night back in our yard. Though it had been south for nearly a year, here it had been gone only overnight. No one had noticed its flight.

But imagine our astonishment in the morning when we found the robin garden brimming with exotic, unfamiliar vegetable plants. All flourishing as though having been planted weeks earlier.

As indeed they had been.

CHAPTER 28

A Growing Family

In late spring, on a day limp with summer warmth, Mack and I received five baby starlings. They had been thoughtlessly removed from the eaves of a house that was being reroofed. If they'd been left for only another week, they'd have fledged under their parents' guidance. Instead, two distraught parent birds were deprived of their brood, and two busy people were catapulted into finding enough bugs daily to satisfy five ever-hungry, clamouring babies.

Mack soon dubbed them "The Little Garburators."

Feeding times erupted into frenzied scrambles. Each nestling had hatched a day later than the one before, so that the oldest, being five days older than the youngest, was considerably bigger and stronger.

And thereby hungrier.

Already their innate competitive nature was in full spate. The older ones, after being fed, felt no compunction whatever at standing on the heads of the younger ones in order to grab their portions as well. When I used my free hand to separate the fed from the unfed, the full babes, never satisfied, would push under my hand and pop up again, bright-eyed and gaping like picnic hampers. But noisier.

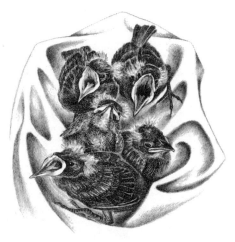

When all the Garburators had finally been fed, they dozed and *chr-r-r*-ed continually in their covered box. But I had only to touch the box to unleash piercing shrieks of hysterical enthusiasm. Every thirty minutes, when I pulled off the towel cover, all the babes screamed, gaped, and trampled each other joyously, their beady eyes riveted on the worms dangling before them.

I could only marvel at the patience of parent starlings. And at their stamina.

"Plucky," being the youngest, and therefore the smallest, had the hardest struggle of all. He was an endearing creature, crowned with wispy down, whose mouth still gaped hopefully – even when two of his siblings were standing on his back demanding his share. I often warmed him inside my shirt when he seemed chilled or sluggish, or perhaps just discouraged at being perpetually under everyone else's feet. Once I dosed him with mineral oil to loosen his bowels.

When we needed to do errands in town, we took the Garburators with us and drove from place to place with our ears ringing. It was so difficult finding enough "wrigglies" for each day's feedings that often we had to drive miles in order to search out other, wormier, gardens. The Garburators became seasoned travellers, riding in the back like royalty and demanding meals with aristocratic authority.

Despite our efforts, the second-youngest mysteriously weakened and died. All the others, Plucky included, flourished and were eventually released.

The season of hatching was rapidly accelerating and we weren't the only parent birds caught in the throes.

We stopped the car one day to let a mother ruffed grouse and her scattering of ten babies cross the road. Like fluffy chicken eggs on matchstick legs, the youngsters milled around their wary mother. A few of them stayed close beside her, but others ran blithely ahead, heedless of danger. One hesitated anxiously back at the roadside and the mother turned her head often, no doubt calling, though we couldn't hear her. Perhaps he finally caught an imperative glint in her eye, for he suddenly burst across the road to her side on legs that seemed to spin like wheels.

Three other babies flew across in a blur, as though propelled by wings with ideas of their own. The mysteries of braking and steering still eluded these daredevils and they crashed awkwardly into the bushes beyond the ditch.

The whole family, tinted in woodland colours, vanished almost immediately into the undergrowth.

The buoyant, fickle nature of spring had even penetrated indoors, and sudden squalls often erupted.

During Bashō's moult, he had rejected all offers to be cuddled. His new spiky feathers, the shafts pink with blood inside, were too tender to be pressed against my hands. He preened constantly, crumbling away the sheath that enclosed each feather. When most of them had finally opened, he again snuggled down gently in my cupped hands, a contented quail – though one still to be handled carefully.

But Chip, too, understood the tender nature of emerging feathers.

One evening, a usually placid Bashō *erupted*. With loud, angry cries, he tore after Chip, chasing her around the furniture and under the woodstove, while she danced mockingly ahead of him, her diabolical eyes gleaming. I tried holding Bashō, but he would *not* be comforted, and immediately scrambled down. Again, the chase was on.

When his legs weren't fast enough, he *flew* after her in short bursts, until finally Chip alighted on the edge of the woodbox. There she remained, taunting him, while Bashō leaped about below her, bristling with fury and crowing.

Chip had deliberately and heartlessly tweaked one of his new, still-pink quills, at its most tender stage.

At times she seemed to regard Bashō as some sort of battery-operated toy. While he was in a quiet doze, she'd poke under his feathers with her long, sharp bill or nip his toes as though trying for the right button to turn him on. When he suddenly roared into life and shot after her, she was as pleased as a kid who'd deciphered a puzzling new plaything, and the game was on.

Mack enjoyed playing with Bashō too, holding him carefully in his hands, swooping him through the air, and then gently tossing him. Bashō, finding himself suddenly airborne, would start up his engine in a staccato of wingbeats and zoom down to the floor, alighting in a short run. Then he'd trot back for another launching.

During the season of moths, when they were clustered on the screens of the porch, Mack had often held Bashō up to catch his own while Chip was snapping up hers. Bashō's quiet air of smug repletion when his crop was full of moths easily equalled Mack's after a liberal second helping of supper.

Now Mack was offering Bashō a succulent mealworm in compensation for Chip's merciless teasing. With squeaks of enthusiasm, Bashō snatched up the mealie and incapacitated it in preparation for eating it. Then, with supreme generosity, he gave it to Mack instead.

In quail parlance, no gift is greater than a favourite food.

Bubble, too, was primed with spring energies. As I lay back in my chair one evening, reading, he lay across my legs, his eyes warm with contentment. But the atmosphere changed when Mack came into the room. He sat down on the couch at the other end of the room and made a face at Bubbs.

Bubble's eyes narrowed. He eyed the other "rooster" with cold disfavour and stood up warningly. Mack, seeing this, deliberately drummed his feet loudly on the floor, a gesture that never failed to provoke.

But Bubbs' reaction this time took even Mack by surprise.

In a sudden wingburst, Bubbs sprang into the air and flew over the coffee table to the couch, a distance of twelve feet, which he covered in a split second. He bounced down beside Mack, eye to eye, hackles bristling and ready to fight.

Mack, saucer-eyed with astonishment and trepidation, froze. I bolted out of my chair and scooped up Bubbs, who was more than an armful even when not dilated with fury. Prattling sweet talk in his ears, I bore him off, rubbing his neck feathers soothingly. The glare I directed at a disgruntled Mack over my shoulder had little effect. Bubble's obvious air of triumph had more impact as he cuddled down in my arms.

After all, it was he who ended up with the hen.

The taunt, however, was not forgotten. Not long after this incident, we were all outside, Bubble scratching for bugs in the earth while I busied myself among the perennials. Mack trudged about on a variety of gardening chores, wearing heavy jeans over sturdy, steel-toed boots. At one point, he passed Bubble on the path.

Each eyed the other suspiciously and, although Mack was ready, Bubbs remained motionless. Mack passed silently. Not until he was a few yards away and just beginning to relax did Bubbs make his move.

He broke into a silent run after his rival and at the last moment leaped, feet and spurs foremost. They struck Mack full strength on one lower leg, and he staggered forward with a bellow which brought me running. Both roosters had recovered their balance and were angrily facing off when I flung myself between them and scooped up Bubbs.

One of his long spurs lay on the ground, broken on impact by the reinforced boot hidden under Mack's pantleg. Drops of blood fell rapidly from the stub as I held him, commiserating with Mack who had removed his boot and was irritably rubbing his calf. Then I carried Bubbs inside, packed the stub with antibiotic paste, and bandaged it.

The next day I marvelled at the dark bruise from Bubble's spur, despite Mack's thick boots and jeans. Though a favoured hen, I was weary of testosterone tantrums.

Hell hath no fury like a rooster scorned.

As she eyed the wild grackles from the windowsills, Chip, too, was full of spring. And springs. She'd leap up a foot or more and bounce down again in the same place over and over in exuberant "Chip Flips." As the days lengthened, her strident calls, as well as

Bubble's crowing, shattered the household stillness earlier and earlier each morning.

Mack, in resignation, found it less irritating to rise earlier himself, despite his night-owl tendencies. One evening I retired, yawning, and left him happily settled for a few hours' quiet reading. Great was my surprise when he climbed the stairs only five minutes later.

Apparently under orders from Chip.

She'd gone to roost when I went upstairs. Then, disturbed presumably by Mack's reading lamp, she'd bounced down beside him with a hideous glare that was unmistakable. Mack was quite perturbed.

Twice, Chip jabbed viciously at the hand that was holding the book. Then she barked out a single undeniable ultimatum and flew back up on her roost, settling herself with an angry shake of her feathers.

Sheepishly, Mack switched off the light and left.

The next morning we fled the demands of our avian garden and the even greater demands of our avian family. Shedding our responsibilities like old clothes, we flitted across the burgeoning meadows to the woods.

Seeking renewal, we barely glanced at the bobolinks calling from the fenceline, at the deer wandering towards the garden, or at the sharp-shinned hawk feasting on the ground amid scattered feathers. We left the shouting world behind and slipped into the dim silence of the trees. Deep within the woods we made our way to a fallen birch and sat down thankfully.

Around us, ferns unfurled in quietness. Moss glowed under long fingers of sunlight. A snail eased slowly across a leaf, exuding a silver trail.

High on a spruce limb a red squirrel dozed, all four legs hanging down limply on either side of the branch. Above the brook, myrtle warblers darted after insects. The melodious rippling of running water soothed us with its timeless music, and we began to feel refreshed.

We felt again the incomparable difference between living a life or living a schedule, as our tightened bodies sighed gratefully and relaxed. When we finally rose from our log, our jangled energies were flowing harmoniously once more.

As we meandered through the woods, we came to the beaver dam, a favourite place to gather wild mint in the summer. In the calm waters above the dam loomed dark, dead trees, their long reflections gently weaving, as a pair of secretive black ducks glided uneasily away into the shadows. Alders surrounding the pond held the sweet carolling of warblers. Plopping frogs disturbed the tranquility as we drew closer.

We stepped carefully onto the dam and began to cross, the silence of still water on one side, and musical cascades on the other, as escaping trickles danced through the tangled twiggery down to the nearby lake.

Beyond the dam, my eye caught a curious movement among the trees. We wandered closer, wondering, and discovered an enormous black eel on the ground. As we approached, he struggled even harder to "swim" away, writhing desperately in the decaying spruce needles.

How did he get there?

The nearest brook, a shallow one flowing from the beaver dam, lay at least twenty-five feet away. If he'd been mysteriously dropped by a predator, he bore no wounds on his body. We shrugged, acknowledging yet another mystery we'd never resolve, and moved in to help him. As the eel watched me pensively, I took off my jacket, slipped it under his handsome, gleaming body, and carried him back to the dam. He lay quietly in his impoverished sling, as though understanding my intentions. Then I gently tipped him out, and we watched in delight as he slid smoothly through the still waters.

I don't know yet what amazed me more – that an eel should appear in the woods, or that those who discovered him in his defenceless state would be those who wished to help, not harm, him.

Both possibilities seemed pretty remote.

When we emerged from our sylvan sanctuary, a cold north wind was sweeping the skies, pushing along huge, portly clouds that seemed unwilling to be harried in such an undignified fashion. As we opened the house door, a note fell out, telling us to look inside the outhouse.

When we did, we found a panic-stricken blue jay that had been mangled by a cat.

CHAPTER 29

ARRIVALS, DEPARTURES, AND MORE ARRIVALS

One of the blue jay's legs dangled loosely near its bloodied body, turning easily, clearly indicating a break. The wing above that leg drooped slightly, and was swollen but not broken.

He calmed down while I held him near the indoor garden so that he might gain reassurance from the other birds. Then I trickled water down his throat, which he obviously relished, followed by tetracycline, which was met with less enthusiasm.

Although I called veterinarians, some were busy at distant clinics and others were out on calls. None who were available felt qualified to deal with a broken leg on a wild bird. Though clearly out of our league, we were on our own.

With awkward but well-intentioned fingers, we packed cotton batting around the knee joint and above, following directions in a book. Then we bound the leg with surgical tape and braced it with light cardboard. Next, we set a box on its side, padding the bottom with thick towels. We added a dish of water treated with tetracycline and avian vitamins, another dish of mixed seeds, grit, and cracked corn, and a jar lid holding mealworms. Finally, we set the jay inside and turned the box against the window, shutting out our human world.

We'd done all we could.

The next morning we peered cautiously into the box, only to discover a very alert blue jay sitting on the edge of his seed dish. Seeds lay scattered about from his rummaging beak, and all the mealworms were gone. We added more mealies and quietly withdrew.

Just as someone knocked on the door.

A Bohemian waxwing was brought in from a town yard, seemingly healthy and unharmed but definitely not strong or able to fly. He'd been frequenting a bird feeder but, not being a seed eater, had remained hungry. Though no wild fruits – standard waxwing food – grew at this time of year, insects were available even in town. His hunger remained a mystery.

"Bandit" was a beautiful bird, sleek and tufted, with yellow-tipped tailfeathers that seemed to have been dipped in sunshine, and a rosy face. Across his eyes he wore a dark mask.

As soon as I released him into the indoor garden among the other birds, he immediately perked up. Bashō, seeing me crouched at the garden's edge, came trotting around a plant, only to encounter a masked stranger, not mealworms as he'd hoped. He instantly doubled in size as his back feathers rose defensively, but in a few minutes he shrank back to normal size. Eyeing the weak stranger, he quickly realized there was nothing to fear.

I set out a dish of thawed raspberries and blueberries, which the waxwing welcomed and cleaned up by dark. Whenever I tossed him mealworms, he devoured them with no hesitation, producing normal droppings.

Clearly, starvation was his only problem.

The next day he began to perch on the trees in the indoor garden, a promising move. Not only was Bandit visibly improving, but "Beejay" the blue jay also seemed stable.

Then someone *again* knocked on the door.

This time we received a male evening grosbeak, resplendent in yellow, black, and white plumage. His thick, pale-green bill had the great strength yet necessary delicacy for hulling and crushing seeds. His dark eyes were deep and bright, an encouraging sign.

Though "Goldie" arrived speechless with trepidation, we knew that hidden within him were soft, high notes of a tremulous sweetness, calls we'd often heard chiming above us in the woods.

He'd struck a window with such force that one wing remained drooping. Though he could beat both wings in a limited way, and even propel himself through the air for a distance of two feet, he'd virtually lost the ability to fly.

The woman who brought him had just finished reading my book *In the Company of Birds* when the grosbeak flew into her window. Horrified, she'd brought him inside and picked up the book again – as a manual this time. For nine weeks she'd tried to help Goldie, shutting off one of her rooms for his sole use and supplying proper food and water, but the grosbeak never improved. Her terrier, too, had hampered her intentions, being determined to seize the bird at any opportunity. Finally, she'd written a letter of desperation to me, which was forwarded from my publisher, and we called her immediately.

Now, after a journey of a hundred miles, she'd arrived.

After examining Goldie carefully, I released him into the garden. Tiny Bashō, encountering yet another – and even larger – stranger, again stood every feather he possessed on end till he resembled a feathered hedgehog. Chip, intrigued, strutted around Goldie, eyeing him from every angle and pointing her beak up defensively whenever he looked at her.

Then she pulled his tail and he shrieked, startling us all.

Though Goldie couldn't fly, he managed to perch in one of the garden trees by hopping up, branch by branch. He also had difficulty with balance, and occasionally fell, plummeting like a rock. Unable to spread his wings and glide down, he usually landed on his back in the soft dirt. After a brief struggle, he'd right himself and begin again. On the windowsill, sadly, he'd patter back and forth, over and over.

Yet his appetite was excellent. Especially for sunflower seeds.

I held out little hope for eventual recovery from such an old and severe injury, but at least we could provide a semi-natural environment in which he could live out his days. For this, the woman who had cared for him was grateful.

When, after a pleasant visit, she'd departed, I walked into the studio, just in time to see Molly land in Desmond's personal loft. Des tried to chase her out as usual, but to my alarm fell heavily to the floor. I scooped him up, horrified, but he felt cool and limp. He lay quietly in my hands, and I realized that Desmond, that gentle pigeon friend of eleven years' standing, was dying of old age.

I cradled him lovingly until he stopped breathing a few moments later. Then I remained standing, numbed.

I turned to Molly on her shelf at the other end of the studio to show her Desmond's body. To communicate about his passing.

But Molly already *knew*.

Far from mourning Desmond, who'd courted her to no avail all his life, she barely glanced at his body. Instead, she eyed his loft – his glorious loft, so much nicer than her own, that she'd coveted for years. Situated above my stored paintings, and running the width of the room, it had always beckoned to her. But Desmond had initially claimed it. Only as his spouse would she have been permitted to share it, an honour Molly had always, and most ungraciously, refused.

No domestic ordeals for her. No endless hours on eggs.

Now, though Desmond's body was still cooling in my hands, she flew to his cherished loft and with pleasure began the cooing and strutting that claimed it as her own. She'd obviously realized he was failing when she'd invaded his space earlier. Desmond's last effort had gone into resisting her onslaught. Though I was appalled at her apparent heartlessness, I had to admit that her personality was certainly consistent.

Only Mack and I mourned Desmond, the gentle recipient of Molly's perpetual rebuffs, as we laid him sadly in the warm spring earth.

As the days passed, all three new arrivals continued to eat well and to remain alert. Indeed, when Bashō was receiving mealworms, Bandit would drop down from his tree for his share, despite my proximity. In the hospice, we finally removed Beejay's box. He flew fairly well, so evidently the bitten wing had not been broken or become infected. He gradually became used to my daily ministrations – adding food, changing water, cleaning droppings. When I entered, he flew onto the branches at the opposite end of the room to wait until I left. Then, pausing a moment outside the closed door, I'd hear him fly back again.

Often he'd respond to the cries of the outside jays, and to one jay in particular. When that jay's voice was heard, Beejay's calls would achieve an ear-stopping stridency he never emitted otherwise, and his anxiety would be trebled. He'd been brought to us by near neighbours, and we had no doubt his mate was outside the window.

Soon a regular routine developed. Every evening, at a time that we could predict with accuracy, Beejay and his mate would call to each other over and over.

Cries of obvious longing. Cries we found heart-rending.

Occasionally they'd break out during the day, but the evening ritual remained punctual. I've read in more than one book that blue jays mate for life. After witnessing Beejay's behaviour, I have no reason to doubt it.

Then, suddenly, Beejay dropped into a decline, as though yielding to his pinings – a depression born of this abrupt change in his life which separated him from the jay world. His appetite dwindled seriously. Then stopped.

Concerned, Mack inflicted his human company on Beejay, refusing to allow him solitude in which to mope. Beejay was forced to fly to the opposite end of the room each time Mack gently, but insistently, approached. Soon Beejay was eating mealworms again, to fuel himself, and watching Mack warily, not listlessly.

Though Beejay was still encumbered with our homemade cast, we released him into the indoor garden, hoping the other birds would create adequate stimulation for him. And so it proved.

He perked up immediately, as did they all with yet another arrival. Bashō again became a temporary hedgehog, and even Chip's eyes widened – Beejay was bigger than she. But to our immense relief, harmony still prevailed.

The garden now blossomed with colourful plumage, each bird different from the next.

Unfortunately, when we finally removed Beejay's splint, we found that, though his leg had fused well, our inexperience had left it very crooked. Instead of a leg with normal usage, he had more of a prop for balance. Whenever he expressed anxiety, the leg shook as though with palsy. Though we tried eventually to release Beejay, he was unable to manage. He still climbed trees branch by branch, being unable to fly upwards into them. Without the needed spring in both legs for a quick take-off, he became easy prey for cats, sharp-shinned hawks, and other predators. His damaged wing, too, remained so weak that a gusty breeze would topple him down to the ground in a tailspin. He was very easy for us to retrieve. Too easy.

Beejay, like Goldie, had become a permanent member of the family. And he was noticeably more contented after his return.

But Bandit, one fair morning, lifted away into blossoming trees, a healthy, strong waxwing again. Insects were plentiful, and the weather more settled.

The rest was up to him.

One evening, we drove to the ocean to meander down a long, secluded shoreline under the gold and blue of a limitless sky. A wonderful sunset began to glow in the west, over the gently breathing ocean. In the east, above a long, still lagoon, rose the full moon. We stood on a narrow beach between both bodies of water, between declining and rising orbs, entranced.

Above our heads, a short-eared owl, hunting in low flights over the bending sea grass, was challenged suddenly by a passing great blue heron and a flock of small but determined shorebirds. They all darted this way and that in a stunning aerial display, only the occasional harsh cry of the heron breaking the wing-woven silence.

Eventually, the owl glided into new territory, the excited shore-birds fluttered back down to the sea, and the heron resumed its stately flight to the roosting trees on the far side of the lagoon. We wandered along the beach in the stillness of sunset and moonrise.

Cast up on the empty sands, we found an evocative twist of driftwood more than six feet long. It curved gracefully around in a semi-spiral, then twisted abruptly back in interesting configurations and stopped – like an immense sea serpent culminating in a dragon's head.

We immediately saw the dragon, but it was Mack who suggested that it be carved to fulfil its potential, then attached to a wall indoors to create a chair. His enthusiasm was contagious, and I readily agreed to carve it if we could lug it to the car, half a mile away.

This proved to be an onerous feat that awakened the latent trickster nature of the dragon-to-be. His awkward shape eluded our grasp. His sinewy form belied its surprising weight, which diabolically increased with each sinking step as we struggled against the soft, sliding sands. Fortunately, when we arrived at the car, the dragon slipped easily inside, as though it had always desired to leave the primal world of the beach.

Lulling us again into believing that it was mere driftwood.

But later, its potent nature surged out once more when I was carving the last of the teeth. The chisel suddenly leaped and sliced through my thumb as though I'd been bitten.

It seemed fitting that his ferocious jaws also appeared to be grinning.

Eventually, the dragon's dense pine body, enriched by linseed oil, was attached firmly – and reprovingly – to a wall, so that it curved out, bearing a soft seat, then swung up alongside the sitter. The head, with bared teeth and enormous, all-seeing eyes, hovered above.

Though the dragon is now immobilized, I sometimes fancy I see a glint in its eye and wonder if, some day, it will casually nibble someone's hair. Or drool into someone's tea. Or gently tip some unsuspecting soul, beguiled by the driftwood façade, onto the floor.

Dragons in various traditions, while full of potential and vitality, are either nourishing or destructive, being associated with life-giving rains or lashing storms. Our saltwater dragon seemed, like all of us, to be possessed of both demure and diabolical personalities.

Admiring his grace and the rich sheen of his wood while changing the bandage on my thumb, I had to agree that he certainly fitted in with our eccentric family.

CHAPTER 30

THE EVE OF SUMMER

The last capricious teasings of spring rapidly dissolved in the steady warmth of early summer. Tremendous energies surrounded us as interwoven life forms, nourished by one another, surged towards fulfilment.

Patterned "plumage" from growing veggies transformed Mack's unique garden into a solid green robin with gigantic wings. On the young pear and plum trees planted near the left wing, we noticed dozens of green caterpillars energetically devouring the new foliage. We gathered them all and fed them to Chip, Bashō, and Beejay, who were thrilled.

On the old apple tree in front of the house, a flock of evening grosbeaks, their soft voices silvery sweet, busied themselves with searching out every caterpillar. Cedar waxwings hunted just as diligently through the chokecherry and serviceberry trees, catching and eating bugs by the hour. Bubble, too, was doing his share, eating fresh young weeds and catching endless bugs and slugs.

Such thorough workers at blossom time guaranteed abundant fruit and vegetables for everyone later in the season.

In a special garden shaped like a crescent moon, strawberry blossoms began to transform into small green berries. On the warm southern slope near the birch tree, wild blueberries flowered. Clusters of tiny rhubarb flowers rose on their mighty stalks. Eagerly awaited hummingbirds, as secretive as ever about their mysterious migratory crossing of the Gulf of Mexico, hovered daintily around the fuchsia blooms. Among the sweet rockets, whose exquisite perfume sweetened the air, dozens of swallowtail butterflies flitted.

As we worked in the garden, we could hear the repeated squawks of a very young raven. Yielding finally to our curiosity, we wandered a short way through the woods, our path twinkling with starflowers, to an area where ravens nest annually. The parents were away foraging when we crept near, trying without success to move quietly over the decaying leafy litter underfoot. Finally we spotted the fledgling out on a branch.

He eyed us with trepidation, but remained quiet, turning his head away as though, by not looking at us, he could eliminate our troubling presence. But at our slightest motion, his eye glinted and he shifted awkwardly and nervously.

Moments passed.

Then he grew suddenly excited, beating his wings and calling as his parents approached. They immediately focused on us and refused to feed their youngster while we remained near. Unwilling to disrupt their lives, we slipped away.

In the trees around the garden, starling fledglings *chr-r-red* monotonously. A pair of robins hunted among the emerging asparagus tips, carrying wrigglies back to their nest at the edge of the woods, and chasing a passing blue jay with sudden fierceness.

One morning the mystery of the missing peas was solved when we spotted a groundhog emerging sleepily from a stack of logs near the garden. Mack grimly set out the live-trap, and by afternoon the culprit was caught. Pausing only to ascertain that we hadn't caught a nursing mother, we carried the trap to the van. Then Bubble and I enjoyed a pleasant drive of several miles to a suitable area with fields, woods, water, and *no* vegetable gardens. Into this paradise, we released the groundhog, and with him many of our gardening anxieties.

Gracing the boardwalk leading to the house, wild roses were in bloom, pale pink and fragrant. As I stopped to savour their aroma, a barn swallow swept above me and dropped a piece of eggshell, white with gold specks. Within the robin garden, appropriately, I picked up a blue eggshell. In such a season of magic, there is so much to see.

From a nearby bridge, we watched a pair of wild Canada geese with youngsters strung behind them like beads, all swimming upstream, the cygnets perky and buoyant, their parents wary and watchful.

At the edge of a singing meadow, a doe and her fawn emerged cautiously, ears and tails twitching. In the woods, a handsome buck melted away noiselessly at our approach. Before us, resting lightly on the rich, spring moss, lay an owl feather beaded with dew.

Deep in the spring mud of an old wood road, moose tracks crisscrossed deer tracks of both fawns and adults as we added our own during a morning walk. Near dense spruce we startled a mother grouse with a flurry of peeping youngsters, already exchanging their downy plumage for feathers of woodland hues. Near us, a northern waterthrush paused, tail bobbing, and over our heads, the young leafing maples cast a greenish glow around us, creating a submarine aura of sunlight falling through seawater.

At a beach on the Fundy Basin, we wandered among red sandstone formations, eroded and sculpted by waves and weather into incredible shapes. Gaping fissures, caves, and arches lent their mysterious gaps to the strange configurations, some free-standing like dissolving castles, each crowned with a tangle of spruce and birches separated forever from their parental forest.

Only the wind and the musical percolating of air bubbles escaping out of the waterlogged sands could be heard as I stood still, drawing.

Cliff swallows flighted in and out of nest holes high above the beach as we ambled at low tide amid miles of closed barnacles. When the tide turned and the waters swept back in, the barnacles would open again, gaping like nestlings, seining the food-rich waves that surged over them in ancient rhythms generated by the moon.

In cultivated bushes dotting a well-kempt lawn, cedar waxwings fed each other. Around them darted yellow warblers catching minute flying insects. Young spotted robins clung to branches, and we heard the unmistakable squalling of baby grackles at regular intervals as food-laden parents returned to the nest only to depart again.

Lupins brightened the roadsides.

On a morning of perfect beauty, we hiked miles into the highlands towards North River Falls, following a winding trail beside a river. Ferns arched gracefully throughout the sun-cloven forest, some fronds still unfurling. A junco darted out of a mossy bank rising on our left. Peeking quickly, we spotted a dainty woven nest cradling five eggs.

Above the falls bloomed delicate lady's slippers. We climbed beyond them to the top of the highlands and paused for a rest, scanning the undulating treetops as they shelved away from us in all directions. Only the wordless winds breathed in the great silence.

A distant eagle floated.

Hot and hungry, we clambered back down to the river's edge and ate lunch on boulders clutched by the strong roots of trees.

From high above our heads the waters fell, with the illusion of slow motion, until they plunged violently into a deep basin. Then they surged out and hurried away towards the sea. A continual breeze of cool mist from the falls freshened us as we sat, absorbing the beauty, the primal solitude.

And the sudden freedom from blackflies who awaited us in the warmer, drier air.

We arrived back home weary, yet reinvigorated, our memories a vivid tangle of moose tracks, sandpipers, ravens, blackflies, and an endless entwining of rocks and trees and musical waters.

In a marsh we spotted a mink approaching us on the path, and paused. He loped along nonchalantly until he suddenly became aware of us, then slipped fluidly into the reeds. Still we could watch his progress as hidden grackles and red-wing blackbirds rose abruptly in alarm. They followed above him, chattering indignantly, until he'd left each of their territories in turn. Then, one by one, they fluttered back down into invisibility again.

Returning from a night walk, we lay on the drumlin in a gentle shower, listening to frogsong and enjoying the drops splashing down on our faces. Passively we yielded to gusts of lashing rain. Melded our bodies with the growing grasses. Inhaled the vibrant aroma of wet earth. Not until we were refreshingly chilled did we finally rise and make our way back to the house.

Beside Grannie's welcoming warmth once more, we found that the primal world of rain and darkness had enhanced familiar indoor comforts. With steaming mugs of cocoa, we snuggled down luxuriously to read in front of the fire, envying no one.

One memorable morning found me at a friend's farm visiting a horse by a fence – rubbing the long hair under the strong jaws, patting the sleek face, feeling his warm breath on my cheek. I leaned closer, stroking the hot neck under the heavy mane, one of his deep purply-brown eyes looming close to mine as his head hung above my shoulder. When I turned away finally, I was stopped, as though my jacket were caught on something.

Then I laughed aloud. *I* may have finished visiting, but the horse hadn't.

In a gentle but firm grip, his teeth were holding my jacket. There was an unmistakable roguish twinkle in his eye as I resumed rubbing his head. His eyelashes drooped contentedly, and he released my jacket while I stroked his neck on both sides, my face laid against his.

Warmth joining warmth.

Who was I to mar such a moment with that deplorable haste that typifies human behaviour?

How often had I noticed holidaying parents striding along designated walking trails of great natural beauty, teaching their youngsters to adopt the same blind pace and not to "lag behind looking at everything or we'll be here all day!" But is leisure and the appreciation of nature not the basis of such a holiday? A *holy*day of reverence in the realm of the gods?

Mindful of that gentle equine admonition, I noticed a moonrise from the window one evening and climbed onto the roof platform to wholly savour the beauty. A nearly full moon hung over the eastern trees, a great globe in an aura of golden cloud. Toads trilled in the distant marsh and the high, pulsing whistles of a white-throated sparrow floated out of the darkness.

Suddenly the sky was split by a magnificent meteorite, igniting an arc of brilliance from the zenith to the southern horizon, as if, through a crack in the darkness, a glimpse were being given of another world. One so vivid that our sunlit earth dimmed in comparison.

An unforgettable response to taking time.

On the eve of summer solstice, after fasting all day, I slipped deep into the woods once more to visit the Tree.

Igniting bound herbs in my hand, I breathed in their pungency, releasing my breath to mingle with the breathing forest around me as I slowly circumambulated the Tree. Then I wiggled down into the concave curve on the eastern side of the great bole, feeling proven strength against my back and on either side of me. And feeling protected.

Patiently, I waited for the dawn.

As darkness deepened around me, the strident hoots of a barred owl startled the stillness. I gazed up out of what seemed a black well to stars glittering among the foliage high above my head. A hidden bird broke into a clear song, briefly warbling cadences of exquisite sweetness.

Time, a human contrivance for convenience, had vanished, leaving only a continuous present. Stars moved slowly across the sky, remote and incurious, on journeys of their own.

The cold intensified as the night grew old. Whenever I became severely stiffened, I rose and slowly circled the Tree again, acknowledging the centre, which is everywhere. Acknowledging mystery.

Another owl called.

Footsteps passed, crackling on the dry, leafy litter beneath the trees. A deer perhaps, but invisible in the darkness.

On a nearby hilltop, coyotes yipped briefly.

After long hours, a grey dimness began to dilute the east, but still I sat, waiting. Shapes of trees began to define themselves, parting from the thick darkness. Despite my heavy clothing, a damp chill pervaded me.

Out of the stillness, a thrush called to the morning. The east responded, growing clearer. I rose stiffly amid dissolving shadows and circled the Tree one more time, grateful for having shared its strength – and its resilience.

Then I bowed.

I emerged from the woods, facing a brilliant flush of pink behind the eastern trees. Still moving stiffly, I passed through dew-laden grasses to the dark house drowsing among the trees.

I had left on a spring night. Now an anxious Mack welcomed me in the yard on the first morning of summer.

CHAPTER 31

ANTICS WITH ANTS

The next day we climbed up on the roof platform after a heavy rain had ceased. We had endured a long, dry spell, so that just breathing the rich fragrance of wet earth and rain-washed foliage exhilarated us. Birdsong harmonized with the dripping trees, and even the robin garden, sparkling from wingtip to wingtip, was singing.

Sunshine, always superb after rain, crept slowly across the meadows, igniting the blossoming greenery. High above us, a short upcurved rainbow smiled.

Later that evening, a friend knocked on the door, bringing a needy bird in his knapsack. He said, grinning, that he'd walked here among swooping birds all heading in the same direction, as though sensing his mission and leading the way!

I opened his pack and lifted out a male adult flicker.

There seemed to be no indication of injury, so perhaps he had struck a window. Unable to fly, he'd been fairly easy to catch. We decided to set up a low table beside a tall window as his base in the hospice, with a plentiful supply of ants and dirt in a bucket beside the table. This arrangement would keep both table and ant-riddled earth at the same level, for easy access. If he fell off the table, he wouldn't fall far, and could regain it by hopping up an angled plank that we propped there for his use. Branches that were nailed permanently at each end of the room would provide natural landing areas when he began to use his wings again, and we added a "tree-hole box" in which he could hide. We also set a long round of firewood upright on his table, so he could hop up it, woodpecker-style, and sit on the top by the window. Then we gently placed him on the table and backed away.

From the first day, the flicker ate well. Since ants are a major part of a flicker's diet, we were hard-pressed at times keeping this fellow well supplied. Black, not red, ants were the desirable ones. We added any bark larvae we could find, pressed a mixture of peanut butter and cornmeal into a crevice in the firewood, and stirred a touch of honey into his water.

He progressed rapidly.

When he was able to fly easily the length of the room, we decided to release him. Unfortunately, though I slid back the hospice door in the living-room wall as gently as I could, it clanged, startling the flicker, who flew hard into the window. I gathered him up quickly, and he struggled with great energy, but when we let him go outside, he took a nose-dive into the shrubbery. Regretfully, we returned him to the hospice, this time pinning heavy, clear plastic sheeting taut across the window casings. Healing would have to begin again.

After another four days, we released the flicker again, this time successfully. With delight and relief, we watched as he swooped easily up into the apple tree. At last he was on his way.

The bucket of earth and remaining ants I dumped into the rooster run, and Bubble scratched happily through the pile, devouring each ant. Hours later, when he was cuddled down blissfully in my lap, a final ant peered furtively out of his plumage, then scuttled away down my leg.

The next day we left home for two days to visit friends in two locations – an innocent plan, intended to give us a brief respite. But fate had other ideas.

The highway traffic was swollen by summer tourists. Ponderous, wide-hipped motorhomes, driven by retired owners, lumbered along at a sedate pace, while local working drivers, harried by pressing anxieties, lined up behind, seeking opportunities to pass. On straightaways, several would burst past with glaring eyes, but on long curves more would line up again.

Tensions rose.

Cars bulging with kids, dogs, and camping gear, or pulling swaying tent trailers, hurried through the beautiful scenery, souvenir lobster traps tied to their roof racks among the bicycles. Those who did slow down and pull over to take a photograph hampered others who couldn't swing around them due to heavy oncoming traffic. Transport trucks on tight schedules bore down menacingly on small vehicles, crowding them off to the shoulders – or swung out boldly into the opposite lane to pass, undeterred by blind curves ahead.

We were beginning to wonder just when our "respite" would begin, when a grackle suddenly darted in front of us and was instantly killed.

We were devastated.

Sadly resuming our journey, and negotiating particularly heavy traffic beside the shore, we suddenly caught a swooping movement on our left in our peripheral vision. There was a barely discernible thud on the side of the fender.

Mack swung off the road, and I ran back to the tiny form, sitting up dazed on the centre line, traffic whizzing past on both sides. Waving off six oncoming cars, two motorcycles, and an eighteen-wheeler, I darted across and scooped up the bird – a beautiful cedar waxwing. We could find no visible injury, and his eyes were bright, but we knew he'd need recovery time. Bruising alone can prevent birds from flying temporarily, sometimes for days.

We took the waxwing with us.

At noon we arrived at our friend's house. We were both weary and frazzled, and I presented a particularly alluring spectacle with a cascade of loose droppings down my front. Mack, after a brief salutation to our friend, disappeared on a bug hunt in her yard, while I sank into a chair, trying to reassure the alarmed waxwing over the shrill barks of a dog.

Our friend rose nobly to the occasion and, despite scuffles and yelps of protest, tied her dog outside. Then she dug a small box out of her basement and laid a clean towel in it. Taking a tiny jar, she filled it with water, stirring in a touch of honey. The waxwing

drank eagerly, ate half a dozen wrigglies that Mack brought in, and bedded down without protest in the little box. We draped another towel across the top and left him to rest.

Only then was I free to wash my hands and change into my remaining clean blouse, which I had planned to wear the following day. As I did so, I was forcibly reminded of my mother's observation years ago when I arrived late for supper and hastily pulled out a chair at the table where she sat.

Waiting.

Unbeknownst to me, a large, loose dropping was trickling down my hair. Eyeing me with disgust, she commented frigidly, "Linda, you are socially unacceptable."

Returning to the living room, clean and freshened, I settled back in my chair, picked up my tea and a cookie, and prepared to enjoy a relaxing visit. We weren't due at our next stop till nightfall, so we had the afternoon before us.

It was then that our friend broke the news to us: a friend of *hers* several miles away was waiting for us with an injured flicker. "I hope she has anthills too," Mack murmured as we bumped down the rutted driveway.

Recalling our friend's verbal directions, we hunted through a maze of back roads and finally emerged at the designated house. The surrounding land, lush with cultivated gardens under a hazy sky, sloped down to the grey sea twinkling below. As we stepped out of the car into sultry silence, a large dog suddenly materialized beside us, barking and bounding, followed by several people all shouting at once. A trail of cats brought up the rear.

After an effusive welcome, we were led to a box beside the garage, in which a terrified young flicker crouched. When I lifted him out, he burst into shrill screams, as though infected by the general mayhem. The dog shouted even louder when he spotted the bird, and everyone else shouted at the dog, who took not the slightest notice.

In the midst of this tumult, I examined the fledgling carefully, but could find no visible injuries. Hunger seemed to be his major problem, and we soon added to the clamorous confusion when we inquired about anthills.

A family bug hunt immediately erupted as everyone fanned out, turning over rocks and boards, and, in their enthusiasm, burrowing through stacked firewood. Each avid hunter ran over to us repeatedly with even the tiniest of bugs clutched hopefully between fingertips. I think the whole group would have pushed over the garage if there'd been an ant underneath. Though ants were scarce, we collected a handful of sowbugs, centipedes, and beetles, most of which I forcefed to the flicker. The rest I fed to the waxwing, which was still crouched in his box inside the car, wide-eyed with alarm.

I continued to hold the flicker, trying to comfort him, but he screamed persistently. This further excited the dog, who needed little incentive, and he barked with renewed vigour, forcing the rest of us to shout at each other in order to be heard. When I bellowed that the gardens were beautiful, we were given not only a tour of the beds but transplants to take home. In the humid warmth, blackflies swarmed frenetically around our heads, and I was bitten near one eye, which began to swell hideously.

After almost mandatory hospitality with tea and cookies, of which I partook still holding the flicker, we returned to the car. A few more bugs were rounded up to feed both birds, then I set the flicker back in his box and placed him on the back seat beside the waxwing. We finally took our leave amid shrill goodbyes, waving hands, and great good humour.

The indefatigable dog still barked.

We drove a couple of miles down the road to a spot described as the one where the flicker had been found. There I climbed up a short bank to the eaves of a forest, carrying both birds against my front. I was hoping that the flicker's calls, which only ceased when he was confined in familiar darkness in his "tree-hole box," would lure his parents to the scene. But though his voice must have carried a fair distance, I waited in vain.

Then I loosed him, speculatively, but he plummeted to the ground. Plainly, he would need prolonged care until he fully fledged. I held out the waxwing, too, but he snuggled down into my hand, reluctant to fly. He wasn't ready either.

I returned to the car, cradling both birds against me, but skidded as I was descending the bank, adding mud and grass stains to my pants. Droppings from both birds already oozed stickily down my blouse, and I had no more clean ones with me. My head ached abominably and my bug-bitten eye was nearly shut.

We arrived at our last visiting spot by dusk and, despite our exhaustion, launched into an intensive bug hunt, aided – or hindered – by two excited children.

And yet another barking dog.

Ants were still scarce, but we forcefed both birds with a few meals of mixed bugs before bedding them down for the night. Then I washed out a blouse for the next day.

Our conversational offerings that evening were undoubtedly meagre, yet we visited until a late hour before crawling into bed, bone-weary. The barking of dogs resounded all night in our dreams.

Dawn found both birds bright-eyed and hungry. We fed them the last of our bugs, then hunted diligently for more to sustain them throughout the day. After an early breakfast we left for home, a large container of wrigglies at my feet. The birds in their boxes sat on the floor in the back of the car, beside both children, who were accompanying us.

Our departure marked the beginning of their overnight stay with the only adults they knew who lived in a house with an indoor garden and free-flying birds. We'd also planned a riding lesson for each child later that day at a stable near our home and some fun at a horse fair the next morning before we returned them to their parents. No wonder both kids had been eagerly anticipating this moment.

With untiring buoyancy that we envied, they chattered and sang, mile after mile. At feeding times, they passed me the bird boxes, one at a time, so I could dole out bugs to the inmates en route.

The young flicker still needed to be forcefed but, thankfully, no longer screamed. He was a striking bird in his colourful plumage, the "moustache" bracketing his bill indicating his gender. Despite his adult appearance, traces still lingered of that irresistible wispiness so characteristic of nestlings – that delightful fusion of devastating dignity clad in ridiculous tufts that *dares* you to laugh.

The waxwing now seized each offering with gentle eagerness, which was enormously helpful. Forcefeeding, especially in a speeding car, is intensive and tricky. He too was a beautiful creature, with sleek feathering, an attractive tuft, and twinkling eyes in his dark mask. He captivated everyone, and graciously accepted food from the children, who were fascinated.

After a two-hour drive, we arrived at the riding stable. Mack parked under a shady tree to avoid overheating the birds, and I gave them a feeding. Then both children had a wonderful, instructive hour with two patient ponies, before it was time to feed the birds again.

We patted every soft muzzle in each of the twenty stalls twice over.

Then fed the birds.

We left the horses and drove home.

Then fed the birds.

I hastily cooked dinner for everyone.

Then fed the birds.

I finally sat down to eat.

Then, of course – fed the birds.

It was not a schedule for the faint-hearted.

Though the birds needed to be fed as often as every thirty to forty minutes at their age, they were given only what would be described as a small quantity. A helpful visualization might be a tablespoon of mixed wrigglies – a tempting ingredient, rarely found in recipes but nevertheless high in protein.

After dinner, I carried the waxwing outside, and he flew eagerly and easily up into the serviceberry tree, ready once more for independence. The kids cheered and we all beamed with delight. Then Mack headed out to the meadow armed with a spade and a bucket to dig up ants for the flicker to eat.

We hated robbing anthills, and no one really wants a bucket of scrambling ants indoors, but the flicker needed natural food. Would that I'd had a flicker some years earlier when I decided to repair a roof leak in the hospice.

A persistent damp trickle after every rain had marred the inside west wall for nearly a year and I had always seemed to be too busy to deal with it. This day, I climbed determinedly up on the roof but couldn't locate the hole, so I decided to pull a panel off the ceiling indoors.

The summer weather was onerously muggy, and I sweated freely as I tried to pry up the reluctant nails. Nearly all were hanging out when I gave the four-by-eight panel a strong pull. It dropped away suddenly, loosing thousands of enormous black carpenter ants, which fell into my hair, down my neck and sleeves, and all over the rest of me.

I howled, dropped the sheathing, and swatted frantically at the equally frantic ants, which were swarming over my skin and biting indiscriminately.

Leaping convulsively, I clawed off my clothes, emptying ants out of unmentionable places. My ravings finally attracted the attention of County, the robin who then lived with me. She appeared suddenly at the threshold of the room, her eyes wide with disbelief – which quickly turned to delight. She bounded over and immediately devoured half a dozen angry ants. Then, satisfied, she left.

Six gone, and thousands to go.

The only answer was a vacuum cleaner, a luxury I didn't possess – but a hysterical phone call to a neighbour brought one within half an hour. The floor, black with milling ants, was thoroughly vacuumed, and ant-riddled insulation was pulled out of the ceiling. The damp wall panel was also removed, and more ants vacuumed. Then I released the horde into a stack of damp wood across the road, amazed at how few had succumbed. Finally, I retreated to the bathroom for a cool, soothing shower.

I still remember trying to sleep that night, my entire body

aflame from ant bites, my energies twittering as though ants by the thousands were galloping through my nervous system.

As indeed they were.

Bubble's size and almost palpable dignity intimidated the children somewhat, but they pushed forward eagerly to stroke his sleek plumage when he lay in my lap. Tiny Bashō, however, entranced them, and they vied for the honour of holding him – to which Bashō graciously agreed. Chip ate tidbits off their protruding tongues during supper but, to their disappointment, refused to be patted – as did Molly, Beejay, and Goldie. But, for the children, the novelty of seeing birds roosting in trees inside a house more than compensated for their aloofness.

With such ongoing entertainment, the television gathered dust and bedtime arrived all too quickly. Only the reminder of more horses in the morning convinced both children to go to bed.

Consequently, after breakfast, we headed for the horse fair. Of necessity, we included the young flicker, setting him inside a large wooden basket draped with a towel – an arrangement we hoped would simulate a tree-hole dwelling. Its woven texture also provided ventilation. The contrivance met with approval, for whenever I peeked through a gap in the towel, the flicker was clinging woodpecker-wise to the side of the basket, a natural position, and his eyes were calm.

At the fair, gleaming horses of every colour floated in all directions over the wide, windy meadow above the ocean. The sun shone out of a cloudless sky with an intensity that warned of even greater heat later in the day. There were no trees under which to park, so I spent most of the morning in the car with the flicker, maintaining a cross-breeze through the windows, while the others sought ringside seats.

To my great relief, instead of having to be forcefed, he began to eat quite readily on his own. When I held a small container of ants or mealworms before him, he snatched them up eagerly. He also began to drink water out of a jar with the ease of a veteran. Despite the strange surroundings into which fate had dropped him, his anxieties had dissolved, and he perched casually on the handle that arched over the basket, watching horses and riders with open-eyed interest.

Later, during the return drive to the children's home, I sat with the basket in my lap. Suddenly, a long tongue emerged curiously from the folds of the towel covering the basket, reaching this way and that like a probing finger. Laughing, I parted the towel and the flicker climbed onto my hand, then up on my shoulder, where he remained, gently exploring my eyes, ears, mouth, and even inside my nostrils with his long tongue.

It tickled hilariously.

In the wild, he'd be probing under loose bark and into crevices searching for larvae and insects, his long sticky tongue pulling them out of their lairs – an all-seeing tongue, from which few would escape.

Now the eyes in his tongue were peering under my shirt, eliciting carefully ambiguous comments from Mack and innocent giggles from the kids. His curiosity satisfied, the flicker leaped down onto the fabric that lined the passenger door and clung there as calmly as though it were a tree trunk, watching the world whiz past beyond the window.

The children were utterly fascinated.

When we had delivered them safely to their home and were departing once more for our own, they watched us as though we were taking an enchanted world back with us – a magical infusion of horses and birds that would always live in their memories.

CHAPTER 32

DIGGER

The following morning, instead of isolating ants in a little dish, I carried the young flicker into the screened porch and set him into a large, shallow tub of earth. Hidden below the surface were hundreds of black ants.

His eyes sharpened with interest when one ant scurried by, and he gave a short squeal. Since he now associated my fingers with food, I also tried to make them bill-like by clenching my fist and probing into the dirt with only my index finger, as an adult flicker would probe into anthills. This excited the ants, and several of them swarmed out.

I pointed at one and imitated the flicker's squeal. He squealed in response and snatched up the ant. Then I pointed at another, and squealed. The flicker squealed too, and seized it. The third ant he chose himself, and the fourth, always emitting the short squeal before eating each one, as though he were counting them.

Perhaps my probing finger stirring up ants also inspired him, for when no ants were left, he dug enthusiastically into the soft earth, churning them up again.

And earning the name "Digger."

I had learned from living with robins that black ants are the edible ones, not red ants. Now from Digger we found that there are *two* kinds of black ants – practical terminology that satisfies birdwatchers, not entomologists. We discovered the difference when we dumped the wrong kind into Digger's tub one evening.

These ants, rather than just milling about when their hill was disturbed, immediately swarmed all over the intruder – in this case Mack's spade. They seemed far more excited when dumped out, and to our horror swarmed all over Digger when he landed in the earth. As he ate them, his usual squeals were accompanied by continual whimpering, no doubt from being bitten. Mack and I looked at each other uneasily, wondering how flickers in the wild handled these ants.

Overnight, the ants settled down in the tub, but in the morning when Digger probed into their earth, they again attacked. Although Diggs ate quite a few, he whimpered steadily. Concerned,

I brushed them off him and carried the ants away. Then I hunted for a hill of the mild-mannered black ants, and dumped these into his tub instead. Diggs threw himself eagerly onto them and suffered no more.

These "attack ants" had black heads and abdomens, separated by tiny reddish thoraxes. With greater awareness, I now noticed that their hills never showed any disturbance from wild flickers as did the other ants' hills.

No wonder.

Digger's personality unfolded rapidly, to our lasting delight. He enjoyed our company and, if we busied ourselves elsewhere, he'd search the house for us, climbing woodpecker-wise up our bodies as if we were tree trunks. He also sought us when his ants were nearly gone and the remainder were so deep in the earth that he needed help dislodging them. Or when he needed a drink of water.

One evening, he hopped from the screened porch, where his ant tub was located, through the living room and kitchen to the dining room, where Mack sat happily playing the guitar. Digger had been hunting fruitlessly through the earth in his tub seeking ants. Hungry and frustrated, he hammered on Mack's foot with his long, hard bill and demanded "FOOD!" Then he hopped up Mack's leg to his knee and glared, speakingly, until Mack carried him back to the porch and stirred up the ants.

Even flickers found us easy to train.

Daily, Diggs rode contentedly on our shoulders and heads, and took tidbits of bread and raisins off our tongue at breakfast. When he became drowsy sitting on our heads, he tucked his head trustingly behind his wing and slept, putting any of our activities temporarily on hold.

Part of one living-room wall was covered with a wide roll of horizontal bamboo strips, and Mack soon devised a game. He'd toss Digger towards the wall, and Diggs would land in perfect woodpecker posture on the bamboo. Then he'd hop up the wall to the top, fly back to Mack, and be tossed again. Since then, we've kept one hospice wall covered with bamboo for any woodpecker clients.

One day we needed to make a journey to a distant city. Our local supply of anthills was seriously depleted, so we also planned to hunt for more on our trip. We knew Digger would run out of ants long before we returned, so we took him with us.

He refused to be ensconced in his basket but rode freely in the car with aristocratic aplomb. En route we stopped for a hitchhiker, a man we knew whose car had been out of commission for weeks, forcing him to thumb rides in order to get to his job. He climbed gratefully into the back seat and was immediately transfixed when Digger flew over companionably and landed on his shoulder.

Fortunately, he liked birds.

Digger began to cry for food, but his new friend didn't understand – until I passed back a dish of mealworms. We sped down the highway, Mack driving, me twisted around in the passenger seat, watching a rough, careworn man feeding mealies to a young flicker with utmost gentleness and good humour. I was reminded of an amusing incident in the local feed store.

I had just entered, one spring day, but all of the staff were in the warehouse. The only person I could see was a large, bow-armed man with an unprepossessing open-mouthed scowl and crooked yellow teeth. His belly hung over his belt, his hair protruded in disarray from under his squashed hat, and his clothes looked as though he spent his days fighting. I swallowed nervously and lingered unnoticed by the door, casting sidelong glances at the man as he lounged moodily down one aisle and up the next.

Suddenly he stopped in front of a large plastic tub on the floor, over which hung a brooder lamp. Musical peepings carolled out of the glowing warmth of the tub. Inside, dozens of tiny yellow chicks milled about busily, pecked at grain in a trough, preened their delicate downy bodies, or dozed delightfully in soft huddles.

With their vulnerability and that pristine beauty of the new-born, the innocent chicks could have presented no greater contrast to the rough-hewn man looming over them.

Then, to my unbounded astonishment and enduring delight, a smile of unmistakable gentleness transfigured his unshaven, corrugated face. Even his battered teeth took on a benevolent look.

He crouched down.

Soft, fatuous sounds like baby talk floated above the golden world of the chicks, and his thick fingers gently stroked their plumage.

I felt justly rebuked and joined him. We both played with the chicks until the sales staff returned from the warehouse.

After terminating our business in the city, Mack, Digger, and I drove to an area of abandoned farmland to hunt for anthills. Luck was with us, and we filled all our buckets, as well as Digger's shallow tub, with thousands of ants. Then we set him down on top of an anthill, and he responded immediately, devouring so many that he dozed in hymenopterous repletion all the way home.

Chip tolerated the newcomer with her usual blend of curiosity and aloofness – and a little jealousy thrown in whenever Digger sat with us. His greater size inhibited her desire to tease him, but she raided his ants in retaliation.

Bubble treated him with cool courtesy and impenetrable dignity, except when Digger saucily pecked at him. Then Bubbs instantly pecked back. My lap he obstinately and consistently refused to share, and he leaped up angrily one evening when Digger climbed up my leg and hopped onto Bubble's broad back.

Undeterred by his mixed reception, Digger explored the house with untiring curiosity, probing into and under dishes, plants, magazines, shoes, clothing, cushions, and hair – any place, likely or not, that might harbour bugs. Once, he landed on a large bag of flour and began probing through it, as though hoping for ants. All pockets and ears were routinely inspected and, at mealtimes, his curious beak would sample every flavour on our plates. He seemed to enjoy the taste of salt, for his long tongue would lick our faces and the backs of our necks whenever we perspired in the summer heat.

He treated each vertical surface as a tree, hopping vigorously up couches, crocheted lampshades, pantlegs, and textured walls, while tiny Bashō watched, fascinated.

When Digger discovered that the end gable of the cathedral ceiling over the living room was covered with brown burlap, he abandoned the side of his "travelling basket," where he'd been sleeping. Now night found him clinging easily to the wall high above us, his head tucked deeply behind his wing, giving him a decapitated silhouette.

When we'd taught Digger the little we knew about being an independent adult flicker, and when he was able to manage his ants and water without assistance, we carried him outside. He responded immediately to the woodland atmosphere surrounding the house, looking eagerly this way and that. We often see wild flickers near the house and felt that he'd make his way.

He flitted up onto the sun-warmed studio roof and sprawled there with outstretched wings and tail, soaking up the sunshine. I lingered nearby, refilling the outside waterdish and putting out more seed for the other birds. Then I glanced up at the roof.

Digger was gone.

We spotted him occasionally through the summer, hunting and finding insects only ten to fifteen feet from us as we worked in the garden. We made no overtures towards him, knowing he'd have to manage on his own. Nor did he approach us, which we felt was a good sign.

Though we felt a tinge of natural regret at ending such an intriguing relationship, we were delighted to see him functioning as a wild flicker.

And even more delighted to remove buckets of milling ants from the household menu. Tanks of mealworms in the closet were enough.

CHAPTER 33

SUMMER BABIES

Summer heaved a fragrant sigh of content and spread herself comfortably, like a hen on eggs, warming and nurturing the land. Trees crowded close to the house in leafy density, shading us from the sun's passion. Spring melt-pools quickly vanished in the woods, and excited brooks dwindled to languid trickles.

Bees and butterflies busied themselves continually in the robin garden, and the plants responded with zeal, blossoms maturing and fading, new veggies forming and growing. Robins and grackles helped their growth by ridding the garden of less desirable insects and feeding them to their families.

Those restless travellers, squash and cucumber plants, scaled the garden walls and crept determinedly across the clearing, steadying themselves with strong tendrils that wound around weeds. Bright orange blossoms began to glow well beyond the garden like beacons, encouraging other plants to follow in their wake.

We gathered aromatic armfuls of lemon balm and hung them in bunches in the kitchen to dry, creating an intoxicating atmosphere. Then we passed through the singing meadow and a more furtive alder thicket, which reluctantly yielded glimpses of silent, secretive warblers, till we arrived at the beaver dam. By the cool water we gathered a basket of wild mint to dry in the kitchen as well. Combined with its cousin lemon balm, mint creates one of our favourite herbal teas.

In the empty bird-feeder box attached to the dining-room window, we discovered two baby raccoons sound asleep in the early morning light. They lolled with the replete indolence of the retired elderly on a tropical beach, bellies like inflated balloons, limp fingers curved as though waiting to be handed a cold drink.

Then the telephone rang.

Out of the uproar of excited children at the other end, a harassed woman spoke. "My children brought home a baby robin. What should we do with it? Oh yes, we've been feeding it . . . bread and milk."

I groaned.

Who started this notion that nestlings are fed bread and milk? Where would they get such food, for heaven's sake? Has anyone ever seen a mother robin slapping together sandwiches? Or a father robin bringing home a quart of milk after a hard day at the office?

Hidden voices suddenly squealed. The woman shouted to her brood with terse parental authority, forgetting to turn aside from the receiver. My ears winced.

"NO! I told you before, keep the cats away from it!"

Cats?

"What's your address?" I demanded, scrambling for a pencil.

When I arrived, as so often happens, I found that the nestling was *not* a robin. Many people seem to feel that any baby bird is a robin, even without that famous speckled breast. In this case, the

black feathering, pale throat, and pointy beak with its extra-broad base proclaimed a starling nestling.

I remember a similar episode in which a whole nest of "robins" had been rescued from a felled tree. One pale-blue egg, which had failed to hatch, was also warming under a lamp beside its downy siblings when I arrived. The lamplit faces of several solemn children encircled the tabletop nest.

"Ah, starlings," I murmured, examining the nestlings. The children shook their heads decisively.

"Robins," they corrected, pointing at the egg.

When I explained that starlings, too, lay the famous blue eggs, they eyed me very doubtfully. Coerced finally by their mother, they reluctantly surrendered the nest and its crying occupants, obviously considering me a blundering old fool who couldn't even recognize a robin when she saw one.

The present starling refugee was exhausted from all the trauma it had absorbed, and difficult to feed when I got home. Mealworms were thrust down its throat only to pop out again as though there were a spring coiled inside. I finally substituted worms, sowbugs, and centipedes hastily unearthed from the garden. When the babe's crop was full, I bedded the little creature down in a small box lined with wool socks. After covering the box lightly with a tea towel, I left it all night beside a lamp for warmth.

In the morning, though the nestling was still sluggish, it gradually brightened. It ate steadily and grew livelier by the hour. The loose, smelly droppings became normal, and by the afternoon the babe was calling lustily for food every twenty minutes. Then the telephone rang.

Out of the uproar of excited children at the other end, a different woman, equally harassed, spoke. "My children brought home a baby robin. What should we do with it? Oh yes, we've been feeding it . . . bread and milk."

This robin, too, turned out to be a starling.

I bedded both babes together that night for warmth and companionship. The next morning found them bounding throughout the indoor garden, tufty headed and stumpy bottomed, their legs pumping like pistons, both mouths gaping rosily for worms, sowbugs, centipedes, and mealworms.

But *not* for bread and milk.

Both starling youngsters were still delighting in all the indoor garden could offer – to Bashō's chagrin, while Beejay, Goldie, and Chip watched curiously from the branches above – when a man and his daughter arrived with a young downy woodpecker. They'd driven a hundred miles to bring us the bird, and still faced a return trip, but they were concerned for his welfare. After he had struck a window, his flight had seemed impaired, but was improving steadily. The downy had been living freely in their bathroom for two days.

"Easier to clean up after it," the man added, bluntly.

The little girl giggled.

After they had departed, we set the woodpecker out in the screened porch. Against the wall we leaned a length of knobby, pitted beech tree for the bird to climb up, woodpecker-style. In the cavities of the tree we packed a mixture of peanut butter, honey, cornmeal, raisins, and shelled sunflower seeds. On the table we set a flat dish of water and another of mealworms.

In this makeshift woodland, the woodpecker thrived, sleeping at the top of the log at night and eating well. His flight strengthened quickly. After a couple of days, we released him in an area of the woods where we'd often sighted woodpeckers. He immediately flew over to a standing dead tree and began probing for bugs under the loose bark.

Later that evening, I glanced into the screened porch and spotted two deermice feasting on the remaining peanut-butter mixture. It would be a clean tree when they were finished.

Two days later we received yet another call about a baby "robin." As I drove into town to collect what I presumed would be another starling, I hoped it would be at the same stage of development as the first two. Then I could release all three together.

"Good heavens, a robin!" I declared, when I entered the house.

"I *told* you it was a robin," retorted the mother, peevishly. Her children eyed me suspiciously. Then I spotted a dish full of worms on the table, always a welcome accompaniment.

"Worms!" I blurted out, brightly.

"That's what baby robins eat," explained the youngest child, patiently. The other children exchanged raised eyebrows at my ignorance.

Unable to dispel the ruinous reputation I was so quickly acquiring, I gathered up nestling and worms and made a hasty departure. As I backed nervously out of the drive, the unwinking eyes of the children watched me from the doorway, sceptical to the last.

The young robin, eight or nine days old, was a delightful creature – a male, characterized by his dark head. From the beginning, "Robb" gaped readily for food, thereby eliminating the tiresome difficulties of forcefeeding. When full and content, he carolled sweetly. His mild disposition eased the addition of yet another occupant for the indoor garden – although, to Chip, every transient provided new opportunities for teasing.

Robb's flight developed quickly, no doubt due in part to Chip's prodding bill, and he often chose to roost on the hanging lamp, loosening his feathers to absorb the warmth. When he discovered the flat waterdish in the indoor garden, he had his first bath, churning the water and beating his wings with great enthusiasm. Flying spray beaded up on plant leaves till they dripped like a rainforest. Bashō shook his feathers fussily, and trotted into the kitchen, buzzing irritably. The other birds sought higher, drier branches. When the youngster finally hopped out of the dish, vibrating his wings and tail to dry them, only half the water remained, rocking wildly. On damp wings, with plastered plumage, he lurched awkwardly through the air to his warm roost on the hanging lamp, where he remained, preening and renewing his feathers to perfection.

In a few days, Robb was in charge of his own feedings. When hungry, he'd jump eagerly into the bug box to probe for worms, or to seize lumbering sowbugs and whizzing centipedes.

Chokecherry bushes flank our home, and we brought in branches loaded with clusters of cherries for all the birds, including young Robb. Everyone except Bashō enjoyed the wild fruits, swallowing them whole and later casting up clean, dry pits. They began to appear everywhere in the garden, as was natural, but also wherever Chip's curiosity led her.

Pits lurked in our salads and sank into our soups. Pits hid inside our boots waiting for tender feet to descend. Pits browned in the toaster or tumbled in the dryer. They fell from our pockets in the stores. One appeared mysteriously in the freezer.

Thanks to Chip, our world was unquestionably "the pits."

As Robb's plumage filled out and his tail lengthened, his confidence also developed. Like any adolescent, he began saucing his elders – and getting away with it. Beejay and Goldie retreated up their trees. Bashō stalked huffily away, swollen with dignity. Retaliation was left to Chip, who refused to admonish the babe directly, but seldom missed the chance to tweak his tail, poke his back, or steal his food, always darting easily out of reach.

Soon all three youngsters were exploring the house, new perplexities enlivening each day. They scrambled ludicrously for footholds among slippery wet plates in the dishrack. They suddenly appeared, flapping awkwardly in the steam over a pot of bubbling soup. Trailing philodendron plants entangled their feet.

The uncovered toilet bowl gaped menacingly. One day, hearing strange sounds within, I opened the stereo cabinet and Robb stepped out into the living room as casually as a caller at the door entering the house.

Their curiosity led them into every room, but hunger and thirst always guided them back to the garden. In the bug box they began to lose interest in the earthworms, but wild bugs and mealworms still remained choice fare.

When we felt all three babes could manage on their own, we released them into the chokecherry bushes beside the house, leaving the door open to the screened porch. Both starling youngsters flitted away with confident maturity to begin their adult lives, but in an hour Robb returned. As soon as the house door opened, he trotted anxiously inside, where he remained for the rest of the day, contentedly enjoying the garden.

More bold the following morning, Robb remained outdoors for most of the day, flying over to us each time we appeared. From the windows, we watched him hunting for food in the rooster run, probing the dirt like a pro, while Bubble lingered nearby, willing to relieve him of any unwanted earthworms. When I climbed up on the roof platform, Robb quickly joined me. Hot sunshine beating down on the asphalt shingles soon lulled him into sprawling luxuriously in the heat, all feathers spread, mouth open and eyes glazed. A true sun-worshipper.

Later, when we offered him a few of the undesirable earthworms, he devoured them without hesitation, so we knew he wasn't catching enough food yet. If we continued only to supplement Robb's daily fare, he'd feel just enough hunger to be stimulated in seeking his own, without being deprived. It was necessary, too, to develop his independence.

At dusk Robb again returned, and cozied down to sleep on the lamp beside my chair. During the night Chip was disturbed, for some mysterious reason, and I awoke groggily to her blundering around in the dark. Then I heard Robb's voice as well. When I switched on the light they both made sudden landings, wide-eyed and panting in the bright glare.

I added my own glare, till they finally flitted off to their roosts, briefly chastened, and peace was restored.

In the early morning, I opened the door and Robb swept past me into the trees, blending amazingly into his surroundings. Throughout the day he hunted for food, preened, and heeded all the alarm calls from the jays near the feeders. Some of the calls must have puzzled him, since they invariably burst out whenever we stepped outdoors. Robb would swoop over to us amidst strident warnings, which scattered all the other birds. Sitting in safety on top of our heads, he'd peer anxiously in all directions for the enemy – not realizing it was us.

No doubt the jays were equally puzzled when we failed to assault him.

Robb slept outside that night for the first time, which delighted us. All the following week he remained out, taking only occasional mealworms or earthworms from us, and we felt he was well on the way to adulthood.

We missed seeing him for a couple of days. Then we had another visit, but he seemed sluggish. Even drowsy. Mack fed him a large earthworm, followed later by a few mealies, but still we were concerned. He left us, flying slowly up into the trees, and disappeared until the next day. When he reappeared, he had a tuft of feathers loose at the back of his neck, his eyes seemed shallow and opaque, and he looked terrible. We fed him mealworms and corn borers and offered water, which he also accepted, but in a short while, he vomited. He refused any other food, but drank a little more water. His droppings were runny, with an odd smell.

After a short while, he died in Mack's gentle hands. We were devastated. Robb had been so woven into our lives in such a brief time.

Since we were unable at that time to have an autopsy done, Robb's death remained a painful enigma. We guessed that he had ingested something poisonous.

Despite the sadness that permeated us after Robb's death, we took pleasure in watching other youngsters as they struggled with the mysteries of growing up.

A young blue jay perched on the rim of the birdbath. Excited by the wind-rippled water, he ducked his head several times, beating his wings and vibrating his tailfeathers repeatedly. Then he hopped over the water to the other side, where he again perched on the rim, demonstrating every movement for bathing correctly. Except one.

He never did get into the water.

On the dining-room feeder, a young grackle was enduring the weaning process under protest. Sometimes he would be fed. Oftener ignored.

On this occasion, he begged and begged his parents for food, fluttering his wings beguilingly, but they continued feeding only themselves. At last, spotting a young jay being fed by its parent, the grackle fledgling flew over and lined up beside the jay youngster, gaping hopefully at the adult jay.

To his despair, even *they* ignored him, and abruptly left.

At dusk one evening, we watched with delight a doe and her two spotted fawns. Despite their mother's obvious wariness and their own inherent caution, the light-footed fawns frisked and bounded with all the forgetful exuberance of youngsters everywhere.

Late the following afternoon, we watched five deer dancing in the meadow. Rimmed with brightness from the sun's low rays behind them, they pranced and pirouetted, tossing their heads and tails and floating above the glowing grasses on delicate legs of pure light.

Their beauty as they danced almost reconciled Mack to the ravages those same deer were making in the robin veggie garden each night. To our dismay, onion, potato, and tomato plants were devoured to the ground. Even many of the onion bulbs were eaten as well, although it was difficult to associate vile onion breath with such otherworldly creatures.

Sometimes we awoke in the mornings to see them knee-deep in the beans, chewing blissfully. Despite our efforts, green peppers, chard, and most of the peas went the way of the rest. But at least the deer did not eat the corn.

The raccoons did.

We harvested what we could from the plundered garden, and gratefully, even eagerly, accepted offerings of excess vegetables from friends with overburgeoning gardens – friends who had dogs to guard veggies against marauding wildlife.

I remember one neighbour struggling with the nightly munchings of what she thought was a groundhog in her garden. Her dog preferred to sleep indoors. Exasperated, she pulled the unused doghouse over beside the garden, then hauled her protesting canine outdoors at dusk and chained him determinedly to the doghouse. Like the rest of us, she wished no harm to the wildlife. She just wanted to be the one to eat the vegetables after having done all the work of planting, watering, and weeding.

However, in the morning the garden had again been raided and her distraught dog was sitting at the very end of his chain, staring back apprehensively at his doghouse.

In the little doorway, a fat – very fat – porcupine lay sleeping the contented sleep of one who has dined well.

I spent a full day in the kitchen chopping my way through mounds of vegetables – at least *some* of which we'd grown ourselves. Cooked suppers of rice and veggies in tofu sauce were set aside to cool before being frozen for the winter. Three large stock-pots simmered on the stove, full to the brim with veggie soup.

Bubble stood on a stool beside me at the counter, daintily eating carrot peelings and the seedy interiors of cucumbers, which I set before him from time to time. When I decided to frost one of the carrot cakes for immediate use and freeze the others, he savoured samplings of penuche icing with eyes of ecstasy – eyes that narrowed menacingly when Mack appeared in the doorway. Without the slightest hesitation, Bubbs hurled himself at him in passionate indignation.

The icing still coating his beak and wattles may have sweetened Bubble's afternoon, but his bitterness towards Mack had lost none of its pungency.

On a warm summery day, a man arrived after a long drive of nearly a hundred miles through holiday traffic. From a small box he lifted out a young kingbird.

Though the bird had been born in the spring, its stunted growth indicated a problem. Its droppings, too, were fluid and of a peculiar colour, and one wing drooped slightly. The feather barbs were so sparse that I could see *through* the tailfeathers. Despite the lack of healthy sheen on the kingbird's plumage, its disposition seemed perky. I offered a mealworm, which he instantly picked up and swallowed.

Over tea, the visitor told us that tourists had picked up the bird at the southern end of the province. They called it an "abandoned nestling," a common description to which I've always objected. I've been closely involved with various mother birds, watching their intensive care of their young, and the notion that they arbitrarily discard their babies from time to time is ridiculous. So many factors can disrupt nesting seasons, from predators to storms, yet always the term is "abandoned." I prefer to say "separated," implying an unknown cause.

The tourists had fed the babe whatever they were eating themselves. When their travels took them to the northern end of the province, they gave the bird to our visitor and his wife.

For two and a half weeks they cared for the bird, but fed it slugs and human food. It quickly became clear to me that, despite good intentions all round, the kingbird had not been correctly nourished during major developmental stages. Nor had it been taught to recognize and search out its natural food.

When the couple tried to release the bird, it remained on a tree branch for hours, crying piteously for food. The woman was tired of droppings in the house. Her husband was at a loss, seeing the young bird's obvious dependence. Frustrated, yet anxious to help the creature, he'd brought it to us.

"Jake" was a beautiful bird, despite his poor condition. His dark head and long, white throat reminded me of a feathered orca whale. Unfortunately, he sang by the hour in shrill warbles that for some inscrutable reason annoyed Molly. Perhaps she was endowed, or cursed, with perfect pitch, and felt that Jake's performances showed no promise whatever.

Though the other birds treated Jake with indifference as he sang on and on, Molly, basking above, began to seethe. She tapped one wing rapidly and warningly, much as an impatient human will drum fingers irritably on a tabletop. When Jake was silent, Molly became still. But as soon as he broke into song, she fumed like a tenant in a thin-walled apartment building forced to listen to another tenant belabouring a violin. Because of a large, delicate clay sculpture in progress in the studio, I was unable to isolate Molly there, so she roosted these days on a shelf in the living room – above the indoor garden.

Her wing-tapping grew louder.

After a couple of days, Molly's patience, never one of her shining virtues, vanished abruptly. She shot menacingly across the room towards Jake, who was singing innocently on a branch. With her great size completely dwarfing him, she looked like a condor after a canary.

Jake dodged her at the last moment, flitting lightly to another branch, while Molly blundered heavily into the tree and fell to the floor in an angry flap. Silenced only briefly by his surprise, Jake quickly resumed his strident trilling, like a smug music-hall singer oblivious to the jeers of an unsympathetic audience.

Molly picked herself up from the floor, glowering ferociously, and I chased her back to her roost, threatening her with various punishments in which graphic descriptions of pigeon pie predominated. Stalking back and forth in her loft, Molly rumbled defiance to all, before finally resettling herself in an angry huff.

Only to bide her time.

Jake quickly became an endearing member of the family. Despite his health difficulties, he always showed a cheery personality, his large, dark eyes bright and wonderfully expressive. A steady diet of bugs, mealworms, and fruit soon brought a slight sheen to his deplorable plumage and restored his droppings to normal consistency.

For such a tiny bird, his capacity for mealworms at one meal was *enormous*. Because kingbirds are classed as flycatchers, I tossed him his mealies one at a time, and Jake snapped them up in mid-air, a method I felt would be psychologically affirming to a grounded flycatcher. He rarely missed.

At least a dozen mealies would be rapidly packed into his spandex crop at one feeding until he'd pause, holding one in his beak instead of immediately swallowing it. Only then did I know that his crop was full. And even so, that last mealie would be crammed inside somehow.

Spiders, centipedes, and sowbugs were set aside for Jake's sole use. For part of each day, we'd shut him into a screened box with his dish of bugs and fruit. In this way, whenever we were busy or absent, Chip and the other birds couldn't steal his food. Jake could learn, by hunger, to feed himself regularly. Despite our efforts, he often waited, sometimes for hours, for one of us to initiate his feedings, so his progress towards independence was slow.

Perhaps, like many of us, he hated to eat alone.

Chip certainly stimulated his feedings, albeit unintentionally, when she discovered the hidden cache of bugs. With persistence I wished Jake would emulate, she tried to force her way into his box at any opportunity, and whenever she succeeded, devoured every bug.

Like Goldie, Beejay, and Chip, Jake possessed the easy skill of swallowing chokecherries whole, casting up clean pits later. We also added a dish of raspberries to his fare, as well as any early blueberries we could find outdoors, ripening quickly in the sunniest locations.

Jake soon became part of daily activities in the indoor garden. Once, when Goldie, the evening grosbeak, was enjoying a bath, Jake drew closer, intrigued. Goldie stopped churning up the water and glared, his enormous bill snapping warnings to Jake to wait his turn. When Goldie finally emerged, shook off the excess water, and climbed back up into his tree, Jake hopped into the water for his own bath. Because of his short legs, I kept the water level lower than usual.

In the evenings, whenever I sat back with a book, Bubble would immediately jump up for hugs before settling himself across my lap, his arched tailfeathers gradually relaxing until they trailed to the floor in an iridescent cascade. Bashō would be snuggled cozily into my shirt, while Chip preened languidly on my head or on one shoulder. On the other shoulder, Jake would sit, dozing contentedly.

At close range, each bird's plumage smelled fragrant, not only from cleanliness but from preening oils, no two alike. Jake, singular to the last, smelled curiously like woodsmoke.

Molly, however, remained unimpressed by the new arrival and still sought opportunities to wreak her wrath upon him. Whenever we shut Jake into his box before driving to town, we'd return to find a scowling Molly standing on top of the box, tearing at the cardboard with a determined beak that I was convinced she spent each night honing.

If we were out of the room and Jake was enjoying the garden, sooner or later we'd hear the loud whirr of Molly's great wings as she hurtled down at him. If she could have contrived silencers for her pinions, I wouldn't have been surprised.

One day, after chasing him into a corner, she jumped on him. Jake screeched and I bounded in to the rescue, grabbed Molly, and flung her savagely onto her shelf. Jake cowered before me, a broken flightfeather protruding from his drooping wing.

At last, frustrated from leaping downstairs, up from meals, or suddenly off the toilet every time I heard Molly take wing, I contrived a shelf in the screened porch and added her food and water dishes. Then I carried an outraged Molly, wings flailing, out to the porch and left her there with only her grievances to warm her.

Unfortunately, a week later, high winds and torrents of rain raged around the house all night. Wakened by explosions of thunder, I opened the porch door to check on Molly. In the lurid flashes of lightning, I found the porch roof spewing water from a dozen outlets like an activated sprinkler alarm. Newspapers that weren't plastered to the floor billowed erratically like rustling ghosts with each gust under the door.

Molly glared accusingly at me. Her plumage was sodden, her waterdish overflowing around her feet, and drips fell steadily into her dish of grain.

Appalled and contrite, I gathered her into my arms – despite her irritable beak snappings – and carried her back into the house. Murmuring apologies, I settled her on her usual shelf with fresh food and water before switching off the light and returning to bed. In the semi-darkness I could see her preening indignantly.

Despite the record-breaking rain, Molly's ire remained unquenched. Morning's light showed great calm after the tempest – but only outdoors. Indoors we seemed to be living in a teacup. Molly rose in an infamous temper, seemingly determined to make up for lost time, and immediately began stalking poor Jake through the indoor garden, cutting short his cheery morning song.

Though he'd been eating proper food for some time, still he remained frail, and slow flights over short distances were all he could manage – an observation not lost on Molly.

Unable to devise earplugs for her to muffle Jake's arias, I finally isolated her permanently back in the studio, the sculpture having been removed to a drying cupboard. There she remained all alone, seemingly contented, militantly unsociable, and responding with warm eyes only to human music from the studio tape deck.

As an enigma, Molly left the Mona Lisa nowhere.

CHAPTER 34

SUMMER SHENANIGANS

Chip, meanwhile, was enjoying the passing summer days. When bored, she possessed more than enough ingenuity to create amusement – though usually by destroying someone else's tranquility. One of her victims was Beejay.

Still maintaining a strong connection with the other jays outside the window of the indoor garden, Beejay would join in their activities. When the wildlings carried off bulging throats of sunflower seeds, Beejay would excitedly load his own throat and busy himself stuffing seeds into secret crevices. When the wild jays rested and preened, so did he. Hopping awkwardly along the windowsill, despite his crippled leg and wing, and eagerly watching the others took up a large portion of his day. However, the instant a wild jay sounded an alarm in shrill screams, Beejay too took cover. Sometimes he added his own alarm calls, as would be natural.

None of this was lost on Chip.

I had vaguely become aware that Beejay was screaming alarm calls more frequently than before. Puzzled, I glanced his way one day and remained rooted to the spot. What I witnessed was only one of many subsequent occurrences.

The wily Chip, seeing Beejay leap eagerly onto the windowsill as the outside jays arrived to feed, suddenly delivered an exact imitation of a blue jay alarm call. Beejay instantly shot under a plant to hide, and moments later Chip took over his windowsill with a triumphant strut, her dark eyes gleaming with insufferable smugness.

Thereafter Beejay's summer was riddled with false alarms from Chip, as she verbally chased him away from the windowsill, only to claim it for herself. Beejay had great difficulty in not automatically heeding such a primal call, and Chip knew that well. Only when he caught her in the act would he contemptuously ignore her, a challenge Chip countered by hiding before she called.

Determined to irritate him, she'd wait until he was comfortably roosted for the night in one of the indoor trees. Then she'd flit to a branch only half a foot away and blast blue jay calls in Beejay's face. Beejay, unable to flounder away in the dusky light with his twisted body, would be forced to endure Chip's sauciness, eyeing her coldly through narrowed eyes. I, too, was helpless to shoo Chip away without alarming Beejay who, unlike Chip, was still a wild bird.

As though to share her new accomplishment, Chip began discharging volleys of blue jay screeches mingled with jocular grackle outbursts on our pillows as the early – *very early* – dawn brightened the eastern sky.

Her shrill vocalizations were only surpassed by our own blasphemous bellows at being hurled so brutally into a new day.

I could only marvel that Chip didn't grow devilish horns. The wedged tail she displayed in flight could certainly have passed for a forked one, and the fact that her dark eyes never attained the pale yellow hue of most grackles' seemed entirely appropriate.

The ingenious minds of wild grackles can often create situations well worth watching. A friend of ours, working at a fish hatchery, spotted a female grackle collecting dead minnows. Another worker had cleaned them out of one of the ponds and tossed them on the grass. The grackle lined them up on one of the paved walkways, with the tail of each fish touching the nose of the next. When she had them all in a row, she began to collect them crosswise in her bill like a puffin, until she could carry no more. Then she flew off to her nest to feed her young before returning for the rest.

Our friend also observed an efficient fishing technique that the wily grackles developed. The fish in the hatchery pools are fed food pellets that are scattered on the surface of the water. Thus anything disturbing the surface immediately attracts their attention. Busy parent grackles, ever searching for food to satisfy their vociferous young, strut up to the water's edge, submerge just the tips of their beaks, and wait. The fish rise curiously and are instantly caught and flicked out onto the bank. When several fish have been lured in this way, the grackles pound their catch in order to kill them, collect them crosswise in their beaks, and fly triumphantly back to their nests.

Chip, though raised with humans, had certainly lost none of this innate grackle ability to fully exploit any given situation.

One morning, as I set an oatmeal-raisin soda bread into the oven to bake, I caught a movement out of the corner of my eye. Spinning around, I spotted an enormous spider that seemed to my electrified eyes to be the size of a fist. It galloped across the floor on thick, striped limbs that presumably passed for legs. Though a confirmed admirer of spiders, I jumped involuntarily at the sight of this Goliath.

Scrambling for a glass in which to capture the creature and release it outside, I suddenly felt Chip land on my shoulder. At the same moment, she spotted the spider, who had paused rather unwisely in the middle of the floor. With heightened eyes the size of dinner plates, she swooped down to do battle, crest feathers on end, tail flared. I fled the scene, unwilling to bear witness, but Chip's radiant expression for the rest of the day betokened the victor. If nothing else, her triumphant encounter with the luckless spider dimmed, if only briefly, her unholy joy in tormenting Beejay, and gave him a welcome respite.

Despite Chip's sly persecution, Beejay enjoyed long moments of repose, which he transfigured with song – not the strident calls so characteristic of jays, but a very soft, melodious rippling of trills and warbles offset with staccatoed "punks" in a blend that sounded utterly enchanting. Often his notes were doubled in harmony, as though two birds were singing. But for the chance of living with a blue jay, I would never have heard such a song. Certainly not in the woods, under the wary gaze of the wildlings. Beejay's song remains one of the most remarkable I've ever heard.

Bubble, too, was enjoying his summer days, despite Squeak's absence. In the dappled sunshine of the rooster run he spent hours luxuriating in dustbaths, or scratching up bugs out of the moist soil and devouring them. His long, iridescent-green tailfeathers danced in the soft breezes that continually teased them.

When he walked, he moved with monumental dignity, daintily closing the toes of each lifted foot, then opening them again as he lowered the foot, placing each step with great precision before him. Royalty glowed in every feather.

The spur he had broken against Mack's leg was pointed once more and growing out well – though Mack seemed strangely disinterested when I informed him of its progress. Now Bubbs was enduring his annual moult, and beautiful feathers, richly coloured, slid loose under my hand whenever I stroked him. Pointed feathers and blunt, long ones and short, curved and straight, soft and stiff, they brightened our floors and drifted through the rooster run like autumn leaves.

Indeed, in colouring Bubble was always my autumn rooster, just as Squeak was my winter one.

Our own foods still held great attraction for Bubbs and, despite his aversion to Mack (or perhaps because of it!), he felt no compunction whatever in grabbing beakfuls of whipped cream off Mack's strawberry shortcake, an accomplishment that left his wattles, even after washing, smelling like sour milk for days. He also gobbled down without remorse half a slice of bread and molasses that Mack had prepared for himself, and strolled regally through the veggie garden, sampling cucumbers, lettuce, and his passion – strawberries.

Despite Bubb's treatment of him, Mack was ever generous to Bubbs, averring that he too, though merely a human rooster, would soundly reject the encroachment of any other rooster on his hen's domain.

I tried to feel flattered.

Even when the strawberry patch dwindled to occasional berries, we shared. If there were three, we each got one. If only one glowed with ripeness, Mack would bite off one third and pass it to me. I'd bite off the second third and pass the last third to Bubbs. All three of us loved strawberries, so all three got a morsel.

Chokecherries were another favourite for Bubble, as for the indoor birds, and when summer waned, I'd hold heads of tiny dark elderberries before him and he'd eat every one.

When I peeled apples for a pie, Bubbs ate the peelings and most of the cores, standing on his stool beside the kitchen counter. When I strained the seeds out of cooked raspberries, he devoured the rosy pulp with clucks of joy.

It soon became clear to Mack that harbouring a gourmet rooster is a serious impediment to creating decent compost for the garden – a situation to which he wisely became resigned.

But Bubble, too, loved to offer treats. Often he'd kill a bug, one that was a particular favourite, and offer it to me so insistently that I'd be unable to persuade him to eat it himself. Conscious of the conferred honour, I'd pretend to comply with his wishes – much to Mack's amusement.

On Bubble's birthday, August the first, we all went for a drive. In town, I gathered Bubbs into my arms, where he always melded cozily to me, exchanging soft clucks, and carried him into the natural-foods store to visit friends while Mack made some purchases. The owner, bluff and welcoming, responded to the auspicious occasion by presenting Bubble with a bag of shredded coconut. Bubbs, although coconut was one of his favourite delicacies, accepted with frigid dignity.

After all, the owner, like Mack, was yet another rooster.

Mack himself had just endured another confrontation with Bubbs. Earlier that day, he'd been working alone in the kitchen when Bubble had casually let himself out of the studio and strolled into the kitchen.

Mack froze.

Bubbs, merely acknowledging the enemy's presence with a withering look, opened his wings and leaped suddenly up onto the kitchen counter. There he crowed in stentorian tones that caused the hanging pots to ring. Then he faced Mack.

Determined to sell his life dearly, Mack seized the broom and held it ready. Had he possessed the wiliness of a woman, he would have grabbed maple cream instead – a treat guaranteed to sweeten any male.

Bubbs and Mack stood eye to eye, neither one moving, till I finally dashed out of the bathroom, sensing a near-calamity. I scooped Bubble up in my arms and bore him off, prattling sweet talk in his ear, to his obvious delight – and Mack's disgust.

Then, for one week, I was obliged to be away from home. When I returned, I opened the door to the rooster run and spoke Bubbs's name. He was right before me and with a joyful squawk leaped several feet straight up into my arms. Hugging him closely, touched to tears by his evident devotion, I wished more people could recognize that chickens, too, if raised with kindness and sensitivity to their needs, can reveal incredible personalities.

Though most people accept the individuality of cats and dogs, even horses, chickens are generally considered a joke. Admirers of chickens are obliged to communicate surreptitiously, lest they be dismissed as intellectually questionable. However, I can attest to the fact that, when chicken aficionados congregate to exchange stories, the results are delightful.

And often astonishing.

One of the most remarkable accounts I've ever heard was related to me by a soft-hearted friend who has an equestrian stable. Her husband, to her distress, one day loaded their meat chickens in the truck and drove them to the local abattoir to meet their intended end. There, one of the hens escaped. Although he searched everywhere, she was nowhere to be seen.

He drove back home and, when he stopped in the yard, the missing hen flew out from under the car. She had ridden home, a distance of *twelve miles*, most of it in heavy traffic on the Trans-Canada Highway, *perched on the truck axle*.

After such a valiant effort to escape being butchered, she was indeed granted a reprieve. "Madeleine" became a revered member of the family for many years, and a familiar figure in the great stable. During cold nights she slept on the horses' backs, sharing their warmth. In the summer, she reciprocated by snapping up barn flies by the dozens.

Not many chickens are treated so well. I was called out one night by a neighbour to examine a sick chicken, and as soon as I saw the creature, I realized there was little hope. She had obviously suffered all her short life from neglect. Her plumage was very dull, her feet scaly and encrusted, her eyes opaque. She was enduring spasms and bore visible external, and probably had internal, parasites. She'd been given the bare minimum to survive, yet was expected to lay large eggs on a daily basis.

I felt a great release for that gentle hen when she died.

Yet often chicken stories are amusing. Years ago, I had half a dozen hens who ranged freely around the house. No trees surrounded that home, and the wary hens always kept a weather eye on the heavens for hawks.

One morning, shortly after I'd let them out of their shed, I realized I had to make a trip to town. The sky was clear, the sunshine mellow, and bugs prevalent after a damp night. The hens flatly refused to be reconfined in their shed. I coaxed and wheedled, filled their treat dish with favourite foods, but to no avail. I tried to *drive* them inside, waving my arms and filling their obstinate ears with gruesome stories of rampaging dogs and bloodthirsty weasels that seek fat, unprotected chickens. I'd shoo them as far as their door but there they'd scatter, insistent upon remaining outdoors. I glared at them in frustration, longing for just *one* hawk to appear.

Then I smiled – wickedly.

I hastened indoors, got out my kite, and slipped around to the opposite side of the house. An ideal breeze was rippling the hayfields as I quickly launched my hawk-shaped kite. From the hens' side of the house I heard sudden squawks of alarm erupt as the kite swooped above them. When I peeked around the corner, the hens had hoisted their skirts and fled into the shelter of their shed.

I sprang out of hiding and bolted them in.

Late one morning at the end of summer, Mack and I climbed up onto the roof platform with our mugs of tea and sat gazing over the fields. Intense cold under a starry sky had silently crystallized our world overnight, but at dawn the early fingers of sunlight had pressed warmth back into the land, reducing the frost to twinkles of moisture. By mid-morning there were patches of earth warm and dry enough for Bubble to create a dustbath.

But the memory of the first frost, though transient and quickly quelled by the sun, remained a sombre, invisible signpost. The leafy undulation of the far hills also seemed to be anticipating autumn's approach in the faint tinge of orange that stained the green maples. Ignoring such rumours, a dragonfly darted about us on glittering wings, swooping after minute insects. Suddenly he wheeled about and landed lightly in my lap, where he remained at rest, his enormous eyes tilting this way and that, his abdomen waxing and waning with each breath.

From a hollow in the big serviceberry tree beside us, a mother squirrel emerged and immediately stopped for a scratch. Unlike the other three female squirrels that had delivered their babies in the spring, she had birthed her young in midsummer. Now they too began to emerge from the nest hole – and they too began immediately to scratch.

Soon six babes and their mother were gambolling before us on various branches, each scratching frantically, with only momentary lapses.

Until then I'd always assumed that only deep luxurious yawns and the hearty laughter of others were contagious – and not just between humans. The natural curved smile of ducks and dolphins always creates a duplicate smile on me. Mack was able to make his cat yawn simply by yawning first in the cat's face. A dog we know welcomes people by lifting his upper lip to expose his small front teeth in a perfect imitation of a human smile – which of course always initiates more smiles in those he welcomes.

Now I discovered that compulsive scratching is irresistible.

Soon Mack and I were summoning all our self-control not to scratch imaginary itches as we watched the squirrels frantically clawing themselves – first with one leg, then the other, contorting themselves as though they were made of spandex.

And all without any visible signs of relief.

As we fled back down the ladder, chased by hordes of imaginary fleas, I resolved to shake rotenone powder into the tree-hole at the first opportunity – before the very tree itself began to scratch.

Late that night we ventured back up onto the roof, lured by the thick glitter of stars hovering above the darkened land. Tiny cries of unseen migrants rang musically above us as they fluttered past, wings following an ancient call to a long journey through mystery.

Somehow, our artificial world of electric lights that eliminate night, of television signals that relay so much trivia, of continual mechanical noise that deadens our sensitivities, seems so meaningless compared to such a primal ritual as starlit birds, like unseen spirits, following the wingbeats of their ancestors.

CHAPTER 35

FAREWELL FROM THE ARK

The autumn days flew past, blown like the whirling leaves around us. Like the wedges of wild geese over the southern hills. Like the flocks of songbirds that appeared, then vanished. Appeared, then vanished. Now, only the calls of blue jays predominated, so familiar in winter.

Colours flared across the hilltops, accented by the dark tips of spruce and fir. Sumacs, not to be outdone, glowed green, yellow, orange, and red all at once. The pale mauve of asters tinged roadsides in an almost melancholy hue. Before long, our feet were scuffling through drifts of dead leaves.

Squirrels stripped the wild hazelnut bushes, leaving only a handful of nuts hanging from the branches. Chuckling at their wasteful ways, I opened each one and found it empty.

Now it was the squirrels' turn to chuckle.

Draped over the woodpile, garter snakes sunned themselves still, though the days were cooler and shorter. They slipped into holes and crevices when the chill of night descended. As wood was wheeled away daily to the woodshed, fewer snakes were seen, till they eventually disappeared for the winter.

A large chunk of twisty firewood caught my eye, suggesting a potential painting. When I lifted it up and turned it around, I discovered a lovely garter snake coiled up in a gaping fissure, watching me warily. Viewed through traditional symbolism, he became Ouroboros, the cosmic serpent encircling and protecting our world but reduced by our persistent environmental decimation to hiding in a remnant of the Tree of Life.

In great contrast loomed the wild-apple trees. They crowded the fencelines, sagging with their rosy or yellow burdens, and every tree boasted abundance.

Even saplings bore impressive apples.

Scatterings of apples dropped from leaning roadside trees and were crushed under passing cars. Apples floated in the lakes. Rolled treacherously under our feet. Appeared outlandishly on high spruce branches after being lugged up by determined squirrels.

Apple pies, apple crisps, apple sauce, and whole apples, stuffed with cinnamon and honey and wrapped in pastry, mounted up in the freezer. We juiced bags of apples, heated the juice with honey and spices, and froze it for cozy winter days around the fire.

When I cut up apples for the mealworms, I placed the wild organic ones on one side of the tanks and, out of curiosity, chunks of a standard grocery apple on the other side. Dozens of mealies clustered around the organic apples, while the sprayed ones remained untouched. And disturbingly unbrowned.

A lesson, surely.

As though in tune with the nostalgic melancholy, that accelerated waning so characteristic of autumn's waxing, we suffered the loss of two of our birds.

On our return from town one morning, we found that Goldie, our flightless evening grosbeak, had fallen upside down into the waterdish and had drowned. Hard on the heels of his death, we returned after a fortnight's absence to discover that, during our last evening away, Smokey, the one-winged pigeon, had been carelessly left out overnight in the rooster run by the person in charge, and killed by raccoons.

The tragic loss of two such gentle creatures, though of little note in the headlong clatter of the modern world, yet created a stillpoint of sorrow in our own lives. Fortunately this was balanced by the ongoing activities of creatures around us.

Jake the kingbird's faulty plumage responded in a unique way to the annual moulting call. All of his tailfeathers, as well as those of his drooping left wing, *broke* off. During the following weeks the unsightly stubs gradually fell out, but only a few replacements grew in singly over the next few months. They invariably broke off live – that is, when the quills were still full of blood and developing.

Never did his feathers grow back en masse, a chronic condition I attributed to incorrect feeding in his nestling days.

With the help of a young vet keenly interested in birds, we adjusted Jake's diet. There followed a marked improvement, in that Jake's tailfeathers grew out once more, and his body plumage thickened, but the left wing still resembled a penguin's. The long flightfeathers were never replaced. Nor did he ever develop plumage of a healthy richness so necessary to maintain a free bird. He became one of our unreleasables, but the rest of our singular family flourished.

One autumn evening we received a phone call from a young couple who lived at least two hundred and fifty miles away. They had scooped up a blackpoll warbler from a city street. The bird had struck a window high up on an office building, bruising itself and temporarily damaging one wing.

Having a natural love of wild creatures, the rescuers were determined to help the warbler. After having it examined by two veterinarians – one of whom returned it minus all its tailfeathers – and still no wiser as to the bird's condition, they'd turned to one of my books for help.

For two and a half weeks they caught sowbugs and spiders, bought mealworms, and minced up kiwis, oranges, and bananas to feed their small guest. The scarcity of wild bugs troubled them, and when they considered the long months until spring, when the warbler could be released, they began to feel anxious about its diet. Their cramped living quarters allowed little flying room, too.

Concerned for the bird's welfare, they called us.

We met them at a town midway between our two homes. The night was dark, cold, and windy, and we accepted the box covered with a towel without peeking. They also contributed a container of mealworms in bran, as well cared for as the bird, with the proper fare of chopped apples.

I was touched by the efforts they'd made, by their evident love for the warbler, which overrode their natural regret at relinquishing it – and by their faith in us.

When we arrived home, I lifted a corner of the towel and to my surprise saw not the blackpoll warbler that I was expecting, but a very restless, immature ovenbird. These birds are so named because of their domed, ovenlike nests, with an entrance on one side, that they build on the ground.

I caught him gently, briefly examined his wing, and then opened my hand. He fluttered up instantly into one of the trees in the indoor garden, a beautifully patterned creature but strangely stumpy without a tail. In the muted lamplight he settled down to

roost only a short distance from Beejay, his dark eyes in their distinctive eye-rings looking enormous.

I remember walking in the woods one exhilarating day in the spring amid a migration of scarcely visible ovenbirds. Bright eye-rings appeared and disappeared around me constantly, like rings in water, as the ovenbirds flitted furtively through the undergrowth. My curious eyes caught only their movements, rarely their forms. Their unusual calls, zigzagging sharply between two pitches, maintained their contact with one another while they foraged.

This little creature, being of the warbler family, needed an insectivorous diet of dozens of mealworms a day – a regime guaranteed to decimate our two mealie cultures in quick order. Through the efforts of the Animal Care Technician at the local university, we received a shipment of five thousand mealies, and a promise of more later if needed. Combined with ground eggshell, powdered vitamins, and all the garden bugs we could scrounge before freeze-up, these would carry the ovenbird through to spring.

The missing tailfeathers grew in quickly and his flight strengthened noticeably. His striped crown soon became tinged with the orange colouring so characteristic of adults. It was his natural gait, however, that unfailingly intrigued us: he sashayed along almost coyly, with dainty steps and teetering tail movements that reminded me humorously of a human walking in anguish across sharp gravel in bare feet.

As always, the other birds showed admirable tolerance of the tiny newcomer, and Bashō in particular often accompanied the stranger in the garden. Both birds were natural ground dwellers, but Mack suggested facetiously that perhaps Bashō enjoyed being near someone smaller than he for a change. A fresh layer of woodland earth riddled with minute wrigglies soon quickened their hunting fervour.

In time, we became aware that most people were not familiar with ovenbirds, which in itself wasn't remarkable. But when a few puzzled folks, particularly around Thanksgiving or Christmas, thought we were referring to a turkey, we laughingly dubbed the little ovenbird "Butterball." Only when we discovered that Butterball preferred to sleep on top of the electric stove at night, and after he flew out of the oven *twice* when the door had been left down to cool, did we find that the joke was on us.

After a few weeks, we began to hear odd flutterings during the nights. Soon we realized that Butterball was "migrating," much as County, the robin with whom I lived in *Sharing a Robin's Life*, also migrated. And, as with County, I left dim lights on till morning to prevent collisions.

Week after week, wings flitted past nightly on their mysterious journey, till I too began to measure the distance to South America not in miles or kilometres but in wingbeats.

And how many wingbeats would bring him back to Canada in time for spring?

As winter gently crept near with succeeding snowfalls and increasing silence, deer began to emerge each day from the woods to forage among the stalks in the veggie garden. Mack began tossing apples out the door and rolling them down the snowy slope towards our shy visitors, who would turn as one and spring for the woods.

Eventually, however, one began to linger, then another, when the apples bounced crazily towards them. Soon the squeak of an opening door or window elicited only heads lifted in anticipation. Apples dropped close to the house were also eaten, though left till the last, and rarely a day passed without several deer, sometimes more than a dozen, feeding or playing only a few feet away from our delighted eyes.

One evening at dusk, Mack spotted a group of deer, opened the door, and sent an apple bouncing down the icy slope towards them. To his astonishment, a saw-whet owl shot out of a nearby spruce, swooped down within inches of the rolling apple, then veered sharply back up to the tree, disappointed in his hopes of an early mouse.

Could the owl have been Doc?

Thereafter at night we often turned on the outside light, only to reveal the saw-whet, and an occasional barred owl, as they perched on branches above the feeding stations, cocking their heads as they heard foraging mice under the snow. Sometimes they'd peer down with suddenly heightened interest, lift their wings slightly, then plunge with outstretched talons deep into the snow.

Other times raccoons, deer, and an owl would all be within the glow of the outside light, creating memorable moments of rare beauty.

As Bashō's birthday approached, we decided to celebrate. He was an endearing favourite with many people and had outlived his less fortunate siblings in the laboratory.

Besides – we welcomed an excuse for a feast.

Drawing on his Japanese origin, we copied out haiku poems by the original Matsuo Bashō – with amusing annotations by his present incarnation. For instance, we struck out traditional words and substituted those appropriate to a Japanese quail. "Ah, the fragrance" would become "Ah, the mealworm." We posted the revised versions all around the living room.

Of the friends we invited on this auspicious occasion, we included one who had lived for a couple of years in Japan. Between us we concocted a delicious Japanese vegetarian meal (Bashō would have to enjoy his mealies later), and we all gathered around the table. Bashō, as the guest of honour, basked cozily in my cupped hand, where he could sample each delicacy off my tongue. We dined by candlelight, with all the indoor lights off and the outside light on in order to watch the wild deer.

They drew close to the glass door beside us, their coats glowing in the lamplight, and began eating apples left for them on the doorstep. Soon they were joined by raccoons, also looking for treats.

The guests, being town-dwellers, were enchanted.

One of them, a poet for many years, read aloud a poem written especially for Bashō, which delighted us all. Then I passed out paper and pencils and, after we toasted Bashō with warm sake, we tried to create haiku ourselves, following the ancient ritual of Japanese poets.

Dessert followed with *kukicha* twig tea and purely Canadian cookies – to signify Bashō's joint Canadian heritage.

Finally, we tucked Bashō into his garden, donned thick outerwear, and trod the new sparkling snow to the top of the drumlin. There under a clear wide sky we embraced the beauty of the full moon – another Japanese tradition. An enormous ring glowed around the moon, augmenting its splendour.

Bashō's "bash" had been a success.

One day, we stepped out of the car to hear what Mack wittily described as a "caw-cawphony" of crows down by the brook. They sounded very upset, and we strode down to investigate. By hissing waters that slipped between icy banks, we stood gazing upward, the centre of a hundred whirling, screaming crows. They circled round and round, only thirty feet above our heads, cawing ceaselessly.

Our fear that they'd found an owl to tease fled, but the mystery remained. Then one crow detached itself from the rest and alighted on the tip of a dead tree directly before us.

He peered at us very speakingly. Very urgently.

We approached the single crow and, as we drew near, became aware of sounds of struggle in a tree beyond his. We quickened our pace, pushed through dense shrubbery, and emerged below a young tree intricately looped with dried wild cucumber vines. Entangled in the vine above our heads, and hanging upside down, was a crow, struggling desperately.

Mack instantly seized the slender trunk of the tree as high as he could reach and began bending it, trying to lower the crow to where we could reach him. At the same time I caught hold of the vine trailers and began to tug each one gently in the hopes of untangling the victim. Crows still whirled around us, and our ears rang with their wild cries.

Suddenly the vines fell apart, due to our efforts, and the crow broke free. After a brief plunge, he flapped wildly up to join the others. The single crow who had guided us also swept away in his wake.

There were a few single cries, then silence. The cloud of crows dissolved back into the woodland.

"It's amazing how creatures find us when they need us," murmured Mack.

Later that evening, I sat before the fire with Bubble drowsing in my lap and Chip preening on one shoulder. Jake lay in Mack's hands nearby, feathers raised in a heatbath. Bashō dozed, tucked snugly into my shirt.

High in his tree in the indoor garden, Beejay slept, his head tucked behind one wing.

Higher still, near the dim cathedral ceiling, Butterball flitted past, still heading for South America.

On her shelf, Molly dozed, looking less malevolent in the flattering firelight.

I thought about Mack's words.

About the crow who beckoned us to help. About the steady procession of creatures who arrive in need, asking us to see them through their eyes. Teaching us how.

Only when they finally set out on their own do we realize how little we give them in comparison with what they give us.

We've begun to see our home as an ark riding the turbulent waves of a disordered world – one small place of safety for creatures.

We're all on the same journey.

We just look a little different from one another.

ABOUT THE AUTHOR

Linda Johns is an artist and writer living in the hills of Nova Scotia. She exhibits regularly in various galleries, and her mediums include acrylic on canvas and paper, brush drawings, pastels, lino-prints, wood engravings, clay sculptures, and carvings in stone, whalebone, and wood. Her artwork has been featured in two television documentaries.

In 1994, her book *Sharing a Robin's Life* won the Edna Staebler Award for Creative Nonfiction and was shortlisted for the Evelyn Richardson's Memorial Literary Prize.